SQL Server Tacklebox

Essential Tools and Scripts for the day-to-day DBA

By Rodney Landrum

First published by Red Gate Books 2009

Technical Review by Shawn McGehee

Cover Image by Paul Beckman

Edited by Tony Davis

Typeset by Gower Associates

Table of Contents

ABOUT THE AUTHOR

Rodney Landrum has been working with SQL Server technologies for longer than he can remember (he turned 40 in May of 2009, so his memory is going). He writes regularly about many SQL Server technologies, including Integration Services, Analysis Services, and Reporting Services. He has authored three books on Reporting Services. He is a regular contributor to SQL Server Magazine and Simple-Talk, the latter of which he sporadically blogs on about SQL and his plethora of geek tattoos. His day job finds him overseeing the health and well-being of a large SQL Server infrastructure in Pensacola, Florida. He swears he owns the expression "Working with Databases on a Day to Day Basis" and anyone who disagrees is itching to arm wrestle. Rodney is also a SQL Server MVP.

ABOUT THE TECHNICAL REVIEWER

Shawn McGehee is a full-time professional DBA and a part-time amateur developer from Pensacola, Florida. He is very active with the local SQL users' group in Pensacola and helps organize / speaks regularly at their events. Shawn is also a contributing writer to popular SQL websites such as Simple Talk and SQL Server Central. He was also a co-author of the book "Pro SQL Server 2008 Reporting Services."

ACKNOWLEDGEMENTS

I would like to thank everyone involved in the making of this book, peripherally and personally, but first and foremost Karla...my love, who has been with me, spurred me on and understood when I needed a fishing or beer respite through 5 books now. I love you.

To all my kids who also sacrificed during the writing of this book. Megan, Ethan, Brendan and Taylor. Well, OK, Ethan did not sacrifice so much, but he did help me understand that "Buffalo buffalo Buffalo buffalo buffalo buffalo Buffalo buffalo" is a legitimate sentence.

Thanks to my Mom and Dad, as always. I love you. There will still be a novel, I promise; just not a Western. Sorry, Mom.

Thanks also to Shawn McGehee, my good friend and DBA colleague, who tech-edited the book. It is much better for it. Also, thanks Shawn, for letting me use snippets of your hard-won code as well.

Special thanks also go to Truett Woods who has opened my eyes in a lot of ways to good coding practices, and for the use of one of his base code queries in Chapter 1.

Thanks to Joe Healy of devfish fame, a straight up bud whose .Net tacklebox is more full than mine. I will be getting the devfish tattoo next.

Finally, I would personally like to thank Throwing Muses, The Pixies and Primus for providing the music that helped me through the many late nights. OK, so they will never read this and offer to come over to play a set at a backyard BBQ, I know, but one can hope.

INTRODUCTION

This book, as with almost all books, started out as an idea. I wanted to accumulate together those scripts and tools that I have built over the years so that DBAs could sort through them and perhaps adapt them for their own circumstances. I know that not every script herein will be useful, and that you might ask "Why are you using this table and not that DMV" or "Why is this code not compatible with SQL Server 2008?" After writing about SQL Server solutions now for the past 10 years, I can expect this criticism, and understand it fully. Everyone has their own ways of solving problems. My goal is to provide useful samples that you can modify as you please.

I wrote the book the way it is because I did not want to bore DBAs to tears with another 500+ page textbook-style tome with step-by-step instructions. I wanted this book to be a novel, a book of poetry, a murder mystery, a ghost story, an epic trilogy, a divine comedy. But realizing that this **is**, after all, a technical book, I compromised by imbuing it with some humor and personality. If you make it as far as the monster at the end of this book, my hope is that you will have been entertained and can use the code from the Tacklebox in some fashion that will make your lives as DBAs easier. Why "The Tacklebox," you might ask, rather than "Zombie Queries," "You Can't Handle the Code" or "You had me at BEGIN?" I think, as I push halfway through my career as a DBA and author, this book is as close as I will ever get to "The Old Man and the Sea"…oh yes, and apparently the "Toolbox" had been copyrighted. Plus, come on! Look at the cover of the book. How can I live here and not go fishing once in a while?

Chapter 1

Here you will find wholesome SQL Server installations on the menu, complete with Express, Continental and Deluxe breakfast choices, depending on your application's appetite. And there will be a little GUI setup support here. This chapter is about automation, and a lengthy script is included that will help you automate SQL installations and configurations. There is some foreshadowing lurking as well, such as code to enable a DDL trigger that I will show later in the book. This is the chapter where your new SQL Server installation is completely yours, having not as yet been turned over to the general populace of developers or users. Enjoy it while you can.

Chapter 2

In this chapter, I introduce the DBA Repository, a documentation tool I have built using Integration Services and Reporting Services. It is easy to manage one, two or three SQL Server instances with the panoramic view the tool gives. It is even easy to work with ten SQL Servers without documentation, but when you have 70 or 100 or 2,000 SQL Servers without an automated documentation solution, you cannot successfully manage your SQL Server Landscape – ironically, that is the name of the chapter, "The SQL Server Landscape."

Chapter 3

I think we can all agree that data at rest never stays that way. No, far from it. The data in this chapter has begun the swim up river to its spawning grounds and will migrate and transform like the intrepid salmon (hey, a fishing reference) from the open ocean, to river, to stream. Here, I look at different ways that data moves about, and I investigate tools such as SSIS and BCP that help facilitate such moves, whatever the reason, be it high availability, disaster recovery or offloaded reporting.

Chapter 4

In this chapter, I describe one of the first hungry monsters of the book, the disk-space consuming databases. The hunger may not be abated entirely, but it can be controlled with proper planning and also with queries that will help you to respond to runaway growth. Here, I will show how to battle the appetite of space-killers with just a bit of planning, tempered with an understanding of how and why data and log files grow to consume entire disks.

Chapter 5

There is a murder in this chapter. Someone or something is killed and most likely you, the DBA, will be the lone killer. Of course, I am talking about processes, SPIDs, that we see every day. Some are easier to kill than others. Some will just not die and I will explain why, using ridiculous code that I hope you never see in real life. The queries here were designed to help you get to the bottom of any issue as quickly as possible without the need for DNA testing. And I am not talking about Windows DNA, if you are old like me and remember this acronym for Distributed Networking Architecture, precursor to .NET. No, no .NET here.

Chapter 6

To sleep...perchance to dream...about failures. Here, I will introduce the sleep killer of DBAs everywhere, where jobs fail in the hours of darkness, and the on-call DBA is awakened from slumber several times a night in order to sway, zombie-like to the computer to restart failed backup jobs. You cannot resolve an issue unless you know about it and here, while discussing notifications and monitoring your SQL Server infrastructure, we will stay up late and tell horror stories. But, in the end, you will sleep better knowing all is well.

Chapter 7

Surely, like me, you are afraid of break-ins. I would not like to come home and find my things strewn about, wondering what all was taken. If you work for a large company that is regulated by one or more government mandates, like HIPAA or SOX (Sarbanes-Oxley) you cannot afford to be without a security monitoring solution. Here, I will introduce a set of scripts to show how to analyze login accounts, the first barrier between the outside world and your data. I will also give pointers to other solutions that will help you track down potential breaches in your outer wall defenses.

Chapter 8

In this chapter I will unveil the monster. It is the Data Corruption beast. Despite advances in hardware, the number one cause of corruption, it does still exist. You will need to first hunt out corruption before you can slay it. And you need to find it early in its lair so as to not spread the corruption to backup files. Here, I will intentionally, though begrudgingly, corrupt a database and show some of the ways to discover and fix it, emphasizing the need for a solid backup strategy.

Code Download

All of the scripts provided in this 'tacklebox', as well as the full DBA Repository solution, presented in Chapter 2, are available to download from:

http://www.simple-talk.com/RedGateBooks/
RodneyLandrum/SQL_Server_Tacklebox_Code.zip.

CHAPTER 1: EATING SQL SERVER INSTALLATIONS FOR BREAKFAST

For many DBAs, choosing an appropriate SQL Server installation is a lot like ordering breakfast at a diner: there is something to suit all appetites, tastes and budgets, and the range of choices can often be mind-boggling. A sample SQL Server breakfast menu might look something like this:

The Express Breakfast (For the cost-conscious)

- 1 SQL Server Express on top of a Windows XP Professional
- 1 large hard drive
- 2 Gig of RAM

The Continental (Enough to hold you over for a while)

- 1 SQL Server Standard Edition 32 bit on Windows Server 2003 Standard
- 1 instance of Reporting Server
- 1 instance of Analysis Server
- 250 Gig RAID 5 Disk Subsystem
- 4 Gigs of RAM

The Deluxe (When cost is no barrier to hunger)

- 1 SQL Server Enterprise Edition 64 bit Clustered
- 2 Windows Server 2003 Enterprise Edition servers
- 1 RAID 10 1TB Data Partition
- 1 RAID 10 200G Log Partition
- 1 RAID 0 100G TempDB Partition
- 64 G of RAM

It is the DBA's task to choose the SQL Server configuration that most accurately reflects the specific needs of a given project, whether it is for cost-conscious deployments, high availability, data analysis or high-performing online transactions for a critical business application. In this chapter, I will investigate the myriad available installation options and propose a custom post-installation script with which to automate the most common configurations.

Specification, installation, configuration

Once the project has been decided, there are many ensuing steps to climb to get from concept to full deployment. Installing SQL Server on the chosen platform is, in reality, only a small part of the overall pre-production setup process. Pre-installation, you have the planning stage, where you need to define the capacity, memory and CPU requirements, and required disk subsystems for your physical server(s) . Post-installation, the true work begins, when it is time for configuration. Fortunately, both of the rote tasks of installation and configuration can be automated, to some degree.

Specifying the physical server

Generally, the size of a given project, in terms of the number of expected users, amount of data to be stored, and so on, will dictate the capacity of the physical server, or servers, that comprise the SQL Server installation. The sort of breakfast that lands on your plate is likely to differ wildly, depending on whether you work for the ubiquitous "mom and pop" shop, or a large enterprise. In the former case, you may well find yourself ordering the parts for the servers yourself, and putting them all together, before moving on to the SQL Server installation. If you are a DBA at the Fortune 100 end of the scale, you may never even get to see your servers, let alone build them! You will just be informed, by way of an e-mail from the server administration team, that your server is powered up, with the base OS installed, and ready to endure your SQL witch-trickery.

In my career, I have sampled both the self-service buffet and the gourmet tasting menu. While I consider it a luxury to no longer have to have to build my own servers, I would not trade that experience. I am often asked how important it is for a DBA to have a technical understanding of networking, storage or even Windows Server systems. In my opinion, it is critical. I could go as far as to say that every DBA should spend two years working in technical support, troubleshooting problems and building systems from the ground up. But that is topic for a different book. Suffice to say here that, regardless of whether you are building your own server or having it delivered on a silver platter, it's vital that a DBA understands a few important components of that physical server, and the factors that affect how you choose these components.

RAM

SQL Server, like any other application, is going to use memory. RAM, like CPU and disk arrays, comes at a cost and how much RAM you are going to need depends on several factors. If you know that you will have 250 users connected simultaneously to a 200 Gigabyte database, then 4G of RAM on SQL Standard 32-bit and Windows 2003 is not going to be enough.

Without wishing to be overly formulaic, I will say that connections come at a RAM cost. More connections equals more RAM. SQL Server will run comfortably in 1G of memory, but you would not want to roll out a production server on that amount. Ironically, one of the most important factors to consider is one that a DBA has very little control over: what application is going to access your beloved database objects? Is it "homegrown" or "third-party"? This is an important question because, if you do not "own" the database schemas, you could find yourself unable to employ basic performance tuning techniques, like adding indexes. In these situations, you are at the mercy of the vendor, whose recommendation is often to "add more RAM," even when all that is required is to add an overlooked index.

At this planning stage, it is always safer to overestimate the need for memory. Get as much as you "think" you will need, and more if performance outweighs cost, which it should. Note though, that buying the additional physical RAM is not the only cost and is seldom the cure. You will also have to purchase software that can support the additional RAM and this might mean, for example, buying Windows Server Enterprise instead of Standard Edition.

CPU

Specifying processor requirements for a SQL Server is a slightly more complex task than specifying RAM. For one thing, software such as SQL Server can be licensed per processor. This can be quite expensive. As a DBA, you must understand the difference between the different processor types. For example, is the processor 32- or 64-bit architecture? Is it single-core or multi-core, meaning you can gain additional virtual processors with one physical processor? If it is multi-core, is it dual-core or quad-core, or octa-core? I'm not even sure if that last one exists yet, but it probably will soon.

Why is it important to know the answer to all these questions? Well, you do not want to be the DBA who relays to your boss that your new 2-proc, quad-core SQL Server is going to require 8 "per proc" licenses when, in fact, it will only require 1 license per "physical" processor, even if SQL Server will use all 8 cores.

The speed of the processor is important as well; what Gigabytes is to RAM, Gigahertz is to processors in determining how your new server is going to perform. Take a little time up front to investigate the server specifications, especially if someone else was responsible for ordering it. It will save you 3 months of pain later on, when the server is ill-performing.

Disk subsystem

The choice of disk subsystem is the most difficult pre-installation hardware decision that the DBA has to make. There are just so many options. Fortunately, you have put together the documentation for your SQL Server infrastructure that will help you narrow down the choices, right? You know, for example, that your performance requirements dictate that you are going to need RAID 1-0 data and log partitions, with a separate volume allocated for TempDB split across as many spindles as possible.

OK, so you don't have that document; not a big deal. If you are able to at least have a RAID 5 configuration then you are off to a good start. It is also worth noting that if you are installing SQL Server in a clustered environment, you will need to have a shared disk array, typically implemented via a Storage Area Network (SAN) back end.

Free tools are available for you to stress test the disk subsystem of the SQL Server installation, prior to moving it to production. One such tool is SQLIO, provided by Microsoft:

http://www.microsoft.com/downloads/details.aspx?familyid=9a8b005b-84e4-4f24-8d65-cb53442d9e19&displaylang=en

Ready to install – almost

So, you have your server built and are ready to install SQL Server. Let's say that you have chosen to install a 32-bit version of SQL Server 2008 Standard, on Windows 2003 Enterprise, with 16 Gigabytes of RAM. You have been given a 350 Gigabyte data partition, and a 200 Gigabyte partition for the logs and TempDB.

One thing you can take comfort in is that this will be your server, at least for the next several hours. If you're lucky, and the project is not as urgent, you may even have a day or two. For this short, precious time, you have total control of this server and can do with it whatever you will. Of course, you want to get the installation right and this is where having an established, standard set of installation procedures is priceless.

The pre-installation checklist

Some DBAs I know look at each server installation as an entirely new experience. It becomes second nature to them to install, prep and release a SQL Server into production. However, mistakes can and will happen. You rattle through the installation process as normal, declare the server live, and then move on to other tasks, not realizing that you have missed a small but important step. Later, or probably sooner, someone discovers that the server is not sending mail, or that a new database has not had a log backup and has filled up the log drive, and all hell breaks loose.

It is a painful experience so, before you hunker down to install SQL Server, you will want to review your *SQL Server Installation Check List*. It will contain multiple instructions for different versions of SQL Server. Many of the configuration options, such as the collation of the SQL Server instance, are best set during installation so it is important to know beforehand what options you need to choose.

Check lists will vary for everyone but there are a few configurations that will be common to all lists. For example:

- Data and Log File Standard Location
    - Data: E:\DataFiles
    - Logs: F:\TLogs
- Service Account: (Created service account and grant local privileges)
- TempDB Location
    - T:\TempDB
- Special Permissions (memory – AWE)
    - Lock Pages in Memory
- Boot.ini
    - Configure for /PAE switch if 32 bit Windows 2003 and SQL Server Standard or Enterprise
- Additional vendor-supplied (Non SQL) applications
    - Defragmentation
    - SQL Backup Compression

Automated command line installation

Having gathered together your pre-installation information, it's time to install. We will place our DVD into the drive, or mount our ISO, and double-click Setup.exe. *Yeah … sure we will.*

Installing SQL Server is, at best, a mundane task. If you do it twice a month then it is probably OK to simply springboard through the GUI installation wizard, manually choosing, clicking, and typing your way to a successful install. However, for me and many other DBAs, standardization and automation are important. A constant theme of this book is that whenever a task can be simplified, automated and repeated, you should make it so.

Installation is no exception. I need a standard install process that can be controlled programmatically, in order to eradicate costly mistakes. As such, I want to avoid the GUI-driven installation altogether. Fortunately, Microsoft continues to support command line installs and that is what I will be demonstrating here: how to automate the installation with setup options, from the command line.

I'll begin by examining some of the installation options available for SQL Server 2008. There are many optional parameters that I'll ignore, but several that are required. I'll show how to string together the command line and execute it on your new server. When it is done, assuming there are no errors, you will be ready for the real fun. If there are errors, then refer to my previous comment about the 2 years spent in Help Desk. They will stand you in good stead, as you will need every ounce of perseverance to solve any issues. I have read volumes in the various SQL Server forums on installation errors and how to overcome them. However, let's assume, as is typical, that there will be no errors.

To get a full list of all of the available command line installation options for SQL Server 2008, including the valuable samples, simply run **Setup /?**, as shown in Figure 1.1.

```
Z:\>setup /?
Microsoft (R) SQL Server 2008 Setup 10.00.1600.22
Copyright (c) Microsoft Corporation. All rights reserved.

Usage:
  setup.exe /[option]=<value> /[option]=<value> ...

Options:
ACTION                        Specifies a Setup work flow, like INSTALL, UNINSTALL,
                              or UPGRADE. This is a required parameter.
ADDCURRENTUSERASSQLADMIN      Provision current user as a Database Engine system
                              administrator for SQL Server 2008 Express.
AGTDOMAINGROUP                Either domain user name or system account
AGTSVCACCOUNT                 Either domain user name or system account
AGTSVCPASSWORD                Password for domain user name. Not required for
                              system account.
AGTSVCSTARTUPTYPE             Either 1 or 0
ALLINSTANCES                  Specifies that all instances are to be included in
                              the Setup operation. This parameter is only supported
                              when applying a patch.
ASBACKUPDIR                   The location for the Analysis Services backup files.
ASCOLLATION                   The collation used by Analysis Services.
ASCONFIGDIR                   The location for the Analysis Services configuration
                              files.
ASDATADIR                     The location for the Analysis Services data files.
ASDOMAINGROUP                 Specifies the Analysis Services domain group name.
ASLOGDIR                      The location for the Analysis Services log files.
ASPROVIDERMSOLAP              Specifies if the MSOLAP provider can run in process.
ASSVCACCOUNT                  The account used by the Analysis Services service.
ASSVCPASSWORD                 The password for the Analysis Services service
                              account.
ASSVCSTARTUPTYPE              Controls the service startup type setting for the
                              service.
```

Figure 1.1: A few of the command line setup options.

Figure 1.2 shows the different, less friendly outcome performing the same step for SQL Server 2005.

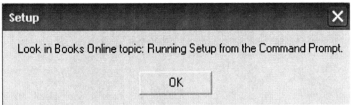

Figure 1.2: If you want the answer look in Books Online.

Once you've picked the options that are right for your install, you simply need to string them together on the command line noting that, for a SQL Server 2008 installation, there are several required options. Listing 1.1 shows a sample command for automating an install.

```
setup.exe /QUIETSIMPLE /ACTION=install /FEATURES=SQL,Tools
/INSTANCENAME=MSSQLSERVER /SQLSVCACCOUNT="Network Service"
/SQLSYSADMINACCOUNTS="domain\username" /AGTSVCACCOUNT="NT
AUTHORITY\Network Service" /SECURITYMODE=SQL /SAPWD="*********"
/SQLTEMPDBDIR="C:\TempDB\\" /SQLUSERDBDIR="C:\SQLData\\"
/SQLUSERDBLOGDIR="C:\SQLLog\\"
```

Listing1.1: A sample command line install.

Most of the options are intuitive. For example:

- **/ACTION** – this is required. It simply specifies whether the action is an install, update or uninstall. In this case, I am going to install.
- **/FEATURES** – determines what SQL Server features to install. The choices are "SQL, AS, RS, IS, Tools". For this install, I chose SQL and Tools, which will install the SQL Database Engine and tools such as SQL Server Management Studio, Business Intelligence Developments Studio and configuration tools. I chose not to install Analysis Services (AS), Reporting Services (RS) or Integration Services (IS).

Each feature also has its own set of properties, such as service account credentials and installation location.

Running the command initiates the installation. If you choose the **/QUIETSIMPLE** option, as I did here, then you will be able to view the progress of the installation. However, there will be no user interaction. If the command executes as expected, you'll see something similar to that shown in Figure 1.3, reporting the progress of the installation.

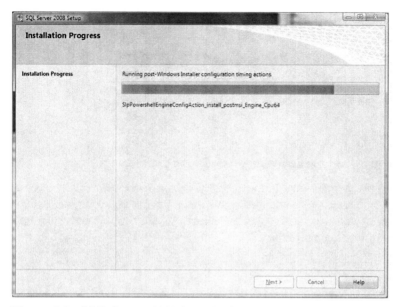

Figure 1.3: SQL Server 2008 installation progress.

When complete, you will have a fully installed SQL Server 2008 instance, complete with tools. There is a good chance that you will not encounter any errors. However, if you do, especially if you chose the silent mode installation, then you can review the **Summary.txt** file, which captures any errors during installation. You'll typically find the file in the **<Install Drive>:\Program Files\Microsoft SQL Server\100\Setup Bootstrap\Log** folder.

As a DBA, you will find that it is par for the course that people bring their troubleshooting installation problems to your door, and you will be looked upon as an expert even though you may not have seen the specific error before. Knowing where to look will at least buy you time to formulate a rational answer. Of course, as DBA, you or your team should be performing all SQL installations anyway, so you can always question why whoever got the error was brazen enough to attempt the install in the first place.

If you have a service pack or hotfix to apply to your SQL Server installation, an obvious next step, then you can automate the service pack installation in the same way, by executing the setup.exe of the service pack with command line options.

NOTE
Starting with service pack 1 for SQL Server 2008, you can now "slipstream" service packs for SQL Server, much like you can do for Windows service packs. See http://msdn.microsoft.com/en-us/library/dd638062.aspx#Slipstream for further details.

Installation done, now to configure

As I said earlier, installing SQL Server is the easy part. Once that portion of your pre-production process is done, you still have many more options to configure. Making the right choices will ensure that your SQL Server performs as you want it to, and play amicably with whatever application will be beating it up every day. Truly, that is what is going to happen. I have heard it said, only half-jokingly, that the one thing you know will hinder the performance of SQL Server is to release it to a production application.

In many organizations there exists a special area, call it staging, QA (Quality Assurance) or Pre Production Modeling, where the entire system is deployed and tested prior to a move to production. If you, as DBA, have the luxury of a QA environment, you will at least know that, functionally, your server configuration is performing as it should. However, often the QA environment is not an exact physical copy of Production. For example, your SQL Server in QA may have only 4 Gigabytes of RAM and not 8. It is important to account for these performance differences.

Standard configuration options

Throughout the version history of SQL Server, several configuration options, though similar in name, functioned differently depending on a number of factors. For example, "AWE enabled", "min server memory" and "max server memory" are all configurable options in SQL Server 2000, 2005 and 2008. However, they behave differently depending on the edition of SQL Server (standard, enterprise or data center), as well as on the operating system on which SQL Server is running. For example, SQL Server 2005 and 2008 Standard Editions allow you to take advantage of all of the memory that the base OS can utilize; for Windows 2003 Server the amount of usable memory is variable depending on whether you have Standard or Enterprise edition, and on whether you have a 32- or 64-bit installation. However, for SQL Server 2000, to take advantage of memory beyond the 4G range, you were required to purchase the Enterprise edition of SQL Server, regardless of the OS version or edition.

With the proliferation of Windows Server 2003, many of these discrepancies have been removed, but they are still very important when setting configuration options. The sample installation being performed here is for SQL Server 2008 but bear in mind that, for each option, there may be a caveat for prior versions.

There are some configuration settings that you will want to change, post-installation, depending on whether you are running a 32- or 64-bit architecture. For example, you will not need to enable AWE for 64-bit architecture, whereas if you do not enable it for 32-bit installations of SQL Server, on Windows 2003 Enterprise, you will not use the memory that you may think you should be using; SQL Server will live within the 2G memory range to which 32-bit applications are generally relegated.

However, there are also options that you will not want to change. Two of these options are "priority boost" and "lightweight pooling". Changes to these options are typically done only with affirmation from Microsoft Support that it will help and not hinder your environment. In general, please do not change a configuration unless you have thoroughly tested it.

The automated SQL Server configuration script

So, what configuration changes can we automate? There are many, and the base script provided in the next section can be extended to support your particular environment. The options fall into three categories:

- **Server-level changes** you can make with `sp_configure`
- **Database-level changes** you can make with `sp_dboption`
- **Custom configurations** that you will apply, specifically custom administrative code, job schedules and DDL triggers.

What follows is the pseudo code for what the configuration script will automate for you. All told, I would estimate that the configuration script will save about 30 minutes of manual configuration effort. More important than the time saving, however, is the fact that this script offers a repeatable and accurate configuration for each server.

- **SQL Server Memory**
    - If 64-bit, do not enable AWE
    - If 32-bit SQL 2008 Standard on Windows 2003 Enterprise and RAM is more than 4G
        - Set max server memory = 2G less than Total Server Memory
    - If 32-bit SQL 2008 Standard on Windows 2003 Standard and RAM is less than 4G
        - Set max server memory = 2G
- **E-Mail**
    - If > 2005 automate setup with DBMail SPs
        - Send Test Mail
    - If < 2005 Document necessity to create MAPI profile
        - Print steps to configure e-mail

- **DDL Triggers**
  - Add Server Trigger to notify upon database create or drop
- **Security**
  - Set to Log Successful and Failed logins
- **DB Maintenance Database**
  - Create the _DBAMain database
  - Create the stored procedures in the _DBAMain database
  - Create and Schedule Maintenance Jobs via stored procedures
- **Other Modifications**
  - Change Model Database Options.

Listing 1.2 displays the actual T-SQL automation script to implement the above steps, which you can execute against your newly installed SQL Server instance. It is documented at stages to distinguish between server, database and custom additions.

```
/* SQL Server Automated Configuration Script
   2009 - Rodney Landrum
*/

--Create Temp table #SerProp. This table will be used
--to hold the output of xp_msver to control server property
configurations

SET NOCOUNT ON
GO

IF EXISTS ( SELECT   name
            FROM     tempdb..sysobjects
            Where    name like '#SerProp%' )
--If So Drop it
    DROP TABLE #SerProp
create table #SerProp
    (
      ID int,
      Name sysname,
      Internal_Value int,
      Value nvarchar(512)
    )

  GO


--Set Show Advanced Option
sp_configure 'Show Advanced Options', 1
Reconfigure
GO
```

```
DECLARE @PhysMem int
DECLARE @ProcType int
DECLARE @MaxMem int

INSERT    INTO #SerProp
          Exec xp_msver

Select    @PhysMem = Internal_Value
from      #SerProp
where     Name = 'PhysicalMemory'

Select    @ProcType = Internal_Value
from      #SerProp
where     Name = 'ProcessorType'

--Set Memory Configuration from server properties
--(memory level and processortype)

If @PhysMem > 4096 AND @ProcType = 8664
BEGIN
   SET @MaxMem = @PhysMem - 3072
   EXEC sp_configure 'max server memory', @MaxMem
   Reconfigure
END

ELSE
IF @PhysMem > 4096 AND @ProcType <> 8664
BEGIN
   SET @MaxMem = @PhysMem - 3072
   EXEC sp_configure 'awe enabled', 1
   Reconfigure
   EXEC sp_configure 'max server memory', @MaxMem
   Reconfigure
END

--Setup Database Mail (SQL Server > 2005 )
--Turn on Mail XPs via sp_configure
--sp_configure (To turn on Mail XPs)

-- Add Profile

If @@microsoftversion / power(2, 24) > 8
BEGIN

EXECUTE msdb.dbo.sysmail_add_profile_sp
        @profile_name = 'Admin Profile',
        @description = 'Mail Profile For Alerts' ;

--Add Mail Account

        EXECUTE msdb.dbo.sysmail_add_account_sp
```

```
    @account_name = 'Admin Account',
    @description = 'General SQL Admin Account for DBA
Notification',
    @email_address = '<Your DBA e-mail account>,
    @display_name = 'SQL Admin Account',
    @mailserver_name = '<Yourmailservername>;

--Add Mail Account to Profile

EXECUTE msdb.dbo.sysmail_add_profileaccount_sp
    @profile_name = 'Admin Profile',
    @account_name = 'Admin Account',
    @sequence_number = 1 ;

--Send Test Mail

EXEC msdb.dbo.sp_send_dbmail
    @profile_name = 'Admin Profile',
    @recipients = '<Your DBA e-mail Account>,
    @body = 'Sever Mail Configuration Completed,
    @subject = 'Successful Mail Test;

  END
  ELSE


--Print Instructions for SQl Server 2000

  BEGIN
  PRINT 'For SQL Server 2000, you will need to
         configure a MAPI client'
  PRINT 'such as Outlook and create a profile to use
         for SQL Mail and SQL Agent'
  PRINT 'mail. Instructions can be found
         at:_____'
  END

--Setup Security Logging
--Enable Successful and Unsuccessful Login Attempts
--SQL Server Services must be restarted to take affect

exec master.dbo.xp_instance_regwrite N'HKEY_LOCAL_MACHINE',
N'Software\Microsoft\MSSQLServer\MSSQLServer',
N'AuditLevel', REG_DWORD,3

--Create Maintenance Database "_DBAMain"

USE [master]
GO

/****** Object:  Database [_DBAMain]
                 Script Date: 02/05/2009 20:41:24 ******/
```

```
IF  EXISTS (SELECT name FROM sys.databases
              WHERE name = N'_DBAMain')
DROP DATABASE [_DBAMain]
GO

/****** Object:  Database [_DBAMain]
                  Script Date: 02/05/2009 20:41:24 ******/
CREATE DATABASE [_DBAMain] ON  PRIMARY
( NAME = N'_DBAMain_Data',
   FILENAME = N'C:\Data\_DBAMain_Data.MDF',
   SIZE = 5120KB,
   MAXSIZE = UNLIMITED,
   FILEGROWTH = 10%)
 LOG ON
( NAME = N'_DBAMain_Log',
   FILENAME = N'C:\Logs\_DBAMain_Log.LDF' ,
   SIZE = 3072KB ,
   MAXSIZE = 2048GB ,
   FILEGROWTH = 10%)
GO

/*
   Run Script To Create Stored Procedures
   In _DBAMain
*/

sp_configure 'xp_cmdshell', 1
Reconfigure

exec xp_cmdshell 'sqlcmd -i C:\Writing\Create_DBAMain_2.sql'

-- Schedule Indexing Stored Procedure

/*
Usage:
spxCreateIDXMaintenanceJob
     'Owner Name'
   , 'Operator'
   , 'Sunday'
   , 0
*/
Create Procedure
     [dbo].[spxCreateIDXMaintenanceJob]
   (
     @JobOwner          nvarchar(75)
   , @ValidOperator       nvarchar(50)
   , @DayToReindex        nvarchar(8)
   , @NightlyStartTime    int --230000 (11pm), 0 (12am), 120000
(12pm)
   )
As
BEGIN TRANSACTION
```

```
DECLARE
    @ReturnCode    INT
  , @jobId    BINARY(16)
  , @MyServer    nvarchar(75)
  , @SQL        nvarchar(4000)
  , @CR        nvarchar(2)

SELECT
    @ReturnCode = 0
  , @CR = char(13) + char(10)

IF NOT EXISTS    (
            SELECT
                name
            FROM
                msdb.dbo.syscategories
            WHERE
                name = N'Database Maintenance'
            AND
                category_class = 1
            )
BEGIN
   EXEC @ReturnCode = msdb.dbo.sp_add_category
        @class = N'JOB'
      , @type = N'LOCAL'
      , @name = N'Database Maintenance'

   IF
        @@ERROR <> 0
   OR
        @ReturnCode <> 0
   Begin
        GOTO QuitWithRollback
   End
END

IF EXISTS    (
            SELECT
                name
            FROM
                msdb.dbo.sysjobs
            WHERE
                name = N'IDX Maintenance'
            AND
                category_id =    (
                        Select
                            category_id
                        From
                            msdb.dbo.syscategories
                        Where
                            name = 'Database Maintenance'
```

```
                                )
              )
Begin
   Exec msdb.dbo.sp_delete_job
         @job_name = 'IDX Maintenance'
End

EXEC @ReturnCode = msdb.dbo.sp_add_job
            @job_name = N'IDX Maintenance'
            , @enabled = 1
            , @notify_level_eventlog = 0
            , @notify_level_email = 0
            , @notify_level_netsend = 0
            , @notify_level_page = 0
            , @delete_level = 0
            , @description = N'Index Tuning'
            , @category_name = N'Database Maintenance'
            , @owner_login_name = @JobOwner
            , @job_id = @jobId OUTPUT

IF
      @@ERROR <> 0
OR
      @ReturnCode <> 0
Begin
      GOTO QuitWithRollback
End

Select @SQL = 'exec spxIDXMaint '
                  + char(39) + @DayToReindex + char(39)

EXEC @ReturnCode = msdb.dbo.sp_add_jobstep
            @job_id = @jobId
            , @step_name = N'Index Maintenance'
            , @step_id = 1
            , @cmdexec_success_code = 0
            , @on_success_action = 1
            , @on_success_step_id = 0
            , @on_fail_action = 2
            , @on_fail_step_id = 0
            , @retry_attempts = 0
            , @retry_interval = 0
            , @os_run_priority = 0
            , @subsystem = N'TSQL'
            , @command = @SQL
            , @database_name = N'_DBAMain'
            , @flags = 0

IF
      @@ERROR <> 0
OR
      @ReturnCode <> 0
```

```
Begin
     GOTO QuitWithRollback
End

EXEC @ReturnCode = msdb.dbo.sp_update_job
          @job_id = @jobId
        , @start_step_id = 1

IF
     @@ERROR <> 0
OR
     @ReturnCode <> 0
Begin
     GOTO QuitWithRollback
End

EXEC @ReturnCode = msdb.dbo.sp_update_job
     @job_id = @jobId
   , @notify_level_email = 2
   , @notify_level_netsend = 2
   , @notify_level_page = 2
   , @notify_email_operator_name = @ValidOperator

IF
     @@ERROR <> 0
OR
     @ReturnCode <> 0
Begin
     GOTO QuitWithRollback
End

EXEC @ReturnCode = msdb.dbo.sp_add_jobschedule
     @job_id = @jobId
   , @name = N'Nightly Index Tuning Schedule'
   , @enabled = 1
   , @freq_type = 4
   , @freq_interval = 1
   , @freq_subday_type = 1
   , @freq_subday_interval = 0
   , @freq_relative_interval = 0
   , @freq_recurrence_factor = 0
   , @active_start_date = 20080101
   , @active_end_date = 99991231
   , @active_start_time = @NightlyStartTime
   , @active_end_time = 235959

IF
     @@ERROR <> 0
OR
     @ReturnCode <> 0
Begin
     GOTO QuitWithRollback
```

```
End

EXEC @ReturnCode = msdb.dbo.sp_add_jobserver
     @job_id = @jobId
   , @server_name = N'(local)'
IF
     @@ERROR <> 0
OR
     @ReturnCode <> 0
Begin
     GOTO QuitWithRollback
End

COMMIT TRANSACTION

GOTO EndSave

QuitWithRollback:
   IF @@TRANCOUNT > 0
   Begin
        ROLLBACK TRANSACTION
   End

EndSave:

GO

--Create Index Maintenance Job

EXEC _dbaMain..spxCreateIDXMaintenanceJob
     'sa'
   , 'sqlsupport'
   , 'Sunday'
   , 0



--Setup DDL Triggers
--Setup Create Database or Drop Database DDL Trigger

/****** Object:  DdlTrigger [AuditDatabaseDDL]
               Script Date: 02/05/2009 19:56:33 ******/
SET ANSI_NULLS ON
GO

SET QUOTED_IDENTIFIER ON
GO

CREATE TRIGGER [AuditDatabaseDDL]
ON ALL SERVER
FOR CREATE_DATABASE, DROP_DATABASE
AS
```

```
DECLARE @data XML,
       @tsqlCommand NVARCHAR(MAX),
       @eventType NVARCHAR(100),
       @serverName NVARCHAR(100),
       @loginName NVARCHAR(100),
       @username NVARCHAR(100),
       @databaseName NVARCHAR(100),
       @objectName NVARCHAR(100),
       @objectType NVARCHAR(100),
       @emailBody NVARCHAR(MAX)

SET @data = EVENTDATA()
SET @tsqlCommand =
EVENTDATA().value('(/EVENT_INSTANCE/TSQLCommand/CommandText)[1]
','nvarchar(max)')
SET @eventType =
EVENTDATA().value('(/EVENT_INSTANCE/EventType)[1]','nvarchar(ma
x)')
SET @serverName =
EVENTDATA().value('(/EVENT_INSTANCE/ServerName)[1]','nvarchar(m
ax)')
SET @loginName =
EVENTDATA().value('(/EVENT_INSTANCE/LoginName)[1]','nvarchar(ma
x)')
SET @userName =
EVENTDATA().value('(/EVENT_INSTANCE/UserName)[1]','nvarchar(max
)')
SET @databaseName =
EVENTDATA().value('(/EVENT_INSTANCE/DatabaseName)[1]','nvarchar
(max)')
SET @objectName =
EVENTDATA().value('(/EVENT_INSTANCE/ObjectName)[1]','nvarchar(m
ax)')
SET @objectType =
EVENTDATA().value('(/EVENT_INSTANCE/ObjectType)[1]','nvarchar(m
ax)')

SET @emailBody = + '--------------------------------' +
CHAR(13)
               + '- DDL Trigger Activation Report     -' +
CHAR(13)
               + '--------------------------------------' +
CHAR(13)
               + 'Sql Command: '
                  + ISNULL(@tsqlCommand, 'No Command Given') +
CHAR(13)
               + 'Event Type: '
                  + ISNULL(@eventType, 'No Event Type Given') +
CHAR(13)
```

```
                + 'Server Name:
                  ' + ISNULL(@serverName, 'No Server Given') +
CHAR(13)
                + 'Login Name: '
                  + ISNULL(@loginName, 'No LOGIN Given') +
CHAR(13)
                + 'User Name: '
                  + ISNULL(@username, 'No User Name Given') +
CHAR(13)
                + 'DB Name: '
                  + ISNULL(@databaseName, 'No Database Given') +
CHAR(13)
                + 'Object Name: '
                  + ISNULL(@objectName, 'No Object Given') +
CHAR(13)
                + 'Object Type: '
                  + ISNULL(@objectType, 'No Type Given') +
CHAR(13)
                + '---------------------------------------------';

EXEC msdb..sp_send_dbmail @profile_name='Admin Profile',
@recipients='<yourmail@yourmail.com>, @subject='DDL Alteration
Trigger', @body=@emailBody

GO

SET ANSI_NULLS OFF
GO

SET QUOTED_IDENTIFIER OFF
GO

ENABLE TRIGGER [AuditDatabaseDDL] ON ALL SERVER
GO


-- Change Model Database Recovery Option from Full to Simple
-- This will prevent unmitigated log file growth.


ALTER Database Model
SET RECOVERY SIMPLE

-- Turn configurations back off

sp_configure 'xp_cmdshell', 0
reconfigure

sp_configure 'Show Advanced Options', 0
Reconfigure
```

```
-- End Script
PRINT 'All Done...Add Server to DBA Repository for further
documentation'
```

Listing 1.2: The SQL Server automated configuration script.

Using the above script you will, in about 3 seconds, have configured many options that might have taken 30 minutes to do manually. Without such a script it is very easy to miss an important configuration such as setting the model database to "simple" recovery mode.

This script is a mere sampling of what you can control and automate, prior to releasing the server into the wild. As we proceed through the rest of the book, I will demonstrate many more scripts that can be used to make your life easier, freeing up more of your time to write or extend your own scripts and then give them back to me so I can use them. Ha!

Bon Appétit

Just because your server installation is now complete, and is stepping out into the real world to be eaten alive by various applications, it is by no means out of your hands. No, now you have the task of protecting it. Every day. The first step toward that goal is to make sure you monitor, maintain and document the server during the course of its life.

Documenting will be the focus of Chapter 2, where I will introduce you to the DBA Repository, a tool that incorporates the combined reporting and data migration strengths of SQL Server Reporting Services and SQL Server Integration Services. It is within the DBA Repository that you will truly come to know your servers.

CHAPTER 2: THE SQL SERVER LANDSCAPE

I started my DBA career working for a small software development company, where I had a handful of SQL Servers to administer. As in many small companies, the term "DBA" was interpreted rather loosely. I was also, as required, a Windows server administrator, network engineer, developer, and technical support representative. I divided my day equally between these tasks and only actually spent a fifth of my professional time managing the SQL infrastructure.

When I moved on to a much larger organization, I found that my first days, as a DBA managing nearly 100 SQL Servers, were daunting, to the say the least. I was astounded by the lack of documentation! Some fragmented efforts had been made to pull together information about the SQL infrastructure, but it was sparse. As a result, my first week found me manually and hastily clicking through server property windows, perusing SQL Server error logs, pouring over reams of stored procedure code, sifting through SQL Agent job failures on each server, and generally just floundering about picking up whatever tidbits of information I could.

I recall feeling very tired that first weekend and, to add insult to injury, also as though I had accomplished very little. With the wonderful benefit of hindsight that I have while writing this book, I can say that what I really needed in those early weeks was a "documentation tool" that would have allowed me to automate the collection of all of the essential information about every server under my control, and have it stored in a single, central location, for reporting.

Over the course of this chapter, I'll describe how I built just such a documentation tool. First, I'll describe the information that I felt I needed to have about each of the servers under my control and the scripts to retrieve this information for each server. I'll then move on to discuss the various ways of automating this data collection process over all of your servers. Finally, I'll demonstrate how I actually achieved it, using SSIS and a central DBA Repository database.

NOTE
The material in this chapter describing how to build a DBA Repository using SSIS and SSRS is adapted with permission from my article "Use SSRS and SSIS to Create a DBA Repository," which originally appeared in SQL Server Magazine, February 2008, copyright Penton Media, Inc.

What information is required?

Before I could even begin to build a documentation tool for my SQL Servers, I had to answer one very important question: what information did I need to gather in order to help me do my job better as a DBA? I am sure that many such lists have been compiled, by numerous DBAs. My list encompasses the categories of information that I saw as pertinent, and was as follows:

- **Server Information** (Server name, SQL Server version, collation information, and so on)
- **Database Management** (Primarily to monitor data and log file growth)
- **Database Backups** (Have backups run successfully? Which databases are in Full recovery mode versus Simple or Bulk-Logged? Are we doing regular log backups of Full recovery databases?)
- **Security** (Who has access to do what?)
- **SQL Agent Jobs** (Which could include those that run your database backups).

Over the following sections, I'll present a series of queries (I like that expression – a series of queries) that I used to collect the required information in each category.

Server information

I needed to retrieve a number of useful pieces of server information for each of my servers, such as:

- The server name
- The physical location of the server
- The SQL Server version, level and edition
- Security mode – Either Windows (Integrated) or Mixed mode
- SQL Server collation.

Listing 2.1 shows the script I developed to return this information (at least most of it) for a given server.

```
SELECT CONVERT(CHAR(100), SERVERPROPERTY('Servername'))
                            AS Server,
        CONVERT(CHAR(100), SERVERPROPERTY('ProductVersion'))
                            AS ProductVersion,
        CONVERT(CHAR(100), SERVERPROPERTY('ProductLevel'))
                            AS ProductLevel,
        CONVERT(CHAR(100),
            SERVERPROPERTY('ResourceLastUpdateDateTime'))
                        AS ResourceLastUpdateDateTime,
```

```
         CONVERT(CHAR(100), SERVERPROPERTY('ResourceVersion'))
                                   AS ResourceVersion,
      CASE WHEN SERVERPROPERTY('IsIntegratedSecurityOnly') = 1
           THEN 'Integrated security'
           WHEN SERVERPROPERTY('IsIntegratedSecurityOnly') = 0
            THEN 'Not Integrated security'
       END AS IsIntegratedSecurityOnly,
      CASE WHEN SERVERPROPERTY('EngineEdition') = 1
                              THEN 'Personal Edition'
            WHEN SERVERPROPERTY('EngineEdition') = 2
                              THEN 'Standard Edition'
            WHEN SERVERPROPERTY('EngineEdition') = 3
                              THEN 'Enterprise Edition'
            WHEN SERVERPROPERTY('EngineEdition') = 4
                              THEN 'Express Edition'
        END AS EngineEdition,
        CONVERT(CHAR(100), SERVERPROPERTY('InstanceName'))
                                      AS InstanceName,
        CONVERT(CHAR(100),
SERVERPROPERTY('ComputerNamePhysicalNetBIOS'))
                        AS ComputerNamePhysicalNetBIOS,
        CONVERT(CHAR(100), SERVERPROPERTY('LicenseType'))
                                      AS LicenseType,
        CONVERT(CHAR(100), SERVERPROPERTY('NumLicenses'))
                                      AS NumLicenses,
        CONVERT(CHAR(100), SERVERPROPERTY('BuildClrVersion'))
                                      AS BuildClrVersion,
        CONVERT(CHAR(100), SERVERPROPERTY('Collation'))
                                      AS Collation,
        CONVERT(CHAR(100), SERVERPROPERTY('CollationID'))
                                      AS CollationID,
        CONVERT(CHAR(100), SERVERPROPERTY('ComparisonStyle'))
                                      AS ComparisonStyle,
        CASE WHEN CONVERT(CHAR(100),
SERVERPROPERTY('EditionID')) = -1253826760
            THEN 'Desktop Edition'
            WHEN SERVERPROPERTY('EditionID') = -1592396055
            THEN 'Express Edition'
            WHEN SERVERPROPERTY('EditionID') = -1534726760
            THEN 'Standard Edition'
            WHEN SERVERPROPERTY('EditionID') = 1333529388
            THEN 'Workgroup Edition'
            WHEN SERVERPROPERTY('EditionID') = 1804890536
            THEN 'Enterprise Edition'
            WHEN SERVERPROPERTY('EditionID') = -323382091
            THEN 'Personal Edition'
            WHEN SERVERPROPERTY('EditionID') = -2117995310
            THEN 'Developer Edition'
            WHEN SERVERPROPERTY('EditionID') = 610778273
            THEN 'Enterprise Evaluation Edition'
            WHEN SERVERPROPERTY('EditionID') = 1044790755
            THEN 'Windows Embedded SQL'
```

```
                WHEN SERVERPROPERTY('EditionID') = 4161255391
                THEN 'Express Edition with Advanced Services'
            END AS ProductEdition,
            CASE WHEN CONVERT(CHAR(100),
SERVERPROPERTY('IsClustered')) = 1
                THEN 'Clustered'
                WHEN SERVERPROPERTY('IsClustered') = 0
                                    THEN 'Not Clustered'
                WHEN SERVERPROPERTY('IsClustered') = NULL
                                    THEN 'Error'
            END AS IsClustered,
            CASE WHEN CONVERT(CHAR(100),
SERVERPROPERTY('IsFullTextInstalled')) = 1
                THEN 'Full-text is installed'
                WHEN SERVERPROPERTY('IsFullTextInstalled') = 0
                THEN 'Full-text is not installed'
                WHEN SERVERPROPERTY('IsFullTextInstalled') = NULL
THEN 'Error'
            END AS IsFullTextInstalled,
            CONVERT(CHAR(100), SERVERPROPERTY('SqlCharSet'))
                                    AS SqlCharSet,
            CONVERT(CHAR(100), SERVERPROPERTY('SqlCharSetName'))
                                    AS SqlCharSetName,
            CONVERT(CHAR(100), SERVERPROPERTY('SqlSortOrder'))
                                    AS SqlSortOrderID,
            CONVERT(CHAR(100), SERVERPROPERTY('SqlSortOrderName'))
                                    AS SqlSortOrderName
ORDER BY CONVERT(CHAR(100), SERVERPROPERTY('Servername'))
```

Listing 2.1: Server information.

As you can see, it's a pretty simple script that makes liberal use of the
SERVERPROPERTY function to return the required data.

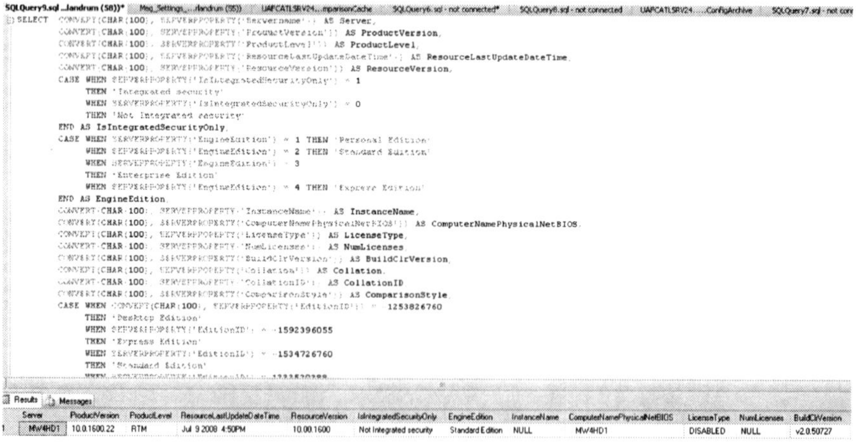

Figure 2.1: Collecting server information.

38

NOTE
All of the various properties of the SERVERPROPERTY function can be found in Books Online or MSDN, see http://msdn.microsoft.com/en-us/library/ms174396.aspx.

If you were to run this query against one of your SQL Servers, you'd see results similar to those shown in Figure 2.1, all of which will be useful in your daily reporting of your infrastructure.

One piece of information that this script does not return is the location of the server. There is no way to glean the location information from a query. Some things, at present, still have to be manually gathered.

Database management

It is obviously important that DBAs know what databases are on each of their servers. While DBAs may not be intimately familiar with every database schema on every SQL Server, it is essential that they are aware of the existence of every database, and at least understand the basic characteristics of each, such as what server they are on, what size they are and where on disk they are located.

You can also gather the information you need to monitor the growth of the data and log files for each database, or answer questions such as "where are the system database files located?" This question brings up the interesting topic of implementing standards across all of your servers. Are the data files for each server stored on the correct, predetermined data drive? The log files on the correct log drive? Are naming conventions consistently enforced? Is each database using the correct default recovery model (e.g. SIMPLE) unless specified otherwise?

You may find that the answer is, generally, "no". It is an unfortunate reality that, often, a DBA will inherit an infrastructure whereby a hodge-podge of different standards have been set and only erratically imposed by a variety of former DBAs. However, once you've got all of this data stored in a central repository, for every server, you can quickly report on how well your current standards have been enforced, and can start the job of pulling the "non-standard" ones into shape. And then, who knows, if you can stay in the position long enough, say ten years, you may actually get to see an infrastructure that properly adheres to all the standards you set forth.

To gather this database management information, you will need to run the same two queries on each SQL 2000, 2005 and 2008 instance. The first of these queries is shown in Listing 2.2. It makes use of the **sp_msforeachdb** system stored procedure, which issues the same query for each database on a server, and saves you the time of writing your own cursor or set-based query to iterate through each database. I create a temp table, **HoldforEachDB** and then populate that table with the results from each database. In this way, I have one result set for all databases on the server, instead of individual result sets for each database, which would have otherwise been the case. Also, since I know that I will ultimately want to get this information from SSIS, and into a central DBA repository, having the temp table pre-defined is ideal.

```
IF EXISTS ( SELECT   *
               FROM      tempdb.dbo.sysobjects
               WHERE    id =
OBJECT_ID(N'[tempdb].[dbo].[HoldforEachDB]') )
    DROP TABLE [tempdb].[dbo].[HoldforEachDB] ;
CREATE TABLE [tempdb].[dbo].[HoldforEachDB]
    (
      [Server] [nvarchar](128) COLLATE
SQL_Latin1_General_CP1_CI_AS
                              NULL,
      [DatabaseName] [nvarchar](128) COLLATE
SQL_Latin1_General_CP1_CI_AS
                              NOT NULL,
      [Size] [int] NOT NULL,
      [File_Status] [int] NULL,
      [Name] [nvarchar](128) COLLATE
SQL_Latin1_General_CP1_CI_AS
                              NOT NULL,
      [Filename] [nvarchar](260) COLLATE
SQL_Latin1_General_CP1_CI_AS
                              NOT NULL,
      [Status] [nvarchar](128) COLLATE
SQL_Latin1_General_CP1_CI_AS
                              NULL,
      [Updateability] [nvarchar](128) COLLATE
SQL_Latin1_General_CP1_CI_AS
                              NULL,
      [User_Access] [nvarchar](128) COLLATE
SQL_Latin1_General_CP1_CI_AS
                              NULL,
      [Recovery] [nvarchar](128) COLLATE
SQL_Latin1_General_CP1_CI_AS
                              NULL
    )
ON  [PRIMARY]
INSERT  INTO [tempdb].[dbo].[HoldforEachDB]
      EXEC sp_MSforeachdb 'SELECT CONVERT(char(100),
SERVERPROPERTY(''Servername'')) AS Server,
              ''?'' as DatabaseName,[?]..sysfiles.size,
[?]..sysfiles.status, [?]..sysfiles.name,
[?]..sysfiles.filename,convert(sysname,DatabasePropertyEx(''?''
,''Status'')) as Status,
convert(sysname,DatabasePropertyEx(''?'',''Updateability'')) as
Updateability,
```

```
convert(sysname,DatabasePropertyEx(''?'',''UserAccess'')) as
User_Access,
convert(sysname,DatabasePropertyEx(''?'',''Recovery'')) as
Recovery From [?]..sysfiles '
```

Listing 2.2: Placing database information into a temporary table.

The second query, shown in Listing 2.3, simply selects from the **HoldforEachDB** temporary table.

```
SELECT [Server]
      , [DatabaseName]
      , [Size]
      , [File_Status]
      , [Name]
      , [Filename]
      , [Status]
      , [Updateability]
      , [User_Access]
      , [Recovery]
   FROM [tempdb].[dbo].[HoldforEachDB]
```

Listing 2.3: Selecting data from the temporary table, HoldForEachDB.

The output of this query can be seen in Figure 2.2, which displays the server name, as well as the database name, size, filename and recovery model.

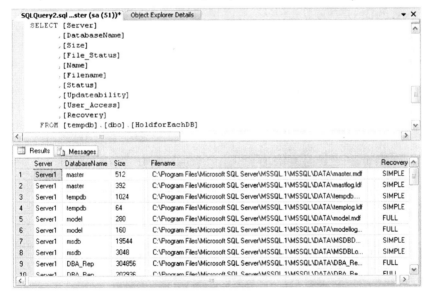

Figure 2.2: Output of database info query.

Database backups

Having backup information is critical for the DBA, especially when working with a large infrastructure. Knowing where the full, differential or log backups are located is more than helpful; it is essential. This type of information can easily be gathered directly from the MSDB database, which has not changed substantially from SQL Server 2000 to 2008. Listing 2.4 shows the driving query for gathering from MSDB the vital database backup information that you need for each server, including information such as backup start date, end data and size. Notice, in the WHERE clause, that this query actually retrieves 30 days worth of history.

```
SELECT   CONVERT(char(100), SERVERPROPERTY('Servername'))
                                              AS Server,
         msdb.dbo.backupmediafamily.logical_device_name,
         msdb.dbo.backupmediafamily.physical_device_name,
         msdb.dbo.backupset.expiration_date,
         msdb.dbo.backupset.name,
         msdb.dbo.backupset.description,
         msdb.dbo.backupset.user_name,
         msdb.dbo.backupset.backup_start_date,
         msdb.dbo.backupset.backup_finish_date,
         CASE msdb..backupset.type
            WHEN 'D' THEN 'Database'
            WHEN 'L' THEN 'Log'
         END AS backup_type,
         msdb.dbo.backupset.backup_size,
         msdb.dbo.backupset.database_name,
         msdb.dbo.backupset.server_name AS Source_Server
FROM     msdb.dbo.backupmediafamily
         INNER JOIN msdb.dbo.backupset ON
msdb.dbo.backupmediafamily.media_set_id =
msdb.dbo.backupset.media_set_id
WHERE    ( CONVERT(datetime,
msdb.dbo.backupset.backup_start_date, 102) >= GETDATE()
         - 30 )
```

Listing 2.4: Query to gather database backup information.

Figure 2.3 shows the output of this backup history query.

Server	logical_device_name	physical_device_name
MW4HD1	Red Gate SQL Backup (5.4.0.55	C:\Documentation\Bulk_Loading_In_Space\LOG_(local)_DBA_Rep_20090217_171344.sqb
MW4HD1	NULL	c:\documentation\dba_log
MW4HD1	Red Gate SQL Backup (5.4.0.55	C:\Documentation\Bulk_Loading_In_Space\LOG_(local)_DBA_Rep_20090217_190408.sqb
MW4HD1	Red Gate SQL Backup (5.4.0.55	C:\Documentation\Bulk_Loading_In_Space\LOG_(local)_DBA_Rep_20090217_192324.sqb
MW4HD1	Red Gate SQL Backup (5.4.0.55	C:\Documentation\Bulk_Loading_In_Space\LOG_(local)_DBA_Rep_20090217_192331.sqb

Figure 2.3: Gathering database backup information.

Security

For security reporting, we essentially want to know who has access to which databases, and with which permissions. A sample query of the kind of information that can be gathered is in shown in Listing 2.5.

```
IF EXISTS ( SELECT   *
            FROM     tempdb.dbo.sysobjects
            WHERE    id =
OBJECT_ID(N'[tempdb].[dbo].[SQL_DB_REP]') )
    DROP TABLE [tempdb].[dbo].[SQL_DB_REP] ;
GO

CREATE TABLE [tempdb].[dbo].[SQL_DB_REP]
    (
        [Server] [varchar](100) NOT NULL,
        [DB_Name] [varchar](70) NOT NULL,
        [User_Name] [nvarchar](90) NULL,
        [Group_Name] [varchar](100) NULL,
        [Account_Type] [varchar](22) NULL,
        [Login_Name] [varchar](80) NULL,
        [Def_DB] [varchar](100) NULL
    )
ON   [PRIMARY]

INSERT  INTO [tempdb].[dbo].[SQL_DB_REP]
        Exec sp_MSForEachDB 'SELECT
        CONVERT(varchar(100), SERVERPROPERTY(''Servername''))
AS Server,
        ''?'' AS DB_Name,usu.name u_name,
            CASE   WHEN (usg.uid is null) THEN ''public''
                   ELSE usg.name
                    END as Group_Name,
            CASE   WHEN usu.isntuser=1 THEN ''Windows Domain
Account''
                   WHEN usu.isntgroup = 1 THEN ''Windows Group''
                   WHEN usu.issqluser = 1 THEN''SQL Account''
                   WHEN usu.issqlrole = 1 THEN ''SQL Role''
                   END as Account_Type,
            lo.loginname,
               lo.dbname AS Def_DB
    FROM
        [?]..sysusers usu LEFT OUTER JOIN
        ([?]..sysmembers mem INNER JOIN
        [?]..sysusers usg ON mem.groupuid = usg.uid)
        ON usu.uid = mem.memberuid LEFT OUTER JOIN
        master.dbo.syslogins  lo ON usu.sid = lo.sid


    WHERE
```

```
       ( usu.islogin = 1 AND
         usu.isaliased = 0 AND
         usu.hasdbaccess = 1) AND
       (usg.issqlrole = 1 OR
        usg.uid is null)'
```

Listing 2.5: Query to return security information about database access.

As for the database management query, a temp table is populated again using **sp_msforeachdb** Ultimately, our SSIS package (**Populate_DBA_Repository**) will read the data from this temp table and then store it in our central repository (**DBA_Rep**).

A simple **Select * from   [tempdb].[dbo].[SQL_DB_REP]**, the output of which is shown in Figure 2.4, delivers a lot of information about security, some of which may be surprising. You might be interested to know, for example, that **"MyDomain\BadUser"** has DBO access to several user databases.

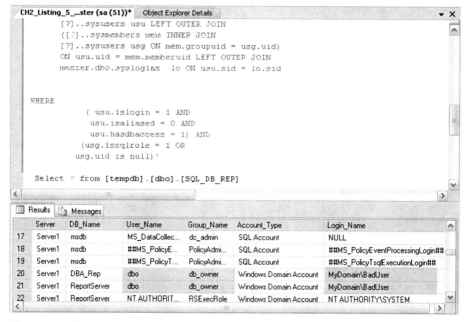

Figure 2.4: Database user access levels.

Over time, policies about who can access production SQL instances inevitably change. You can use this data to formulate a new policy, or bolster your existing policy, to guarantee that only users that you are aware of have access to your database.

SQL Agent jobs

Finally, it is critical that a DBA monitors closely the status of any SQL Agent jobs running on their servers so that they are aware of any failed jobs, unscheduled jobs, disabled jobs, notifications and so on. In most large shops, failed jobs will notify the on-call DBA and they will be expected to respond immediately, especially in the case of failed backup jobs.

When using SQL Agent to schedule your jobs, it is very important that you know how the jobs are performing. Over time, jobs are added and modified and these changes need to be known to the DBA team in case any issues arise. Also, some jobs, such as business processes scheduled to move data, will not be owned by the DBA. Any delay or failure of these jobs would be unsettling for business users waiting to make decisions on the loaded data.

For these reasons, I make sure to collect almost every piece of information about SQL Agent jobs, for storage in the repository. Listing 2.6 shows the query I use. As you can see, it returns many fields from the system database, MSDB. Unfortunately, the MSDB schema changed from version 2000 to 2005, primarily for the job schedule information, so you'll need two different versions of the query depending on whether you're using SQL 2000 or 2005/2008. Listing 2.6 shows the SQL Server 2005/2008 version. The SQL 2000 version will be available in the script download file for the book (see http://www.simple-talk.com/RedGateBooks/RodneyLandrum/SQL_Server_Tacklebox_Code.zip).

```
SELECT   CONVERT(nvarchar(128), SERVERPROPERTY('Servername')) AS
Server,
         msdb.dbo.sysjobs.job_id,
         msdb.dbo.sysjobs.name,
         msdb.dbo.sysjobs.enabled AS Job_Enabled,
         msdb.dbo.sysjobs.description,
         msdb.dbo.sysjobs.notify_level_eventlog,
         msdb.dbo.sysjobs.notify_level_email,
         msdb.dbo.sysjobs.notify_level_netsend,
         msdb.dbo.sysjobs.notify_level_page,
         msdb.dbo.sysjobs.notify_email_operator_id,
         msdb.dbo.sysjobs.date_created,
         msdb.dbo.syscategories.name AS Category_Name,
         msdb.dbo.sysjobschedules.next_run_date,
         msdb.dbo.sysjobschedules.next_run_time,
         msdb.dbo.sysjobservers.last_run_outcome,
         msdb.dbo.sysjobservers.last_outcome_message,
         msdb.dbo.sysjobservers.last_run_date,
         msdb.dbo.sysjobservers.last_run_time,
         msdb.dbo.sysjobservers.last_run_duration,
         msdb.dbo.sysoperators.name AS Notify_Operator,
         msdb.dbo.sysoperators.email_address,
         msdb.dbo.sysjobs.date_modified,
```

```
            GETDATE() AS Package_run_date,
       msdb.dbo.sysschedules.name AS Schedule_Name,
       msdb.dbo.sysschedules.enabled,
       msdb.dbo.sysschedules.freq_type,
       msdb.dbo.sysschedules.freq_interval,
       msdb.dbo.sysschedules.freq_subday_interval,
       msdb.dbo.sysschedules.freq_subday_type,
       msdb.dbo.sysschedules.freq_relative_interval,
       msdb.dbo.sysschedules.freq_recurrence_factor,
       msdb.dbo.sysschedules.active_start_date,
       msdb.dbo.sysschedules.active_end_date,
       msdb.dbo.sysschedules.active_start_time,
       msdb.dbo.sysschedules.active_end_time,
       msdb.dbo.sysschedules.date_created AS
Date_Sched_Created,
       msdb.dbo.sysschedules.date_modified AS
Date_Sched_Modified,
       msdb.dbo.sysschedules.version_number,
       msdb.dbo.sysjobs.version_number AS Job_Version
FROM   msdb.dbo.sysjobs
       INNER JOIN msdb.dbo.syscategories ON
msdb.dbo.sysjobs.category_id =
msdb.dbo.syscategories.category_id
       LEFT OUTER JOIN msdb.dbo.sysoperators ON
msdb.dbo.sysjobs.notify_page_operator_id =
msdb.dbo.sysoperators.id
       LEFT OUTER JOIN msdb.dbo.sysjobservers ON
msdb.dbo.sysjobs.job_id = msdb.dbo.sysjobservers.job_id
       LEFT OUTER JOIN msdb.dbo.sysjobschedules ON
msdb.dbo.sysjobschedules.job_id = msdb.dbo.sysjobs.job_id
       LEFT OUTER JOIN msdb.dbo.sysschedules ON
msdb.dbo.sysjobschedules.schedule_id =
msdb.dbo.sysschedules.schedule_id
```

Listing 2.6: SQL Agent Job Information query.

Figure 2.5 shows the output of the SQL Agent Job Information query.

```
CH2_Listing_5_...ster (sa (51))*    Object Explorer Details                          ▼ X
   SELECT  CONVEPT(nvarchar(128), SEPVERPROPERTY('Servername')) AS Server,
           msdb.dbo.sysjobs.job_id,
           msdb.dbo.sysjobs.name,
           msdb.dbo.sysjobs.enabled AS Job_Enabled,
           msdb.dbo.sysjobs.description,
           msdb.dbo.sysjobs.notify_level_eventlog,
           msdb.dbo.sysjobs.notify_level_email,
           msdb.dbo.sysjobs.notify_level_netsend,
           msdb.dbo.sysjobs.notify_level_page,
           msdb.dbo.sysjobs.notify_email_operator_id,
           msdb.dbo.sysjobs.date_created,
           msdb.dbo.syscategories.name AS Category_Name,
```

	Server	job_id	name	Job_Enabled	description	notify_level_eventlog
1	Server1	94313CEF-...	ETL Process with Restore from UNC	1	No description available.	0
2	Server1	7998E108-...	Run Long	1	No description available.	0
3	Server1	D3C17A95...	SSIS Long Running Jobs	1	No description available.	0
4	Server1	46006216-...	Load All Data From UNC and Backup	1	No description available.	0
5	Server1	07DA5C75-...	Backup - Full [All]	1	No description available.	0
6	Server1	F2D18604-...	syspolicy_purge_history	1	No description available.	0
7	Server1	CECE9CA...	collection_set_1_noncached_collect_...	1	Data Collector job for c...	2
8	Server1	83F61220-...	collection_set_2_collection	0	No description available.	2
9	Server1	4CCFC9E2...	collection_set_3_collection	0	No description available.	2

Figure 2.5: SQL Agent Job Information query output.

Automating information retrieval

The information provided by these scripts, regarding database backups, SQL Agent jobs, data file management, security and so on, is moderately useful when examined on a server-by-server basis. However, the real power comes when you can automate the collection of this data, from multiple servers, and store the output centrally, for reporting. It really does make finding potential issues orders of magnitude faster.

There are several options for building a "repository of DBA information". All of them would require you to create a central database to store all the data, but there any several different ways in which you can automate the collection of this data across all your servers. The following list shows some of the tools or techniques I have reviewed that provide solutions to the problem of gathering and centrally storing SQL Server administrative data.

- **SQL Server Health and History Tool** – though quite dated now, this is one of the first free tools I found that would collect information from numerous databases and store it in a central database for reporting. It also includes a separate report download. The tool can still be downloaded from:

> http://www.microsoft.com/downloads/details.aspx?FamilyID=eedd10d
> 6-75f7-4763-86de-d2347b8b5f89&displaylang=en

- **PowerShell** – while I am not necessarily a developer, I do aspire, occasionally, to expand my knowledge base and find tools that will make my life easier. One of these tools is PowerShell, which has been incorporated into SQL Server 2008 and promoted extensively by Microsoft. While I have not used this tool to build DBA solutions, others have and it is worth reviewing some of their solutions. One such solution, by Allen White, can be found at: http://www.simple-talk.com/sql/database-administration/let-powershell-do-an-inventory-of-your-servers/

- **SQL Server 2008 Data Collector** – this is a new feature in SQL Server 2008 that you may choose to use in your day-to-day DBA data gathering tasks. Once such technique, performance data gathering, is described by Brad McGehee at: http://www.simple-talk.com/sql/learn-sql-server/sql-server-2008-performance-data-collector/.

In addition to free tools and technologies, you could certainly acquire a vendor application that will provide some form of out-of-the-box "DBA repository". There is no shame in that whatsoever. Many DBAs think that the only way they will get the solution they really want is to build it themselves, often believing that they will save their company lots of money in the process. While this attitude is admirable, it is often misguided. For one, it is unlikely that you'll be able to create a documenting solution that will match the capability of a vendor product, the most obvious reason being that you are one person and your time will be limited. If your time can be given full bore to such an endeavor, you will then have to weigh the man-hours it will take you to build, test, and deploy and maintain the solution.

Even without huge time constraints, a vendor-supplied solution is likely to have features that a home-grown one will never have, plus updates are regularly dispersed and features continually added. In general, my advice to DBAs is that it's certainly worth researching vendor tools: if you find one that works for you, then that's probably the best route to go down.

However, despite the apparent advantages of going down the Microsoft or vendor tool route, that is not the way that I went and here is why: I reasoned that as a DBA I would need to use SSIS often, either because I would be directly responsible for data loading/ transfer tasks that needed SISS, or I would have to work with developers who used SSIS.

In short, a considerable fringe benefit of building my own repository solution would be that it would require me to expand my knowledge of creating all kinds of

SSIS packages and use objects I would not normally use. Also, I did not want to be in a position where I did not know more than the developer. That is just me.

So, in fact, I set out on the project primarily to gain valuable experience in SSIS. Fortunately for me, and many other DBAs with whom I have shared the solution, it turned out to be quite useful. For the remainder of this chapter, I will focus on how to create and use the DBA Repository, how to load it with all of the previously-described database information, using SSIS, and finally how to generate reports on the assembled data using SSRS.

The DBA repository solution

The DBA Repository solution consists of three components:

- A SQL Server database call **DBA_Rep**
- An SSIS package that contains data flow tasks designed to query a list of SQL Servers and store the results in the **DBA_Rep** database
- A series of Reporting Services reports and queries that the DBA team can use to make important decisions about their SQL Server infrastructure.

I will introduce each piece of the solution individually and then marry them together to show how a DBA can use this solution every day. The code download file for the book (http://www.simple-talk.com/RedGateBooks/RodneyLandrum/SQL_Server_Tacklebox_Code.zip) includes all the components of this solution, so that you can deploy and extend as you see fit.

The DBA_Rep database

If you are going to store all of this information centrally in SQL Server, you need a database. When I designed the **DBA_Rep** database, I decided to link each category of information, such as Server, Database Management, Security, and job information, using the SQL Server name as the key field.

With hindsight, the database design could have been a bit more normalized, with key columns other than the server name, for example, but for the most part it has worked as I intended and performs well. Many of the joining queries you will see, when reporting off the **DBA_Rep** database, use this SQL Server Name key field. Figure 2.6 shows the tables in the **DBA_Rep** database, as well as the columns specific to the **SQL_Servers** table.

As you can see, the **DBA_Rep** database is fairly straightforward in terms of the scope of information it stores. There are tables for logins (**SQL_Logins**), Databases, (**Database_Info** and **Databases**), SQL Agent job information (**Jobs**), server-specific data (**SQL_Servers**) and the server location (**Server_Location**). In this case, location refers to the geographical location of the server, like Beijing or Houston or even Pensacola (shameless hometown plug). This is the one piece of information that will need to be manually identified for the DBA repository.

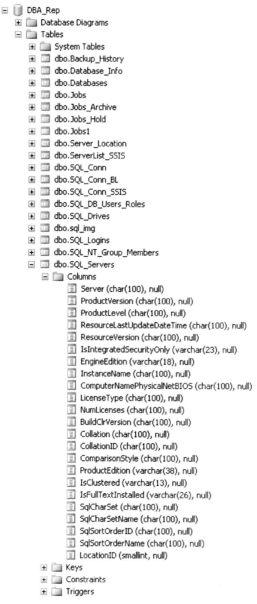

Figure 2.6: DBA_Rep sample schema.

On this note, it is a pity that Microsoft, at present, does not offer "Extended Server Properties", in the same way that they provide Extended Properties for the internal documentation of database objects. For example, I can create a table in a database and add an extended property that explains the purpose of the table but I cannot do the same at the server level. If there was an extended Server property that held the location of the server, and its primary function, I could automate the collection of this data and store it in the **SQL_Servers** table, which is designed to store the bevy of Server information that we have collected about our SQL servers, including version, edition, collation and so on.

To demonstrate how the DBA repository works, I will walk through an example using the **SQL_Servers** table, and how it is populated using the SSIS package. The other tables in the database, aside from **Server_Location**, are populated in the same way.

The SSIS package to load the DBA_Rep database

When I embarked on this project, the only previous attempt to consolidate and document server information had taken the form of a fairly primitive DTS package. The main problems with it were:

- The package had to be updated manually with each new server addition
- It became unwieldy when more than 10 servers existed because every server connection was manually created and maintained.

With over 100 servers for which to gather information, it was clear that this DTS package was not up to the job.

SQL Server Integration Services contains three objects that make the process of gathering information from multiple servers clean and efficient: **Variables**, **Foreach Loop Containers** and **Expressions**. These three objects provided the basis for the entire **DBA_Rep** documentation solution.

When I want to add or remove a server, all I need to do is add this server to, or update a bit flag on, a driving table, called **ServerList_SSIS** (more on this shortly).

The SSIS package that populates the **DBA_Rep** database is called **Populate_DBA_Rep**. Figure 2.7 shows several of the tasks that comprise the SSIS package.

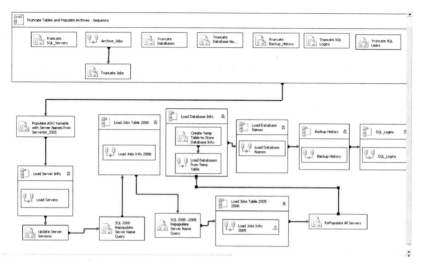

Figure 2.7: Populate_DBA_Rep SSIS package.

Over the following sections, I'll walk through every step that is required to retrieve Server information from your SQL Server instances, and store the data in the **SQL_Servers** tables of **DBA_Rep**. Once you've seen how this section of the package works, you'll understand how the others work too.

The only information the package needs in order to do its work is the names of the SQL instances that we wish to document. In a way, this is a manual discovery process. If you were to shell out to a command prompt where you have SQL Server installed and execute **"sqlcmd /Lc"**, you may see something similar to that shown in Figure 2.8.

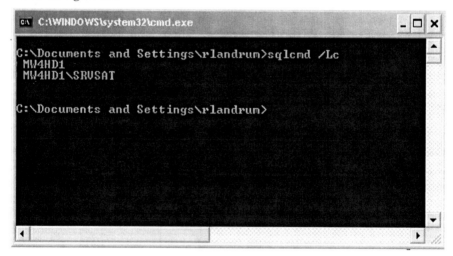

Figure 2.8: List of SQL Servers using SQLCMD.

In this simple example, we have discovered one server, with two instances of SQL Server, **MW4HD1** and **MW4HD1\SRVSAT**. The former is a version 10, or SQL Server 2008, instance, and the latter a version 9, or SQL Server 2005, instance. This is a simple scenario, but the principles would be exactly the same were the instances installed on two separate servers on the network, or if there were hundreds of instances distributed across 10, 50 or 200 servers on your network. In short, this solution will work with any number of servers.

All I need to do is place these server instance details into a table, called `ServerList_SSIS`, which can then be used to "seed" the `Populate_DBA_Repository` SSIS package. The `ServerList_SSIS` table is shown in Figure 2.9.

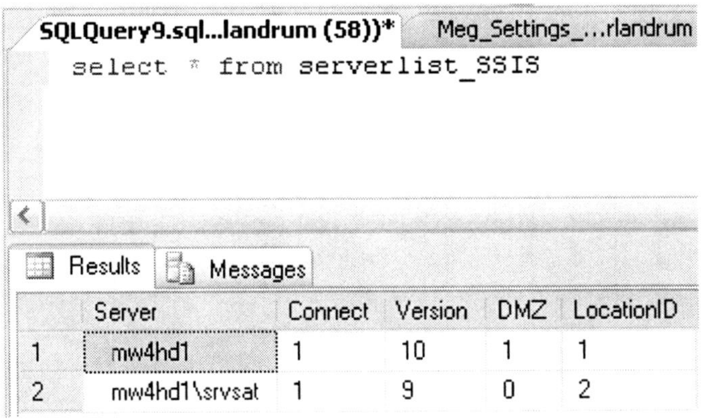

Figure 2.9: The Serverlist_SSIS table.

As you can see, the Server column stores the instance names. The other columns in the table are as follows:

- **Connect** – a smallint data type. If it has a value of "1" for the server, the SSIS package will attempt to connect otherwise it will skip the server.
- **Version** – version of the SQL Server instance, 8, 9 or 10 for SQL Server 2000, 2005 and 2008 respectively. This field is used after the package execution to update the servers that are added to the `SQL_Servers` table that contains the information for each SQL Server from Listing 2.1 of this chapter.
- **DMZ** – used for specific connection types where SQL Authentication has to be employed.
- **LocationID** – denotes the geographic location of the server. A join to the Server_Location table, on `LocationID`, will reveal the location details, such as a city name or region.

53

We are now ready to walk through the steps that comprise the SSIS package. The basic objective is to have the package load, and "spin" through, the list of SQL Server instances in our Serverlist_SSIS table and, one by one, connect to the appropriate server, execute the queries, and then store the results in the DBA_Rep database.

Truncate tables in DBA_REP

The top portion of the package, shown in Figure 2.7, simply truncates all of the tables so that you can subsequently insert fresh, clean data. So, in this case, we will simply have a "Truncate SQL_Servers" control flow task that truncates the **SQL_Servers** table. While there is no archival process for the **SQL_Servers** table, there is simple archiving functionality for the Jobs query. If you need to maintain archival information for your server information all that is required is that you add another data flow to append data to an archive table, prior to performing the truncate.

Populate ADO variable with server names from Serverlist_SSIS

This task populates an ADO System Object variable, called **SQL_RS**, with the server instances names, which it retrieves from the **ServerList_SSIS** table. The query that is used to populate the **SQL_RS** object variable is shown in Listing 2.7.

```
SELECT LTRIM(RTRIM(Server)) AS servername
FROM ServerList_SSIS
WHERE (Connect = 1) AND (DMZ = 0)
ORDER BY LTRIM(RTRIM(Server))
```

Listing 2.7: Populating the SQL_RS variable.

In SSIS you can use many types of variables, such as a String variable and a System Object variable. In order to iterate through each server in the **ServerLIst_SSIS** table, I had to use both. The ForEachLoop container that iterates through the list of server requires the ADO object source type of variable. However, the Expressions that dynamically control the actual connection string of the target servers (explained shortly) require a string variable. Figure 2.10 shows the "Populate ADO Variable with Server Named from **Serverlist_SSIS**" task, as well as the list of variables that I use.

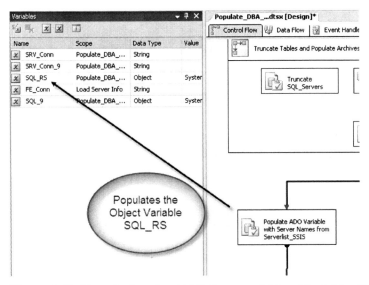

Figure 2.10: Populating the ADO System Object Variable, SQL_RS.

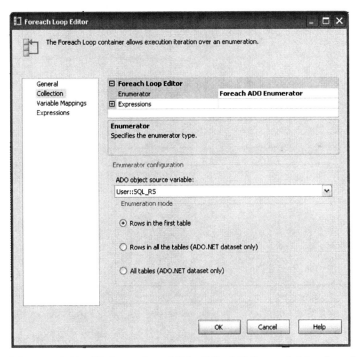

Figure 2.11: Using the SQL_RS ADO variable in the Foreach Loop container.

Load server info

Once the **SQL_RS** Object variable is populated with a list of servers from the **ServerList_SSIS** table, which in this case will be two instances, this ADO variable is fed into the next task, "Load Server Info". In this task, a Foreach Loop Container object enumerates through the list of servers in the **SQL_RS** variable, as shown in Figure 2.11.

Notice that the **SQL_RS** variable is referenced now as **User::SQL_RS**. If you click to the "Variable Mappings" tab of the Foreach Loop editor, you will see that this object variable will be used to populate a string variable called **SRV_Conn**, as shown in Figure 2.12.

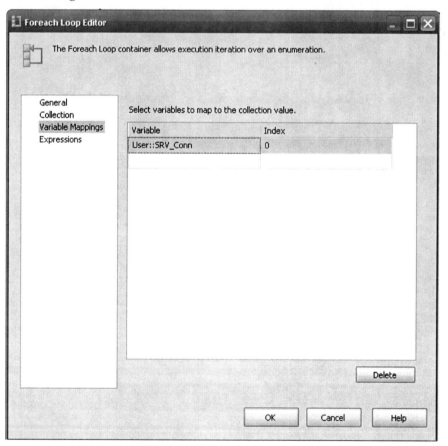

Figure 2.12: Mapping the ADO Object variable to a string variable, SRV_Conn.

This mapping of Object-to-String ultimately leads to the final dynamic association, and that is to the Connection Manager object.

Connection manager

The Connection Manager object, called **MultiServer**, controls which servers to connect to in order to execute the underlying SQL code, in this case the script shown in Listing 2.1. In other words, the **Multiserver** Connection Manager object is used to connect to each listed SQL Server instance, for every Foreach Loop Container in the **Populate_DBA_Rep** package. You can see other Connection Manager objects, as well as the **MultiServer** object, in Figure 2.13.

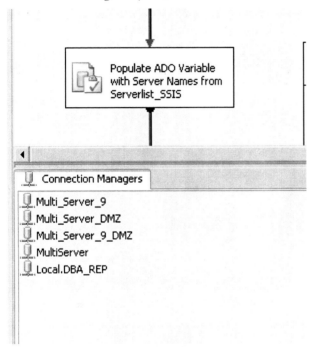

Figure 2.13: Connection Manager objects in Populate_DBA_Rep SSIS package.

All of the **Multi_Server_XXX** objects are used in the same way as **Multiserver**, but control connections to various locations and versions; **Multi_Server_9**, for example, is for connections to SQL Server 2005 instances, and **Multi_Server9_DMZ** connects to SQL Server 2005 instances in the DMZ, and thus knows to use SQL authentication and not Windows authentication in cases where cross domain authentication may not exist for the account executing the package. The **Local.DBA_Rep** object is the Connection Manager for the **DBA_Rep** database, where the gathered server information will be stored.

Figure 2.14 shows the Properties window for the **MultiServer** Connection Manager object.

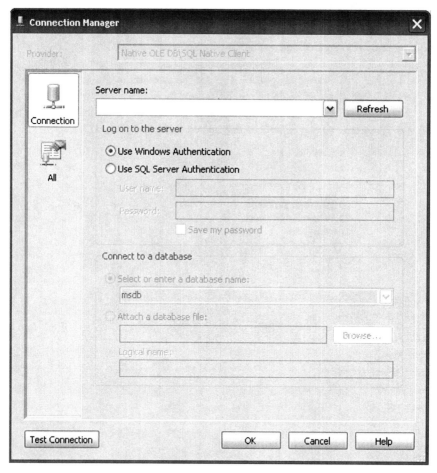

Figure 2.14: Connection Manager property with blank Server name.

Notice that the Server name property value is blank. This is because this value is populated at runtime from the **SRV_Conn** string variable, from every Foreach Loop Container object in the SSIS package.

So how do you populate the server name property with the values stored in the **SRV_Conn** string variable? That is easy. SSIS, along with other Microsoft technologies like Reporting Services, allows you to use Expressions, which are very useful in controlling object properties including, in this case, the server name. Figure 2.15 shows the Properties window for the **Multiserver** object.

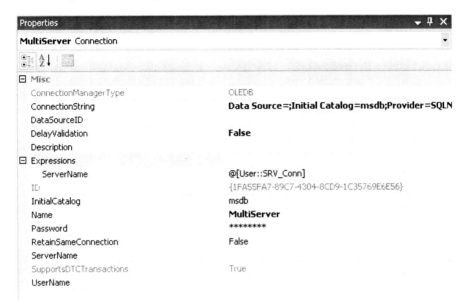

Figure 2.15: Assigning the User::SRV_Conn variable to the ServerName property.

Notice that the expression @[User::SRV_Conn] variable is assigned to the ServerName property. At runtime the ServerName Expression, which is part of the Connection Manager, is populated with the current value of the SRV_Conn variable. As the Foreach Loop container iterates through the server list that was derived from the Populate_ADO Variable From ServerList_SSIS task, the value for the expression changes dynamically and the next server in the list is assigned to variable, and queried. This continues until there are no more servers in the list. All that is required is that you know that they are in the ServerList_SSIS table and have the Connect field set to 1.

Executing the package

Now that we know how to populate DBA_Rep, via the SSIS Populate_DBA_Rep package, let's execute the package and review the results. Figure 2.16 shows the Populate_DBA_Rep package executing in real time (the task to populate the SQL_Servers table is on the left).

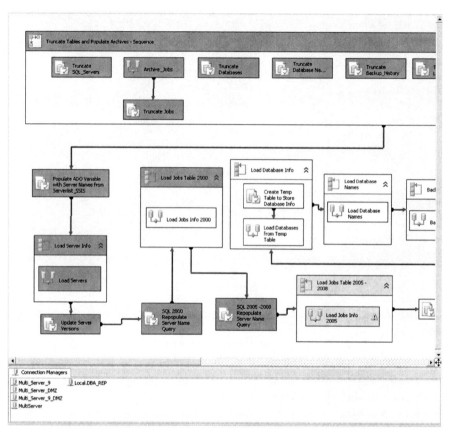

Figure 2.16: Populate_DBA_Rep package executing.

At the start of this chapter, I ran a script that retrieved Server information for a single server. With this package, I can execute this script, and all the others, against as many servers as necessary, and return all the results to the central **DBA_Rep** repository.

Listing 2.8 shows a typical reporting query against the recently-populated repository.

```
select   SQL_Servers.Server,
         SQL_Servers.ProductVersion,
         SQL_Servers.ProductLevel,
         SQL_Servers.ResourceLastUpdateDateTime,
         SQL_Servers.ResourceVersion,
         SQL_Servers.IsIntegratedSecurityOnly,
         SQL_Servers.EngineEdition,
         SQL_Servers.InstanceName,
         SQL_Servers.ComputerNamePhysicalNetBIOS,
         SQL_Servers.LicenseType,
```

```
         SQL_Servers.NumLicenses,
         SQL_Servers.BuildClrVersion,
         SQL_Servers.[Collation],
         SQL_Servers.CollationID,
         SQL_Servers.ComparisonStyle,
         SQL_Servers.ProductEdition,
         SQL_Servers.IsClustered,
         SQL_Servers.IsFullTextInstalled,
         SQL_Servers.SqlCharSet,
         SQL_Servers.SqlCharSetName,
         SQL_Servers.SqlSortOrderID,
         SQL_Servers.SqlSortOrderName,
         SQL_Servers.LocationID
from     SQL_Servers
```

Listing 2.8: Selecting rows from the DBA_Rep table SQL-Servers.

The output, as you can see in Figure 2.17, shows data for the two SQL Server instances, **MW4HD1** and **MW4HD1\SRVSAT**.

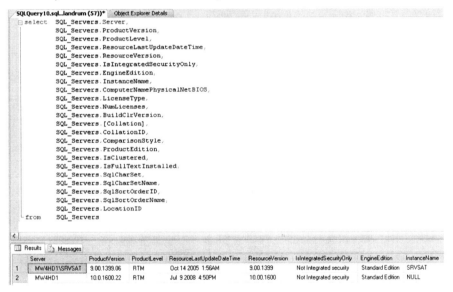

Figure 2.17: Output of multiple servers in the DBA_Rep database.

After assuring that all is successful, you can schedule this package to run via SQL Agent. I have done this in my environment and I find that running it during production hours, say once every 3 hours, has no overhead and keeps data relatively fresh for immediate viewing. I have seen it run in about 15 minutes for 70 servers.

SSRS reporting

More powerful than ad hoc querying of **DBA_Rep** is designing fully fledged Reporting Services reports that can be scheduled and subscribed to. You can also offer a level of historical data viewing via SSRS execution snapshots.

While I have created and written about many SSRS reports that I have developed for the **DBA_Rep** solution, one SSRS report, in particular, stands out for me, as I use it daily for many tasks. It is the Job Interval Report and it allows me to filter out SQL Agent Job information by a range of criteria, including whether or not the job is scheduled or enabled, if it is a database backup job, and also if it failed or succeeded on the last run. Additional details tell me how long the job ran, at what time and even how many jobs exist on each monitored server.

Figure 2.18 shows the Job Interval Report listing all jobs that are labeled as "backups", based on the parameter "Backup Jobs Only". This helps me narrow down my search criteria, for server, location and job status. While a detailed description of creating such reports is outside the scope of this chapter, I've included several of them in the code download for the book.

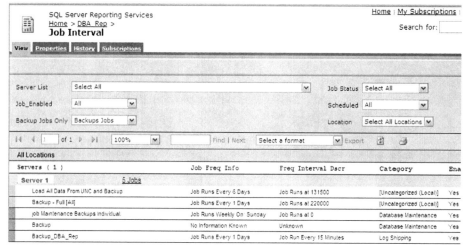

Figure 2.18: SSRS Job Interval report based on DBA_Rep database query.

Summary

Whether you build your own, deploy someone else's, or purchase one from a vendor, having a documentation solution is critical for a DBA, especially when dealing with more than 20 servers. In this chapter, I dove headlong into how to document a SQL Server infrastructure, using some T-SQL scripts, a DBA Repository, SSIS and SSRS. If you are interested in deploying this solution in your environment, it is available to download from:

http://www.simple-talk.com/RedGateBooks/
RodneyLandrum/SQL_Server_Tacklebox_Code.zip.

It can easily be modified to suit your needs.

With this repository, or something similar, in place you will have a means to easily get to know, and monitor, your SQL Server environment. Next, it is time to consider the sort of tasks that this SQL Server environment needs to do, and what others want it to do. A common request, just when you've got the environment nice and settled down, is to move the data around a bit. The migratory data, as it is often referred to, at least by me, is the subject of the next chapter.

CHAPTER 3: THE MIGRATORY DATA

When someone, usually a developer or project manager, enters my office and states, "We are going to need to move data from X to Y ..." there usually follows a short inquisition, starting with the question, "Why?" Of course, I can probably guess why, as it is such a common request. As a data store grows, it often becomes necessary to "offload" certain processes in order to maintain performance levels. Reporting is usually the first to go, and this can involve simply creating a mirror image of the original source data on another server, or migrating and transforming the data for a data warehouse. QA and Dev environments also need to be refreshed regularly, sometimes daily.

As a DBA, I have to consider many factors before deciding how to allocate the resources required in building a data migration solution. As Einstein may have posited, it is mostly a matter space and time or, more correctly, space time. The other, less scientific, variable is cost. Moving data is expensive. Each copy you need to make of a 1.5 Terabyte, 500-table production database is not only going to double the cost of storage space, but also the time required for backup and restore, or to push the data to target systems for reporting, and so on.

In this chapter, I am going to cover the myriad ways to push, pull, or pour data from one data store to another, assessing each in terms of space, time and cost criteria. These data migration solutions fall into three broad categories:

- **Bulk Data Transfer solutions** – this includes tools such as Bulk Copy Program (BCP) and SSIS.
- **Data Comparison solutions** – using third party tools such as Red Gate's SQL Data Compare, a built-in free tool such as TableDiff, or perhaps a homegrown T-SQL script that uses the new MERGE statement in SQL 2008.
- **"High Availability" solutions** – using tools for building highly available systems, such as log shipping, replication, database mirroring and database snapshots.

I'll review some of the available tools in each category, so that you're aware of the options when you come to choose the best fit for you, and your organization, and I will provide sample solutions for BCP, SSIS and TableDiff. I will also cover log shipping in some detail as, in my experience, it continues to be one of the most cost effective data migration solutions, in terms of cost, space and time.

Mapping out the data migration solution

As always, the most appropriate solution will depend on your exact requirements, and each option varies in terms of complexity and the time it will take you as DBA to plan and implement it. A common mistake of the novice DBA is to declare recklessly to a manager, on receiving a relatively straightforward data migration request, that moving the data "should only take 10 or 15 minutes". I can say, with utmost confidence, that there is absolutely no data migration solution that takes 10-15 minutes to design, document and implement.

There is also the question of monetary cost. Some of the tools are comparatively expensive whereas others, such as Log Shipping and BCP, are essentially "free". However, that can be misleading too. Free is never really free. There is no free lunch, no free data. One thing is for sure though: regardless of cost, most data migration requests are approved because they satisfy an important business need and this means that a DBA will be tasked with moving data at some point, regardless of cost, space or time.

When the topic of moving data from one location to another arises, I turn to my trusty wall-sized whiteboard and plethora of dry erase markers. I quickly assess the data migration needs with a series of probing questions, which I map out in a flowchart format on the white board. Here are some of the typical questions, with some typical answers:

- **"How much data are we talking about?"**
  ["Roughly 15 Gigs worth of data a month"]
- **"How often do you need the data refreshed?"**
  ["Daily"]
- **"Do you need the whole database(s) or a subset of data?"**
  ["A subset of data."]
- **"Who is going to need access to the data?"**
  ["Developers/Analysts"]
- **"Does the data need to be modified on the target, or do we need to apply indexes on the target?"**
  ["We need to apply indexes independent of the source"]
- **"What version SQL are you using on the source, and can the target be a different version and edition?"**
  ["SQL Server 2000 and 2005 … unclear on the edition … that is your job Mr. or Mrs. DBA"]

At this point, I have the information that I need. There are several possible solutions, in this case, and which one you choose largely depends on cost.

Log Shipping is a solution that has served me well in my career, across the space, time and cost boundaries. However, this solution would not allow us to add indexes on the target system. In addition, it is not possible to log ship between different versions of SQL Server, say SQL 2000 to 2005, and reap all of the benefits for a reporting instance because you will be unable to leave the target database in Standby mode and therefore can not access the database. There are many potential solutions to the "once-a-day refresh" requirement. Database snapshots may be a viable option, but require Enterprise Edition and that the snapshot resides on the same SQL Server instance as the source database.

While, on our imaginary whiteboard, we might cross off Log Shipping and Snapshots as potential solutions, for the time being, it would be a mistake to rule them out entirely. As I mentioned before, log shipping has served me well in similar scenarios, and it's possible that some future criteria will drive the decision toward such a solution. Bear in mind also that, with log shipping in place, it is possible to use your log shipped database target instance as both a hot standby server for disaster recovery as well as a server to offload reporting processes.

However, for now let's assume that another solution, such as SSIS, BCP or TableDiff, would be more appropriate. Over the following sections, I'll demonstrate how to implement a solution using these tools, noting along the way how, with slight modifications to the criteria, other data migration solutions could easily fit the need.

The data source

Most of the examples for data migration will use the DBA repository database, **DBA_Rep**, discussed in the previous chapter, as the data source. The data that I will be working with for bulk loading via BCP, and data comparisons using TableDiff.exe, comes from the table, whose schema is defined in Listing 3.1.

```
CREATE TABLE [dbo].[SQL_Conn] (
    [Run_Date] [datetime] NULL,
    [Server] [varchar] (100) NULL,
    [spid] [int] NULL,
    [blocked] [bit] NULL,
    [waittime] [int] NULL,
    [name] [nvarchar] (128) NULL,
    [lastwaittype] [nvarchar] (150) NULL,
    [cpu] [int] NULL,
    [login_time] [datetime] NULL,
    [last_batch] [datetime] NULL,
    [status] [nvarchar] (50) NULL,
    [hostname] [nvarchar] (128) NULL,
    [program_name] [nvarchar] (150) NULL,
    [cmd] [nvarchar] (60) NULL,
```

```
    [loginame]  [nvarchar](128)  NULL,
    [duration]  [datetime]  NULL
)  ON  [PRIMARY]
```

Listing 3.1: Schema for the SQL_Conn table.

This table is a heap; in other words it has no indexes. It is populated using an SSIS job that collects connection information from each SQL Server instance defined in the DBA Repository, and merges this data together.

NOTE
For a full article describing the process of gathering this data, please refer to:
http://www.simple-talk.com/sql/database-administration/using-ssis-to-monitor-sql-server-databases-/

I chose this table only because it provides an example of the sort of volume of data that you might be faced with as a DBA. Over time, when executing the scheduled job every hour for many tens of servers, the table can grow quite large. However, as a side note, it is worth gathering as the data offers many insights into how your servers are being utilized.

TIP
If you would like to view the data from a sample data file that might be otherwise too large to open in Notepad, I use tail.exe to view the last n lines of the data file. Tail.exe is available in the Windows 2003 Resource Kit.

Bulk data transfer tools

The bulk loading of data is not a new concept. It has been around since the very early days of SQL Server. Loading data in bulk typically involves taking a subset of data, say all of the data in one or more tables, dumping it out to a flat file and subsequently loading it into a secondary source, such as another database on a secondary server. Though the terminology has changed somewhat, from "bulk loading" to "fast loading", this basic concept remains the same across all versions.

Such a process is generally effective both in terms of cost and time; in the former case, because the tools that are available to do it, such as BCP and SSIS, are freely distributed with SQL Server and in the latter case because these methods have the ability to bypass logging, in certain circumstances, and so are extraordinarily efficient. You can expect as much as 20K records per second in some cases, depending on what the hardware subsystem that performs the reads and writes of data from source to target can accommodate, and on the speed of your network link.

The two bulk transfer tools that we'll consider here are:

- **Bulk Copy Program (BCP)** – This tool has been around for nearly as long as SQL Server itself. DBAs have a hard time giving it up. It is a command line tool and, if speed of data loading is your main criteria, it is still hard to beat. There are several caveats to its use, though, which I will cover.

- **SQL Server Integration Services (SSIS)** – I have found that SSIS is one of the best choices for moving data, especially in terms of cost, and in situations where near real-time data integration is not a requirement, such as you may achieve with native replication or Change Data Capture technologies. Transforming data is also a chore that SSIS handles very well, which is perfect for data warehousing. I will show how to use SSIS to load data from a source to destination, and watch the data as it flows through the process.

Whether you choose to use BCP or SSIS will depend on the exact nature of the request. Typically, I will choose BCP if I receive a one-time request to move or copy a single large table, with millions of records. BCP can output data based on a custom query, so it is also good for dumping data to fulfill one-off requests for reports, or for downstream analysis.

SSIS adds a level of complexity to such ad-hoc requests, because DBAs are then forced to "design" a solution graphically. In addition, many old school DBAs simply prefer the command line comfort of BCP. I am not sure how many old school DBAs remain, but as long as Microsoft continues to distribute BCP.exe, I will continue to use it and write about it, for its simple and fast interface.

SSIS has come a long way from its forebear, Data Transformation Services (DTS) and, in comparison to BCP, can be a bit daunting for the uninitiated DBA. However, I turn to it often when requested to provide data migration solutions, especially when I know there may be data transformations or aggregations to perform, before loading the data into a data warehouse environment. SSIS packages are easy to deploy and schedule, and Microsoft continues to add functionality to the SSIS design environment making it easy for developers to control the flow of processing data at many points. Like BCP, SSIS packages provide a way to import and export data from flat files, but with SSIS you are not limited to flat files. Essentially any ODBC or OLEDB connection becomes a data source. Bulk data loads are also supported; they are referred to as "Fast Load" in SSIS vernacular.

Over the coming section, I'll present some sample solutions using each of these tools. First, however, we need to discuss briefly the concept of minimally logged transactions.

Minimally logged transactions

When bulk loading data using BCP or SSIS, it is important to know how this massive import of data will effect data and log growth. In this regard, it is important to review the concept of "minimally logged" transactions. If the database to which you are bulk loading the data is using the Full recovery model, then such operations will be "fully logged". In other words, the transaction log will maintain a record for each and every inserted record or batch. This transaction logging, in conjunction with your database backups, allows for point-in-time recovery of the database.

However, if you were to load in 50 million records into a database in Full recovery mode this could eventually be a nightmare for the DBA. Transactions in the log file for a Full recovery database are only ever removed from the log upon a transaction log backup and so, in the absence of frequent log backups, log file growth would spiral out of control.

As such, you may consider switching to one of the other available recovery models, Simple or Bulk-logged, for the duration of the bulk import operation. In these recovery modes, such operations (and a few others) are only minimally logged. Enough information is stored to recover the transaction, but the information needed to support point-in-time recovery is not written to the transaction log. Note, however, that there are a few caveats to this exemption from full logging. If, for example, there is a clustered index on the table that you are bulk loading, all transactions will be fully logged.

So, for example, in order to minimize logging for bulk activities, such as those used by BCP.exe, you can temporarily switch from Full recovery mode to Bulk-logged mode, while retaining the ability to back up the transaction log. One downside of Bulk-logged mode, however, is that you lose the ability to restore to a point in time if there are any bulk transactions, though you can still restore the entire transaction log in Bulk-logged mode.

Alternatively, you can set the database to Simple mode, in which bulk operations are also minimally logged. By definition, the Simple mode does not support point-in time recovery, since the transaction log cannot be backed up, and is truncated each time a checkpoint is issued for the database. However, this "truncate on checkpoint" process does have the benefit that the log is continually freed of committed transactions, and will not grow indefinitely.

The dangers of rampant log file growth can be mitigated to some extent by committing bulk update, inserts or delete transactions in batches, say every 100,000 records. In BCP, for example, you can control the batch size using the batch size flag. This is a good practice regardless of recovery model, as it means that the committed transaction can be removed from the log file, either via a log backup or a checkpoint truncate.

The model in normal use for a given database will depend largely on your organization's SLAs (Service Level Agreements) on data availability. If point-in-time recovery is not a requirements, than I would recommend using the Simple recovery model, in most cases. Your bulk operations will be minimally logged, and you can perform Full and Differential backups as required to meet the SLA.

However, if recovering to a point in time is important, then your databases will need to be in Full recovery mode. In this case, I'd recommend switching to Bulk logged mode for bulk operations, performing a full backup after bulk loading the data and then subsequently switching back to Full recovery and continuing log backups from that point.

> **NOTE**
> I cover many tips and tricks for monitoring file growth in Chapter 4, on managing space.

BCP.EXE

BCP has been a favorite of command line-driven DBAs ever since it was introduced in SQL Server 6.5. It has retained its popularity in spite of the introduction of smarter, prettier new tools with flashy graphical interfaces and the seeming ability to make data move just by giving it a frightening glare. I have used BCP for many tasks, either ad hoc, one-off requests or daily scheduled loads. Of course, other tools and technologies such as SSIS and log shipping shine in their own right and make our lives easier, but there is something romantic about BCP.exe and it cannot be overlooked when choosing a data movement solution for your organization.

Basic BCP

Let's see how to use BCP to migrate data from our **SQL_Conn** table in the **DBA_Rep** database. We'll dump the 58K rows that currently exist in my copy of the table to a text file, and then use a script to repeatedly load data from the file back into the same **SQL_Conn** table, until we have 1 million rows.

Knowing that the table **SQL_Conn** is a heap, meaning that there are currently no indexes defined for the table, I rest easy knowing that I should be minimally logging transactions, as long as the database is set for the Bulk logged or Simple recovery model.

With BCP, just like with SSIS dataflow, data is either going in or coming out. Listing 3.2 shows the BCP output statement, to copy all of the data rows from the **SQL_Conn** table on a local SQL Server, the default if not specified, into a text file.

```
bcp dba_rep..SQL_Conn out "C:\Writing\Simple Talk
Book\Ch3\Out1.txt" -T -n
```

Listing 3.2: BCP output statement.

After the **bcp** command, we define the source table, in this case **dba_rep..SQL_Conn**. Next, we specify **out**, telling BCP to output the contents of the table to a file, in this case, "C:\Writing\Simple Talk Book\Ch3\Out1.txt". Finally, the **-T** tells BCP to use a trusted connection and **-n** instructs BCP to use native output as opposed to character format, the latter being the default.

Native output is recommended for transferring data from one SQL Server instance to another, as it uses the native data types of a database. If you are using identical tables, when transferring data from one server to another or from one table to another, then the native option avoids unnecessary conversion from one character format to another.

Figure 3.1 shows a BCP command line execution of this statement, dumping all 58040 records out of the the **SQL_Conn** table.

According to Figure 3.1, BCP dumped 17 thousand records per second in a total of 3,344 milliseconds, or roughly 3 seconds. I would say, from first glance, that this is fast. The only way to know is to add more data to this table and see how the times change. Remember that at this point, we are just performing a straight "dump" of the table and the speed of this operation won't be affected by the lack of indexes on the source table. However, will this lack of indexes affect the speed when a defined query is used to determine the output? As with any process, it is fairly easy to test, as you will see.

Let's keep in mind that we are timing how fast we can dump data out of this sample table, which in the real world may contain banking, healthcare or other types of business critical data. 58 thousand is actually a miniscule number of records in the real world, where millions of records is the norm. So let's simulate a million records so that we may understand how this solution scales in terms of time and space. I roughly equate 1 million records to 1 Gigabyte of space on disk, so as you are dumping large amounts of data, it is important to consider how much space is required for the flat file and if the file will be created locally or on a network share. The latter, of course, will increase the amount of time for both dumping and loading data.

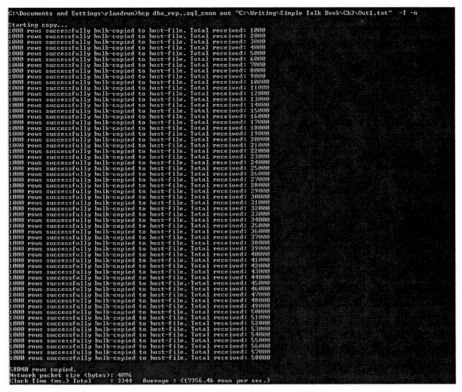

Figure 3.1: Dumping 58K records out of the SQL_Conn table.

In order to simulate a million or more records, we can load up the 58,000 records into a table multiple times so that we cross the plateau of 1 million records. I have created a batch file to do this, which is shown in Listing 3.3. In this case, I am loading the data back into the same table from which it came, **SQL_Conn**.

```
set n=%1
 set i= 1
 :loop
 bcp dba_rep..SQL_Conn in
       C:\Writing\Simple Talk Book\Ch3\Out1.txt"
                          -n -b 50000 -T -h "TABLOCK"
 if %i% == %n% goto end
 set /a i=i+1
 goto loop
  :end
```

Listing 3.3: Batch file to load 1 million records from 58,000.

You will see that the main difference between this BCP statement and the previous one is that instead of out I am specifying in as the clause, meaning that we are loading data from the text file back in to the **SQL_Conn** table, which currently holds 58K rows.

The **-h TABLOCK** hint forces a lock on the receiving table. This is one of the requirements to guarantee minimally logging the transactions. The **-b** option tells BCP to batch the transactions at n rows, in this case every 50,000 rows. If there are any issues during the BCP load process, any rollback that occurs will only rollback to the last transaction after the n load. So, say I wanted to load 100,000 records, and I batched the BCP load every 20,000 records. If there were an issue while loading record 81,002 I would know that 80,000 records were successfully imported. I would lose 1,002 transactions as they would roll back to the last 20,000 mark, which would be 80,000 records.

The batch file takes one parameter, which is the number of times to run the BCP command in order to load the required number of rows into the table. How did I choose 20 iterations? Simple math: 20 * 58,040 = 1,160,800 records.

As you can see in Figure 3.2, this is exactly the number of rows that is now in the **SQL_Conn** table, after 20 iterations of the BCP command, using the 58,040 records in the **fl_out.txt** file as the source.

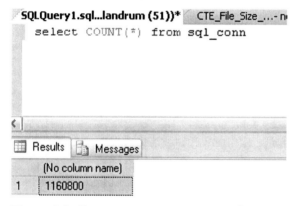

Figure 3.2: Query to count SQL_Conn after loading over 1 million records.

NOTE
For what it is worth, I have also used this batch file to load a Terabyte worth of data to test how we could effectively manage such a large data store.

If you re-run the BCP command in Listing 3.2, to output the query results to a file, you will find that the process takes more than a minute for a million rows, as opposed to the previous 3 seconds for 58K rows, indicating that the time to output the records remains good (58,040 / 3 = 19,346 records per second * 60 seonds = 1.16 million). I am still seeing nearly 20,000 records per second times(?) despite the increase in data, attesting to the efficiency of the old tried and true BCP.

Filtering the output using queryout

Rather than working with the entire table, you can use the **`queryout`** option of BCP to limit the data you will be exporting, by way of a filtered T-SQL query. Suppose I want to export data only from a particular time period, say for a **`run_date`** greater than October 1st of 2008.The query is shown in Listing 3.4.

```
Select * from dba_rep..SQL_Conn where run_date > '10/01/2008'
```

Listing 3.4: Query to filter BCP output.

There are many duplicate rows in the **`SQL_Conn`** table, and no indexes defined, so I would expect that this query would take many seconds, possibly half a minute to execute. The BCP command is shown in Listing 3.5.

```
bcp "Select * from dba_rep..SQL_Conn
        where run_date > '10/01/2008'"
  queryout
  "C:\Writing\Simple Talk Book\Ch3\bcp_query_dba_rep.txt" -n -T
```

Listing 3.5: BCP output statement limiting rows to specific date range, using the `output` **option.**

As you can see in Figure 3.3, this supposedly inefficient query ran through more than a million records and dumped out 64,488 of them to a file in 28 seconds, averaging over 2,250 records per second.

```
1000 rows successfully bulk-copied to host-file. Total received: 48000
1000 rows successfully bulk-copied to host-file. Total received: 49000
1000 rows successfully bulk-copied to host-file. Total received: 50000
1000 rows successfully bulk-copied to host-file. Total received: 51000
1000 rows successfully bulk-copied to host-file. Total received: 52000
1000 rows successfully bulk-copied to host-file. Total received: 53000
1000 rows successfully bulk-copied to host-file. Total received: 54000
1000 rows successfully bulk-copied to host-file. Total received: 55000
1000 rows successfully bulk-copied to host-file. Total received: 56000
1000 rows successfully bulk-copied to host-file. Total received: 57000
1000 rows successfully bulk-copied to host-file. Total received: 58000
1000 rows successfully bulk-copied to host-file. Total received: 59000
1000 rows successfully bulk-copied to host-file. Total received: 60000
1000 rows successfully bulk-copied to host-file. Total received: 61000
1000 rows successfully bulk-copied to host-file. Total received: 62000
1000 rows successfully bulk-copied to host-file. Total received: 63000
1000 rows successfully bulk-copied to host-file. Total received: 64000

64488 rows copied.
Network packet size (bytes): 4096
Clock Time (ms.) Total     : 28578  Average : (2256.56 rows per sec.)

C:\>
```

Figure 3.3: BCP with queryout option.

Of course, at this point I could fine tune the query, or make recommendations for re-architecting the source table to add indexes if necessary, before moving this type of process into production. However, I am satisfied with the results and can move safely on to the space age of data migration in SSIS.

SSIS

We saw an example of an SSIS package in the previous chapter, when discussing the DBA Repository. The repository is loaded with data from several source servers, via a series of data flow objects in an SSIS package (**Populate_DBA_Rep**). Let's dig a little deeper into an SSIS data flow task. Again, we'll use the **SQL_Conn** table, which we loaded with 1 million rows of data in the previous section, as the source and use SSIS to selectively move data to an archive table; a process that happens frequently in the real world.

Figure 3.4 shows the data flow task, "SQL Connections Archive", which will copy the data from the source **SQL_Conn** table to the target archive table, **SQL_Conn_Archive**, in the same **DBA_Rep** database. There is only a single connection manager object. This is a quite simple example of using SSIS to migrate data, but it is an easy solution to build on.

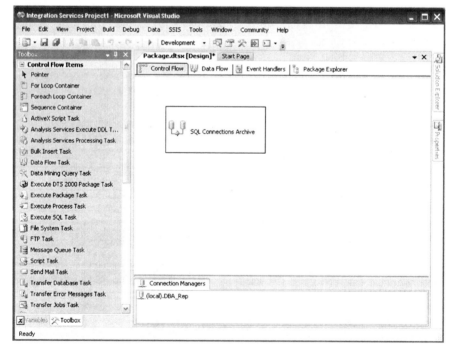

Figure 3.4: Simple SSIS data flow.

Inside the SQL Connections Archive data flow, there are two data flow objects, an OLE DB Source and OLE DB Destination, as shown in Figure 3.5.

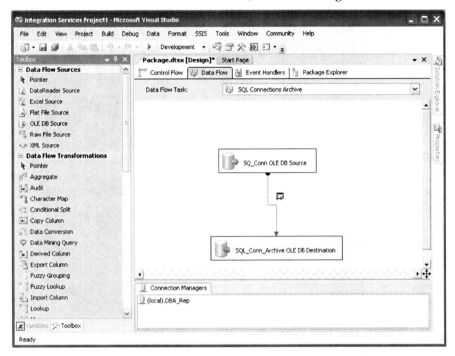

Figure 3.5: Source and destination OLE DB objects in SSIS.

We'll use the OLE DB source to execute the query in Listing 3.4 against the source **SQL_Conn** table, to return the same 64,488K records we dumped out to a file previously. Instead of a file, however, the results will be sent to the OLE DB destination object, which writes them to a **SQL_Conn_Archive** table. Figure 3.6 shows the Source Editor of the OLE DB source object, including the qualified query to extract the rows from the source table, **SQL_Conn**.

For the **Data Access Mode**, notice that I am using "SQL command"; other options are "Table or view", "Table Name or View Name Variable" and "SQL Command from variable". I am using SQL command here so as to have control over which fields and subset of data I wish to move, which is often a criteria for real world requests. Notice that I am filtering the data with a **WHERE** clause, selecting only transactions with a **run_date** greater than '10/01/08'.

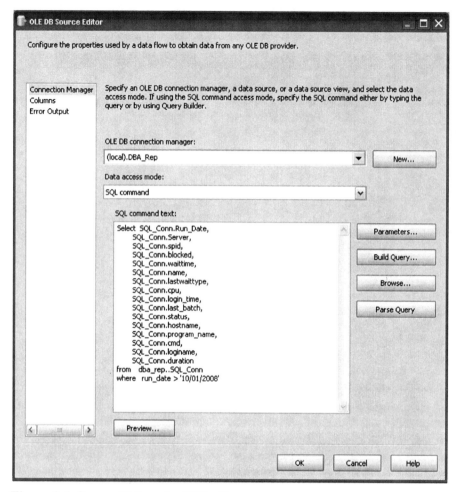

Figure 3.6: Source Editor for SQL_Conn query.

Figure 3.7 shows the Source Editor for the OLE DB Destination object, where we define the target table, **SQL_Conn_Archive**, to which the rows will be copied.

There are a few other properties of the destination object that are worth noting. I have chosen to use the **Fast Load** option for the data access mode, and I have enabled the **Table Lock** option, which as you might recall from the BCP section, is required to ensure minimally logged transactions.

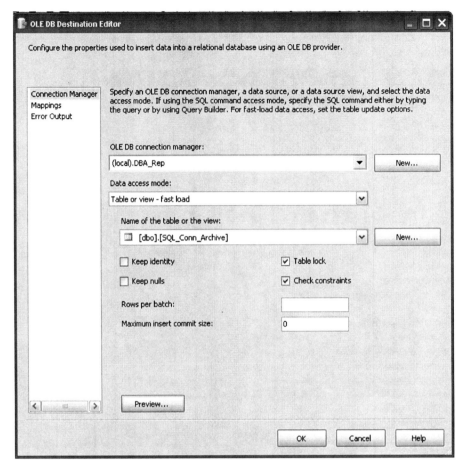

Figure 3.7: OLE DB Destination Editor properties.

Although I did not use it in this example, there is also the **Rows per batch** option that will batch the load process so that any failures can be rolled back to the previous commit, rather than rolling back the entire load.

It is worth noting that there are other **Fast Load** options that you cannot see here. In SSIS, these options are presented to you only in the Properties window for the destination object. Additional fast load properties include:

- **FIRE_Triggers**, which forces any triggers on the destination table to fire. By default, fast or bulk loading bypasses triggers.
- **ORDER**, which speeds performance when working with tables with clustered indexes so that the data being loaded is pre-sorted to match the physical order of the clustered index.

These properties can be manually keyed into the **FastLoadOptions** property value. In this example, I also used the **FIRE_TRIGGERS** fast load option, as shown in Figure 3.8.

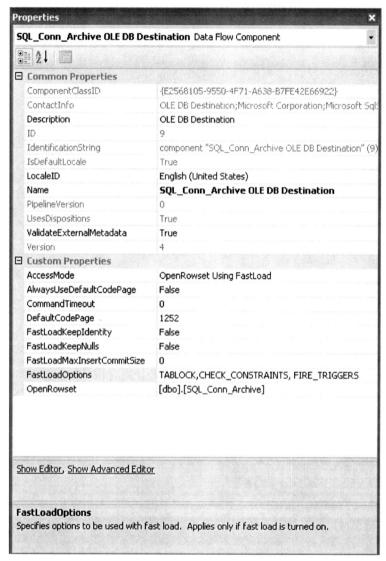

Figure 3.8: Additional options for Fast Loading data within SSIS destination objects.

It is almost time to execute this simple data migration package. First, however, I would like to add a data viewer to the process. A data viewer lets you, the package designer, view the data as it flows through from the source to the destination object. To add a data viewer, simply right-click on the green data flow path and select "Data Viewer". This will bring up the "Configure Data Viewer" screen, as shown in Figure 3.9. The data viewer can take several forms: Grid, Histogram, Scatter Plot and Column Chart. In this example, I chose **Grid**.

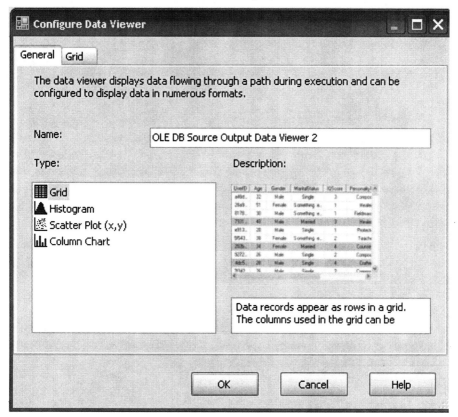

Figure 3.9: Selecting a data viewer.

When we execute the package, the attached data viewer displays the flow of data. You can detach the data viewer to allow the records to flow through without interaction. The data viewer is useful while developing a package to ensure that the data you are expecting to see is indeed there. Of course, you will want to remove them before deploying the package to production, via a scheduled job. Figure 3.10 shows the data viewer, as well as the completed package, as the 64,488 records are migrated.

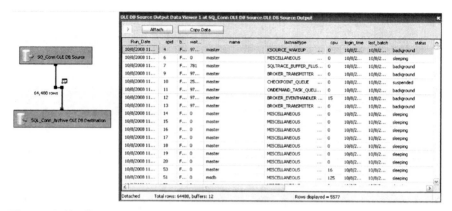

Figure 3.10: Completed package execution with data viewer.

If this was indeed an archive process, the final step would be to delete the data from the source table. I will not cover this step except to say that it too can be automated in the SSIS package with a simple **DELETE** statement, matching the criteria we used for the source query when migrating the data.

I am always careful when deleting data from a table, not because I am fearful of removing the wrong data (good backup practices and transactions are safety measures) but because I am mindful of how it might affect my server. For example, how will the log growth be affected by deleting potentially millions of records at a time? Should I batch the delete process? Will there be enough space for log growth when accounting for each individual delete? How long will it take? These are all questions the answers to which have, over the years, taught me to tread carefully when handling the delete process.

Data comparison tools

Now that we have investigated how to bulk load and move data with BCP and SSIS, it is time to turn our attention to the other very popular and efficient ways to get selected data from source to target. Sometimes you do not have to resort to the truncate and load processes that are prevalent in many data load facilities like BCP or SSIS. Sometimes, merging the data from one location to another is a much quicker way of synchronizing two data stores.

Some third party tools that perform these comparisons incur cost but offer substantial savings in terms of space and time because you do not need to store multiple Gigabytes of data in output files, or transfer those same large files across slow network connections.

With data comparison, you are migrating a much smaller subset of transactions, for example those that have occurred over the last day, or even hour for that matter. This is similar in nature to log shipping in the sense that only new transactions are migrated, but with the added benefit of maintaining much more control over the target data. For example, once the data is migrated from source to target, via a data comparison tool, you can add indexes to the target that did not exist on the source. This is not possible with log shipping, as I will discuss shortly.

Several tools come to mind immediately, for performing this data comparison and "merge" process:

- **Native Change Data Capture** (SQL Server 2008 only) – this new technology allows you to capture date changes and push them to a target in near-real time. I have been anxiously awaiting such a technology in SQL Server but I would have to say that I have not found CDC to be fully realized in SQL Server 2008, and I don't cover it in this book. Don't get me wrong, it is there and it works but, much akin to table partitions and plan guides, it is a bit daunting and not very intuitive.
- **T-SQL Scripts** – Pre SQL Server 2008, many DBAs developed their own ways of merging data from one source to another, using T-SQL statements such as **EXCEPT** and **EXISTS**. Essentially, such code tests for the existence of data in a receiving table and acts appropriately upon learning the results. This was not difficult code to produce; it was just time consuming.
- **TableDiff** – this is another tool that has been around for many years. It was designed to help compare replication sets for native SQL Server replication but it is also a handy tool for comparing and synchronizing data.
- **Third party Data Comparison tools** – there are several available on the market, but I am most familiar with Red Gate's SQL Data Compare. Where tablediff.exe is excellent for comparing one table to another, SQL Data Compare allows you to compare entire databases, or subsets of objects, and data therein. The process can be scripted and automated to ensure data is synchronized between data sources. It is particularly valuable for synching your production environment to your test and dev environments, or for reporting.

I will cover TableDiff.exe in this chapter. While I do not cover SQL Data Compare here, I would highly recommend trying it out if you do a lot of data migration and synchronization:

http://www.red-gate.com/products/SQL_Data_Compare/index.htm.

However, before I present the sample solution, using TableDiff, we need to discuss briefly the concept of uniqueness.

Guaranteeing unique data

Regardless of the data comparison tool you use, you will need to guarantee uniqueness in your source and target data sources, in order for these techniques to work. Heretofore, in a frenzy to load data as fast as possible, I have not been concerned with duplicate data rows or indexes. For this next section, however, I need to start with a clean slate and refactor the SQL_Conn and SQL_Conn_Archive tables in such a way that we can guarantee uniqueness of data.

The SISS package that populates the SQL_Conn table runs every 15 minutes, and captures the date and time that the package ran as a field value, so this "run time" would be a good candidate for a unique column. However, to truly guarantee uniqueness, the clustered index will be a composite of the package run date and several other fields. I will also add an identity column (ID) to the tables.

Since the tables currently contain duplicate rows, in this example, I will first need to clean up a bit by truncating both the SQL_Conn and SQL_Conn_Archive. I can then run the package to populate the SQL_Conn table with current process information. Figure 3.11 shows the new record count for the SQL_Conn table, a mere 32 records.

Figure 3.11: Repopulated SQL_Conn table ready for merging data.

The SQL_Conn_Archive table currently holds zero records, as we would expect, clean slate and all. Figure 3.12 shows the empty table, in preparation for the prestidigitation to follow.

Figure 3.12: Empty SQL_Conn_Archive table.

So, now I am going to add the clustered index and an identity column (**ID**) to both tables. Figure 3.13 shows the 5 fields from the **SQL_Conn** table that I used to guarantee uniqueness. I am heartened by the fact that, as this table fills up over time, the clustered index will also benefit me when running interrogative queries for reports of sever activity.

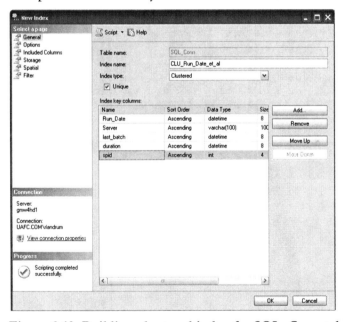

Figure 3.13: Building clustered index for SQL_Conn table.

With the newly built index and identity column on both source (**SQL_Conn**) and target (**SQL_Conn_Archive**), it is time to introduce Tablediff.exe, which we will use to keep the two tables in sync.

Tablediff.exe

Tablediff.exe is a little known and free tool that comes with SQL Server, and has done so for many releases. It was designed to assist with comparing replication sets for native SQL Server replication. However, even if you are not using SQL replication, it can be put to good use in comparing and synchronizing source and target tables.

It compares one table at a time and displays the differences between the two tables. Further, it can generate scripts that will sync the two tables, if there are differences. For SQL Server 2005, Tablediff.exe can be found in the C:\Program Files\Microsoft SQL Server\90\COM\ folder. It has options that allow you to define the source and destination servers, as well the required databases and tables.

Listing 3.6 shows the command line execution that will compare the freshly loaded **SQL_Conn** source table and the destination **SQL_Conn_Archive**. The options **-q** and **-t 200**, respectively, tell tablediff to do a simple record count rather than a full blown compare, and to timeout after 200 seconds. You also have the ability to lock the source and target tables, as I am doing here with **-sourcelocked** and **–destinationlocked**.

```
C:\Program Files\Microsoft SQL Server\90\COM\tablediff.exe" -
sourceserver MW4HD1 -sourcedatabase DBA_Rep -sourcetable
SQL_Conn -sourcelocked -destinationlocked -destinationserver
MW4HD1 -destinationdatabase DBA_Rep -destinationtable
SQL_Conn_Archive -q -t 200
```

Listing 3.6: Tablediff with source and destination options.

Figure 3.14 shows the 32 records that are different in **SQL_Conn** and **SQL_Conn_Archive** tables, by doing a simple row count. It took less than a tenth of a second to deliver the results.

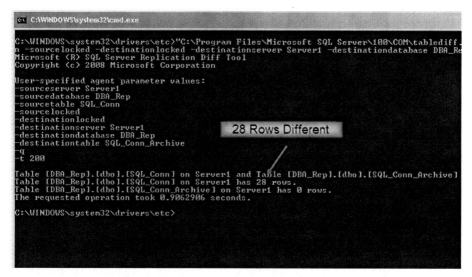

Figure 3.14: Tablediff.exe row count differences.

Without the `-q` option, you will get a list of differences, by **ID** column, as shown in Figure 3.15. This comparison took 0.15 seconds for the 32 records.

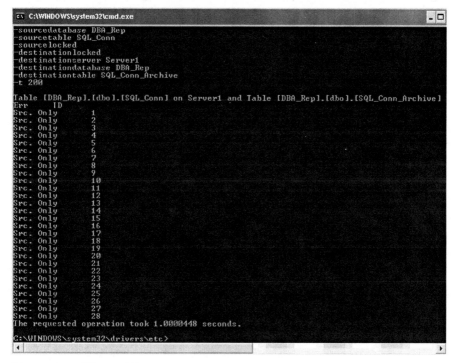

Figure 3.15: Tablediff showing detailed differences.

The best thing about Tablediff.exe is that it will generate a script that will bring the two tables in sync. That option is **-f** which takes a filename and path, as shown in Listing 3.7.

```
C:\Program Files\Microsoft SQL Server\90\COM\tablediff.exe" -
sourceserver MW4HD1 -sourcedatabase DBA_Rep -sourcetable
SQL_Conn -sourcelocked -destinationlocked -destinationserver
MW4HD1 -destinationdatabase DBA_Rep -destinationtable
SQL_Conn_Archive -q -t 200 -f C:\Output\SQL_Conn.sql
```

Listing 3.7: The tablediff comand to synch the two tables.

Running this tablediff command, with the **-f** option, generates a file containing all of the T-SQL statements to make the two tables identical. Figure 3.16 show the **SQL_Conn.sql** file that the command created.

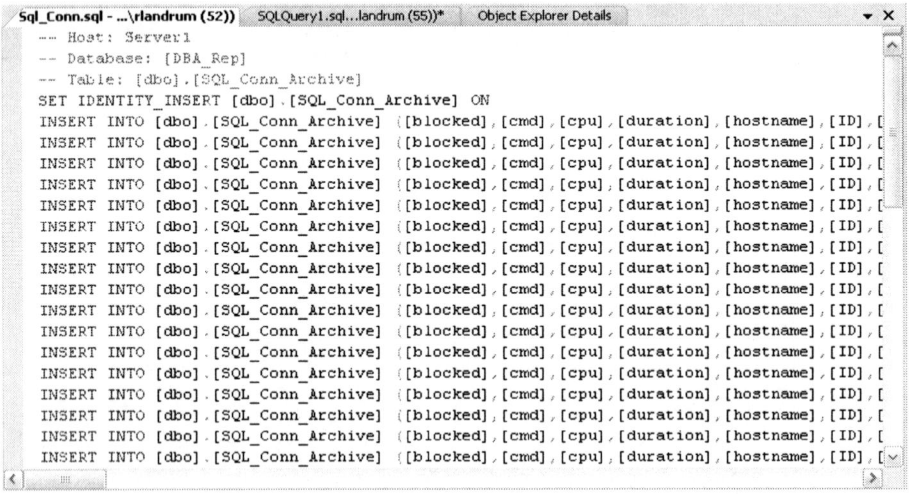

Figure 3.16: Output of fix file for Tablediff.exe

Executing the script against the **SQL_Conn_Archive** table and then re-running the tablediff.exe will show that the two tables are now identical.

"High Availability" tools

Finally, we move on to a discussion of what I have termed "high availability" data migration tools, simply because these tools generally form part of an organizations strategy in minimizing downtime and maximizing the availability of its data.

Up to now we have been working with single source tables, whereas these techniques are more applicable when whole databases need to be migrated, and the data in them needs to be regularly resynched with the source. The added benefit of using a tool such as log shipping is that you can segregate reporting processes from transactional processes, which can offer performance gains in some scenarios.

Log shipping vs. mirroring vs. replication

There are three main tools that you can choose from, when implementing a "HA" solution for data migration:

Log Shipping – I have used log shipping for a variety of data migration tasks and it is probably the most reliable mechanism that I have found. However, it does have its downsides and a big one is that refreshing the data requires everyone to be out of the target database, and data is only as fresh as the last restore on the target.

Log shipping can be setup natively, or using third party tools like RedGate SQL Backup, which sets up all of the automated schedules for you and also compresses the backed up logs, making for much faster data loads. In terms of financial cost, the only significant consideration is the secondary server instance, though you can also log ship to the same server, as I will show. The space required to store log backups is much less than the space required to implement a solution that performs a full backup and restore of a database, and the time to synch two databases, via log shipping, is drastically lowered.

Native SQL Server Replication – This is one of the few solutions that provide near-real time data on a target. However, to be quite honest, I have avoided native SQL replication for a long time. It is not so much the overhead of maintenance or administration that has prevented me from deploying it to production, but the learning curve of the technology and need for "compliant schemas". In order to use native replication, the database schema has to fit into a normalized structure, with unique primary keys defined for each replicated table. For whatever reason, many third party vendors do not always adhere to this requirement.

Database Mirroring (SQL Server 2005 and Database snapshots) – This technology was introduced in SQL Server 2005. Mirroring is a way of introducing high-availability to SQL Server by allowing the secondary server to become the main server, instantly. In a mirrored setup, the secondary database is never online, or accessible to the end user, until failure occurs on the source. The only way to get around this, if you wish to offload reporting to the secondary server, is to set up database snapshots. Unfortunately, snapshots are only available in Enterprise editions of SQL Server so cost is definitely a factor for this solution. As such, Database Mirroring is primarily used for high availability, rather than as a more casual data migration technique.

It is when you start using these techniques that the issues of cost, space and time really come to the fore and it is important to understand what problems each will solve, compared to their cost. Native replication and database mirroring, while certainly valid solutions, come with a higher price tag if you want to cross breed a high availability solution with a reporting solution.

While I may choose replication or mirroring as options at some stage, so far I have found that, in my career as a stolid, bang-for-the-buck DBA and manager, log shipping has come out ahead of the three solutions nearly 100% of the time, when considering cost, space and time. Therefore, it is the solution I will focus on here.

Log shipping considerations

Log shipping is a method, based on SQL Server Agent jobs, by which the transaction log backups from a primary server are applied to secondary servers. In this way, one can keep one or more spare "warm standby" servers in a state of readiness to take over in the event of failure of the primary server.

Log shipping is a solution that sounds like it would be a breeze to set up, but there are often complications. Let's reconsider our (slightly modified) original requirements:

- Migrating roughly 15 Gigs worth of data a month
- Data needs to be refreshed daily
- Need to migrate the whole database
- Developers/Analysts need access permission to the target database
- Indexes do not need to be applied independent of the source
- Source databases are both SQL Server 2005

In this case the log shipping solution sounds straightforward until … you discover that the source database is in Simple recovery mode, so you can't take log backups. Also, wait a second, how are we going to add permissions that are different from the source, as the target database will be in read-only/stand mode, so I cannot add users to it. This has gotten a bit more complex than I may have anticipated.

The time required for log shipping is not insubstantial. On a 1 Gigabit network, where both the source and target are on different servers, or even if the source and target databases are on the same SQL Server instance, it is going to take time to backup and restore the data on the target. However, this time is negligible if done in off peak hours, like in the early AM before the start of business operations. Also, it is easy to gauge the time it takes to backup, transfer and restore the log file. Furthermore, you can reduce the required time by incorporating a scheduled, compressed log shipping solution with, say, Red Gate's

SQL Backup. However, of course, one then needs to add the cost of this tool to the overall cost of the solution.

However, what if there were 2 G worth of log data, and the target server was reached via a 3MB WAN connection? What if the request was for more than one target? What could have taken 15 minutes, on first analysis, is now taking 45 minutes or more, and pushing past the start of business. DBAs constantly find themselves making accommodations based on unexpected changes to the original requests. Proper communication and expectations need to be set upfront so that planning follows through to execution as seamlessly as possible, with contingencies in circumstances of failure.

Don't forget also that if the target database ever gets out of synchronization with the source logs for whatever reason (it happens), then the entire database needs to be restored from a full backup to reinstate the log shipping. If the full database is over 200G and you have a slow WAN link, then this could be a big issue. Those 45 minutes just became hours. No one likes seeing a critical, tier 1 application down for hours.

Finally, there will be a need to store this redundant data. As you add servers to the mix, the amount of space required grows proportionately. Soon, the 200G database, growing at a rate of 2G per day, becomes a space management nightmare. It is always best to perform upfront capacity planning, and over estimate your needs. It is not always easy to add disk space on the fly without bring down a server, which is especially true of servers with local disk arrays not SAN attached. If you have SAN storage, the process is more straightforward, but comes with issues as well. Also, consider if the disk subsystem is using slower SATA drives (often used for QA and Dev environments) or faster SCSI drives, which are more expensive per Gig, to the tune of thousands of dollars.

Setting up log shipping

With all of the considerations out of the way for log shipping, I want to take a quick look at how to setup a log shipping solution. Fortunately, Microsoft SQL Server has made it very easy to implement. One requirement is that the source database must be in Full recovery mode. As you can see in Figure 3.17, showing the Properties dialogue of the **DBA_Rep** database, Transaction Log Shipping has its own set of properties including the backup setting for the source database.

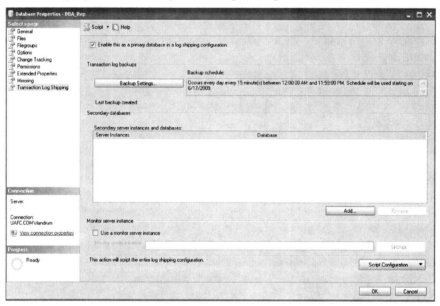

Figure 3.17: Transaction log shipping for DBA_Rep database.

If you click the backup Settings button, you can specify:

- A network share to store the transaction log backups for the source database.
- A retention policy, expressed as the number of hours to keep the backup log files.
- A backup job name and schedule. Transaction Log Shipping uses the SQL Agent service to schedule both the source log backups and target server (can be the same as the source) restores.

The settings I chose are shown in Figure 3.18.

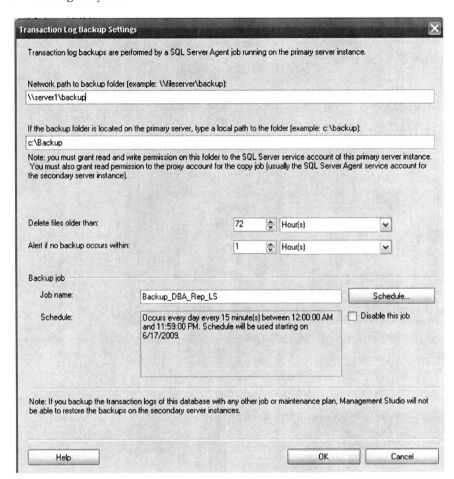

Figure 3.18: Selecting Transaction Log Backup settings.

Having specified the backup location, it is time to add the information for the secondary database, where the source transaction logs will be applied. A nice feature, when setting up log shipping for the first time, is the ability to let Management Studio ready the secondary database for you, by performing the initial backup and restore, as seen in Figure 3.19. The secondary database, non-creatively enough, is **DBA_Rep1**.

Most often, you will want to transfer the log files to a different server from the source. By selecting the "Copy Files" tab in Figure 3.19, you can specify where the copied transaction log backup files will reside for the subsequent restores to the target database. However, in our simple example, both the backup and restore will reside on the same server, as shown in Figure 3.20.

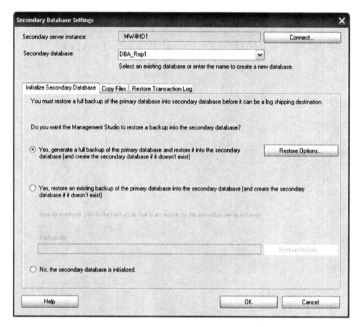

Figure 3.19: Setting up initial restore of secondary database for Log Shipping.

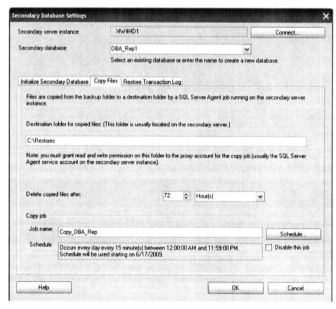

Figure 3.20: Setting up Copy Files options for Transaction Log Shipping.

The next and final, "Restore Transaction Log", tab is very important. This is where you set the database state to either "No Recovery" or "Standby" mode. You will want to use Standby mode if you are planning on using the target database as a reporting database, while still allowing subsequent logs to be applied. The other important option is "Disconnect users in the database when restoring backups", seen in Figure 3.21. Without this important option, the log restore would fail because the database would be in use.

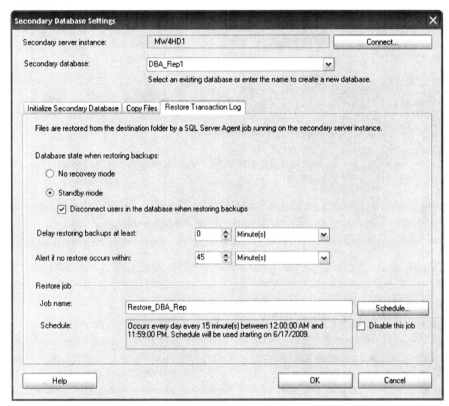

Figure 3.21: Checking Standby Mode and Disconnect Users.

Once all of the backup and restore options are set, you can choose whether or not you want to use the log shipping monitoring service. Essentially, this is an alerting mechanism in case there are any issues with the log shipping process. I do not typically set up the monitoring service, though it may be useful in your environment. Once you are happy with the backup and restore options, select OK, and everything else will be done for you, including backing up and restoring the source and target databases, and setting up all SQL Agent jobs to backup, copy and restore the transaction logs on an automated schedule. Figure 3.22 shows the completion of these steps.

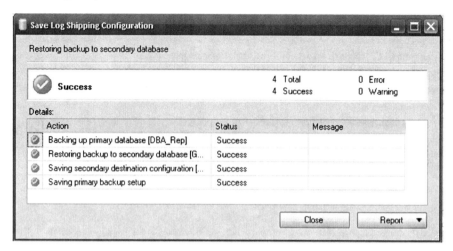

Figure 3.22: Log Shipping setup completed.

With log shipping setup and configured for Standby mode, you have conquered two very important DBAs tasks:

- Separating source data from transaction data for reporting to reduce the risk of contention with online processes on production
- Assuring a secondary backup of the source data in case there is disaster.

As I mentioned earlier, however, there are downsides to log shipping, such as the difficulty in creating indexes on the target and assigning specific permissions to users (both hard to do when the database is read only).

There is one final trick I will leave you with for log shipping and security. You can assign a login and user on the source, so that the user is created in the database, and then delete the login on the source but not the database user. Next, create the login on the target system, preferably a Windows account which will always sync up login to user. If it is a SQL authenticated account you are trying to align on the target, you will need to insure that the account Security ID (SIDs) are the same. This is where you will want to use the ultra-handy **sp_help_revlogin** stored procedure (http://support.microsoft.com/kb/246133). Because user permission assignment is a logged transaction in the source database, it will move with the next log restore and the user and login on the target system will align. Thus, you have no access on the source and the access you desire on the target.

Summary

In this chapter, we covered several tools that will facilitate the migration of data from a source to a target, or multiple targets. Data is moved for several reasons, the main ones being either for Disaster Recovery, High Availability, or to offload reporting from the source to increase performance of an application. There are as many reasons to move data as there are ways and means. Fortunately, you and I, as DBAs, can make informed decisions that will ultimately equate to cost savings for the companies we work for. Speaking of saving money, the next chapter is devoted to storing all of this migratory data. It is sometimes challenging to capacity plan for new projects, and even more challenging, as your SQL infrastructure grows, to force adherence to standards that would mitigate many storage issues. I will show you how I try to do this daily, in the next compartment of our SQL Server tacklebox.

CHAPTER 4: MANAGING DATA GROWTH

When I look back over my career as a SQL Server DBA, analyzing the kinds of issues that I have had to resolve, usually under pressure, nothing brings me out in a colder sweat than the runaway data, log or TempDB file. I would estimate that for every time I've had to deal with an emergency restore, including point in time restores using transaction log backups, I've probably had to deal with a hundred disk capacity issues. Overall, I would estimate that such issues account for around 80% of the problems that a DBA team faces on a weekly basis.

Occasionally, the cause of these space issues is just poor capacity planning. In other words, the growth in file size was entirely predictable, but someone failed to plan for it. Predictable growth patterns are something that should be analyzed right at the start, preferably before SQL Server is even installed. In my experience, though, these space issues are often caused by bugs, or failure to adhere to best practices.

In this chapter, I'll delve into the most common causes of space management issues, covering model database configuration, inefficient bulk modifications, indexes and TempDB abuse, and how to fix them. I will finish the chapter by describing a query that you should store securely in your the SQL Server tacklebox, **SizeQuery**. I use this query on more or less a daily basis to monitor and track space utilization on my SQL Server instances. Used in conjunction with the DBA repository to query multiple SQL Servers, it has proved to be an invaluable reporting tool.

I have given a name to the time in the morning at which a DBA typically staggers in to work, bleary eyed, having spent most of the previous night shrinking log files and scouring disks for every precious Gigabyte of data, in order to find enough space to clear an alert. That name is **DBA:M** (pronounced D-BAM), and it's usually around 9.30AM. My main goal with this chapter is to help fellow DBAs avoid that DBA:M feeling.

Common causes of space issues

The following issues are among the most-common of DB space-related sorrow:

- **Poorly configured Model database** – meaning that subsequent databases adopt properties (AutoGrowth, Recovery Model and so on) that are inappropriate for their intended use.
- **Inefficient Delete, Insert or Bulk Insert statements** – such processes, plus those that create temp tables, can very quickly fill the log file with unnecessary data. The situation is exacerbated by incorrect Model database configuration.
- **Indexes and large row counts** – clustered indexes can take up a lot of space for tables that contain millions of rows of data. However, you simply need to plan for this because the consequences of not having these indexes can severely impact performance.
- **Blatant misuse of TempDB** – Temporary tables often play an important role when developers are tasked with comparing millions of rows of data, to return a small subset of results. This practice can have unwanted consequences, such as inadvertently filling the TempDB database. It is our job, as DBAs, to make sure this does not happen, often by performing a code review and offering an alternate solution.

Over the coming sections, I am going to delve into each of these issues, and discuss the techniques I have used to analyze and fix each one, where possible. I say "where possible" because sometimes data growth really does exceed all expectation and confound even the most rigorous capacity planning. The only course of action, in such cases, is to expand disks or add additional SAN space, things only peripherally known to many DBAs.

I want to stress that this chapter is not going to shine a light on SQL Server internals. I will not be taking you on a journey to the heart of the database engine to explore the esoteric concepts of leaf level storage. Every DBA needs to understand where and how objects, such as tables and indexes, use up space on your servers, and be very familiar with core concepts such as pages, extents, fill factors, as well as internal and external fragmentation. However, I will leave those details to Books Online. Here, I intend to drive the All Terrain Vehicle of my experience right to the source of the space allocation issues that wreak havoc on the waking and sleeping life of the on-call DBA.

Being a model DBA

This chapter is about space utilization in SQL Server and there is no better place to begin than with the Model database. The first thing I will say about the Model database is that, if it were up to me, I would rename it. Out of the box, there is nothing "model" about it; it is not a "model" citizen nor should it be considered a "role model" for other databases. Nevertheless, it is the template upon which all subsequent databases are based, including TempDB. In other words, new databases created on the server, unless otherwise specified, will inherit the configuration settings of the model database.

The full list of options for the Model database, including their default settings, can be found at http://technet.microsoft.com/en-us/library/ms186388.aspx. The defaults for most of the options are fine for most databases. Most significantly, however, the model database settings determine the following:

- Autogrowth properties for the data and log files
- Recovery model for the database

The default settings for each of these are definitely **not** appropriate for all databases, and it's easy for new DBAs, or even us old haggard DBAs, to forget to check these settings especially where we're working with a server configured by a previous DBA.

Beware of default autogrowth and recovery

By default, the data file (**modeldev**) for the Model database, for both SQL Server 2005 and 2008 will be roughly 3MB in size initially, and is set to autogrow in 1 MB (1024 K) increments, unrestricted, until the disk is full. The log file is set at an initial size of 2MB and is set to grow in 10% increments, again until the disk is full. These settings are shown in Figure 4.1.

> **NOTE**
> **Microsoft SQL Server 2008 Books Online states: "The sizes of these files can vary slightly for different editions of SQL Server." I am using Standard Edition for the examples in this chapter.**

In SQL Server storage terms, 1024K is 128 pages; pages are stored in 8K blocks. For applications that are going to potentially load millions of records, growing the data file of a database every 128 pages incurs a large performance hit, given that one of the major bottlenecks of SQL Server is I/O requests.

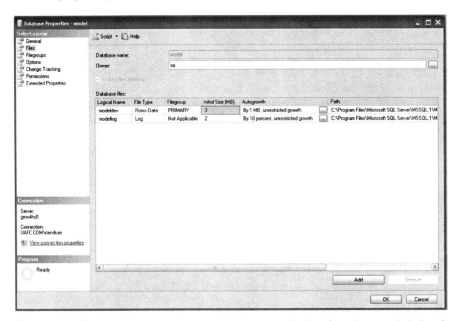

Figure 4.1: Initial sizes and growth characteristics for the model database data and log files.

Rather than accept these defaults, it is a much better practice to size the data file appropriately at the outset, at say 2G. The same advice applies for the log file. Generally, growth based on a percentage is fine until the file reaches a threshold where the next growth will consume the entire disk. Let's say you had a 40G log file on a 50G drive. It would only take two 10% growths to fill the disk, and then the alerts go out and you must awake, bleary-eyed, to shrink log files and curse the Model database.

Coupled with the previously-described file growth characteristics, our databases will also inherit from the default model database a recovery model of **Full**. Transactions in the log file for a Full recovery database are only ever removed from the log upon a transaction log backup. This is wonderful for providing point in time recovery for business critical applications that require Service Level Agreements (SLAs), but it does mean that if you do not backup the transaction log, you run the risk of eventually filling up your log drive.

If you have a database that is subject to hefty and /or regular (e.g. daily) bulk insert operations, and you are forcing the data file to be incremented in size regularly, by small amounts, then it's likely that the performance hit will be significant. It is also likely that the size of your log file will increase rapidly, unless you are performing regular transaction log backups.

To find out how significant an impact this can have, let's take a look at an example. I'll create a database called **All_Books_Ever_Read**, based on a default model database, and then load several million rows of data into a table in that database, while monitoring file growth and disk I/O activity, using Profiler and PerfMon, respectively. Loading this amount of data may sound like an extreme case, but it's actually "small fry" compared to many enterprise companies, that accumulate, dispense and disperse Terabytes of data.

> **NOTE**
> I just happen to own a file, Books-List.txt, that allegedly contains a listing of all books ever read by everyone on the planet Earth, which I'll use to fill the table. Surprisingly the file is only 33 MB. People are just not reading much any more.

The first step is to create the **All_Books_Ever_Read** database. The initial sizes of the data and log files, and their growth characteristics, will be inherited from the Model database, as described in Figure 4.1. Once I've created the database, I can verify the initial data (mdf) and log file (ldf) sizes are around 3 and 2 MB respectively, as shown in Figure 4.2.

Name ▲	Size	Type	Date Modified	Attributes
SQLLogs		File Folder	4/2/2009 9:49 PM	
SQLTempDB		File Folder	11/16/2006 3:13 PM	
All_Books_Ever_Read.mdf	3,072 KB	SQL Server Databa...	4/2/2009 9:49 PM	A
All_Books_Ever_Read_log.ldf	2,048 KB	SQL Server Databa...	4/2/2009 10:02 PM	A

Figure 4.2: Data and log files sizes prior to data load.

The next step is to back up the database. It's important to realize that, until I have performed a full database backup, the log file will not act like a typical log file in a database set to Full recovery mode. In fact, when there is no full backup of the database, it is not even possible to perform a transaction log backup at this point, as demonstrated in Figure 4.3.

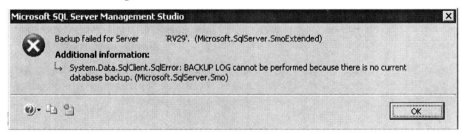

Figure 4.3: Can't backup log if no full database backup exists.

Figure 4.3: Can't backup log if no full database backup exists.

Until the first full backup of the database is performed, this database is acting as if it is in Simple recovery mode and the transaction log will get regularly truncated at checkpoints, so you will not see the full impact of the data load on the size of the log file.

With the database backed up, I need to set up Profiler and PerfMon so that I can monitor the data load. To monitor auto growth behavior using Profiler, simply start it up, connect to the SQL Server 2008 instance that holds the `All_Books_Ever_Read` database, and then set up a trace to monitor Data and Log file Auto Grow events, as shown in Figure 4.4.

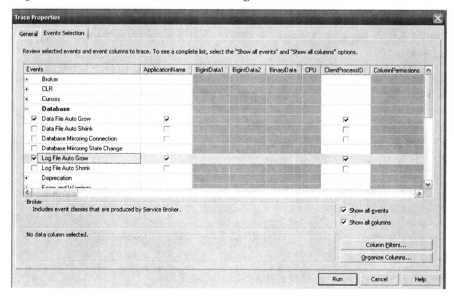

Figure 4.4: Setting SQL Server Profiler to capture data and log file growth.

All you have to do then is click "Run".

Next, I'll set up Perfmon (Administrative Tools |) in order to monitor disk I/O activity. Click on the "+" button in the toolbar of the graph; Perfmon will connect to the local server by default. Select "Physical Disk" as the performance object, as shown in Figure 4.5, and then select "% Disk Time" as the counter and click" Add".

Next, change to the Physical Disk object and select the "Average Disk Queue Length" and "Current Disk Queue Length" counters. These settings will capture the amount of disk activity, to review after the data load.

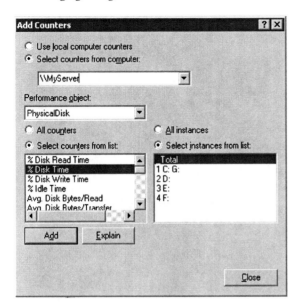

Figure 4.5: Physical Disk performance object in Perfmon.

With all monitoring systems a go, I am ready to load up a heap table called
book_list that I created in the **All_Books_Ever_Read** database. The **Books-
List.txt** file has approximately 58 thousand records, so I'm going to use the BCP
batch file technique (see Listing 3.3, in Chapter 3) to iterate through the file 50
times, and load 2.9 million records into the database. Now it is time to begin the
load. A quick peek at Perfmon, see Figure 4.6, shows the current absence of
activity prior to executing a hefty query.

PhysicalDisk	_Total
% Disk Time	0.000
Avg. Disk Queue Length	0.000
Current Disk Queue Length	0

Figure 4.6: Perfmon low disk activity.

Executing Load … now! Please don't turn (or create) the next page …!!

Sorry! I could not resist the Sesame Street reference to *The Monster at the End of
This Book*. In fact, the load proceeds with little fanfare. Imagine this is being done
in the middle of the afternoon, perhaps after a big lunch or, worse, early in the
AM (DBA:M most likely) before your second sip of coffee, with you blissfully
unaware of what's unfolding on one of your servers. Figure 4.7 shows the BCP
bulk insert process running.

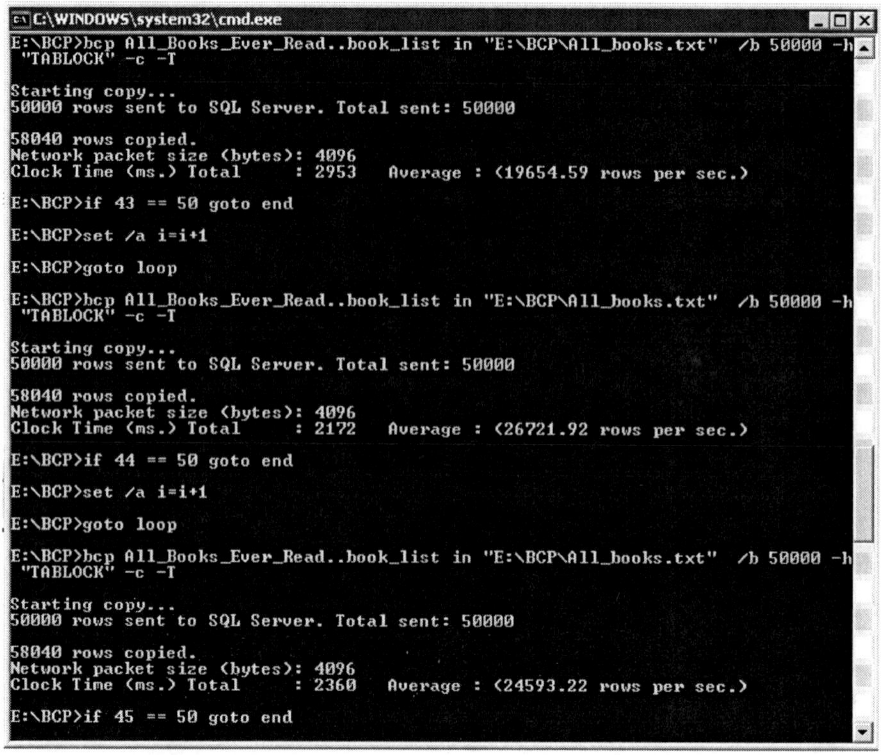

```
C:\WINDOWS\system32\cmd.exe                                    _ □ ×
E:\BCP>bcp All_Books_Ever_Read..book_list in "E:\BCP\All_books.txt"  /b 50000 -h
"TABLOCK" -c -T

Starting copy...
50000 rows sent to SQL Server. Total sent: 50000

58040 rows copied.
Network packet size (bytes): 4096
Clock Time (ms.) Total     : 2953    Average : (19654.59 rows per sec.)

E:\BCP>if 43 == 50 goto end

E:\BCP>set /a i=i+1

E:\BCP>goto loop

E:\BCP>bcp All_Books_Ever_Read..book_list in "E:\BCP\All_books.txt"  /b 50000 -h
"TABLOCK" -c -T

Starting copy...
50000 rows sent to SQL Server. Total sent: 50000

58040 rows copied.
Network packet size (bytes): 4096
Clock Time (ms.) Total     : 2172    Average : (26721.92 rows per sec.)

E:\BCP>if 44 == 50 goto end

E:\BCP>set /a i=i+1

E:\BCP>goto loop

E:\BCP>bcp All_Books_Ever_Read..book_list in "E:\BCP\All_books.txt"  /b 50000 -h
"TABLOCK" -c -T

Starting copy...
50000 rows sent to SQL Server. Total sent: 50000

58040 rows copied.
Network packet size (bytes): 4096
Clock Time (ms.) Total     : 2360    Average : (24593.22 rows per sec.)

E:\BCP>if 45 == 50 goto end
```

Figure 4.7: BCPing data into the `All_Books_Ever_Read` database.

You can see that the batch process ran 50 times at an average of 2.5 seconds a run, with a total load time of roughly 2 minutes. Not bad for 2.9 million records. Now for the bad news: Figure 4.8 shows how much growth can be directly attributed to the load process.

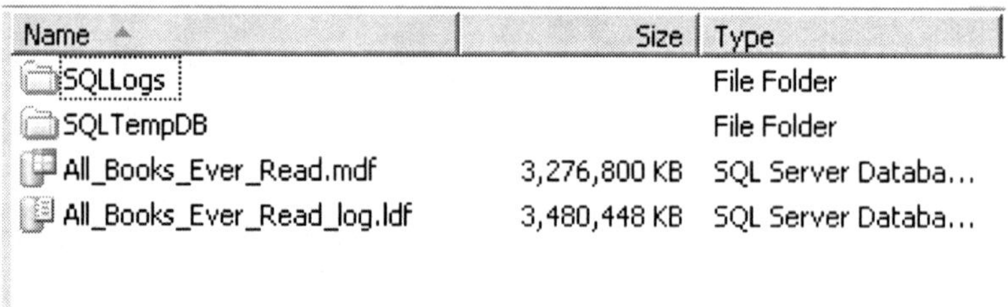

Name ▲	Size	Type
SQLLogs		File Folder
SQLTempDB		File Folder
All_Books_Ever_Read.mdf	3,276,800 KB	SQL Server Databa...
All_Books_Ever_Read_log.ldf	3,480,448 KB	SQL Server Databa...

Figure 4.8: Log file growth loading millions of records into table.

NOTE
For comparison, in a test I ran without ever having backed up the database, the data file grew to over 3 GB, but the log file grew only to 150 MB.

106

Both the data file and the log file have grown to over 3GB. The Profiler trace, as shown in Figure 4.9, reveals that a combined total of 3291 Auto Grow events took place during this data load. Notice also that the duration of these events, when combined, is not negligible.

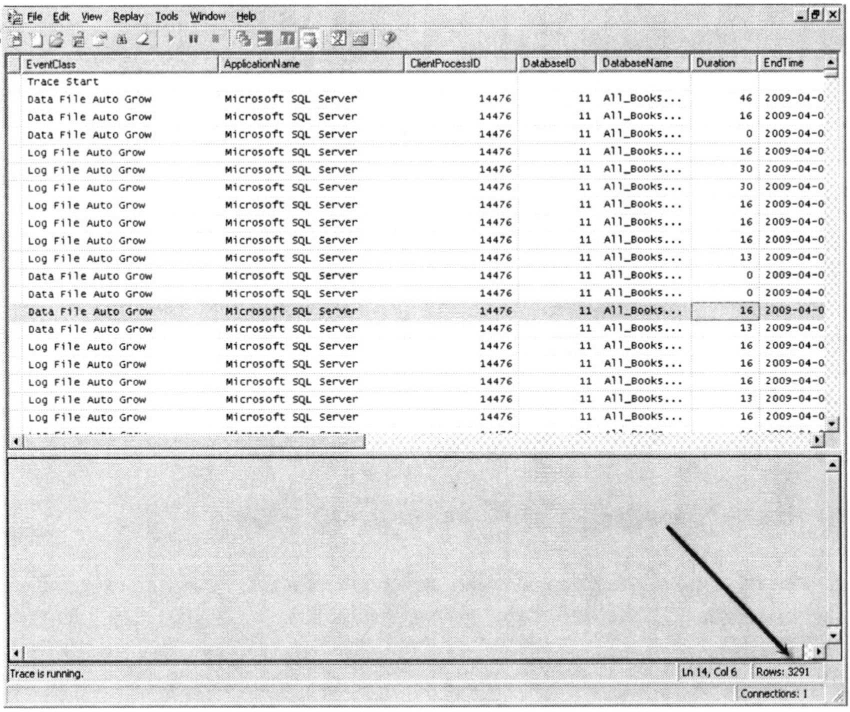

Figure 4.9: Data and log file growth captured with Profiler.

Finally, Figure 4.10 shows the Perfmon output during load. As you can see, **% Disk Time** obviously took a hit at 44.192 %. This is not horrible in and of itself; obviously I/O processes require disk reads and writes and, because "Avg Disk Queue Length" is healthily under 3, it means the disk is able to keep up with the demands. However, if the disk being monitored has a **%DiskTime** of 80%, or more, coupled with a higher (>20) Avg Disk Queue Length, then there will be performance degradation because the disk can not meet the demand. Inefficient queries or file growth may be the culprits.

PhysicalDisk	_Total
% Disk Time	44.192
Avg. Disk Queue Length	1.768
Current Disk Queue Length	0

Figure 4.10: Perfmon disk monitor.

Average and Current Disk Queue Lengths are indicators of whether or not bottlenecks might exist in the disk subsystem. In this case, an Average Disk Queue Length of 1.768 is not intolerably high and indicates that, on average, fewer than 2 requests were queued, waiting for I/O processes, either read or write, to complete on the Disk.

What this also tells me is that loading 2.9 million records into a heap table, batching or committing every 50,000 records, and using the defaults of the Model database, is going to cause significant I/O lag, resulting not just from loading the data, but also from the need to grow the data and log files a few thousand times.

Furthermore, with so much activity, the database is susceptible to unabated log file growth, unless you perform regular log backups to remove inactive log entries from the log file. Many standard maintenance procedures implement full backups for newly created databases, but not all databases receive transaction log backups. This could come up to bite you, like the monster at the end of this chapter, if you forget to change the recovery model from Full to Simple, or if you restore a database from another system and unwittingly leave the database in Full recovery mode.

Appropriately sizing your data and log files

Having seen the dramatic impact of such bulk load operations on file size, what I really want to know now is how much I could reduce the I/O load, and therefore increase the speed of the load process, if the engine hadn't had to grow the files 3291 times, in 1 MB increments for the data file, and 10% increments for the log file.

In order to find out, I need to repeat the load process, but with the data and log files already appropriately sized to handle it. I can achieve this by simply truncating the table and backing up the transaction log. This will not shrink the physical data or log files but it will free up all of the space inside them. Before I do that, take a look at the sort of space allocation information that is provided by the sp_spaceused built-in stored procedure in Figure 4.11.

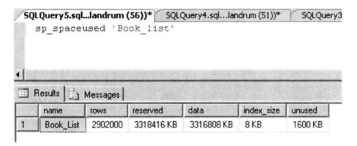

Figure 4.11: Output of sp_spaceused for the loaded Book_List table.

As you can see, the **Book_List** table is using all 3.3 GB of the space allocated to the database for the 2.9 million records. Now simply issue the **TRUNCATE** command.

```
Truncate Table Book_List
```

And then rerun **sp_spaceused**. The results are shown in Figure 4.12.

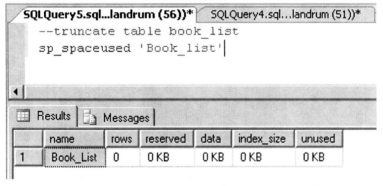

Figure 4.12: sp_spaceused after truncation.

You can verify that the data file, although now "empty", is still 3.3GB in size using the **Shrink File** task in the SSMS GUI. Right click on the database, and select "Tasks |Shrink | Files". You can see in Figure 4.13 that the **All_Books_Ever_Read.mdf** file is still 3.3 GB in size but has 99% available free space.

What this means to me as a DBA, knowing I am going to load the same 2.9 million records, is that I do not expect that the data file will grow again. Figure 4.14 shows the command window after re-running the BCP bulk insert process, superimposed on the resulting Profiler trace.

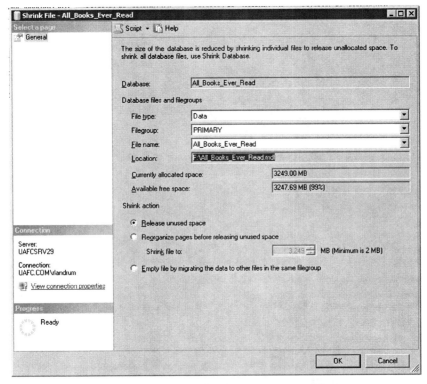

Figure 4.13: Free space in data file after truncate table statement.

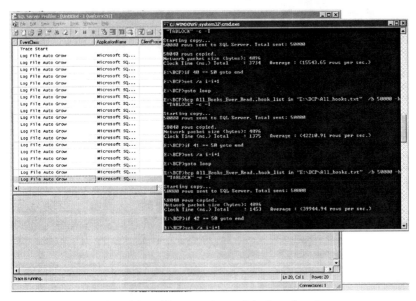

Figure 4.14: Minimal log file growing with data load.

This time there were no Auto Grow events for the data file, and only 20 for the log file. The net effect is that the average time to load 50,000 records is reduced from 2.5 seconds to 1.3 seconds. A time saving of just over 1 second per load may not seem significant at first, but consider the case where the same process normally takes an hour. Just by ensuring log and data growth was controlled, you have cut the process down to under 30 minutes, and saved a lot of I/O processing at the same time.

Handling space problems

I've shown that having incorrectly sized data and log files and inappropriate Auto Grow properties, both inherited from the model database, can significantly increase the I/O load during bulk insert processes. I've also demonstrated the dangers of unabated log file growth, unless you change the default recovery model or perform regular log backups.

Even for a database that is subject to as few as 50K transactions per day, I have seen the database log file grow to over 220G over the course of a few months, because no log backups have been taken. The reason for this is that, generally, there are databases with low level SLAs, meaning that a full nightly backup is all that is required.

As I've stressed previously, handling these space issues is mainly about planning. The DBA needs to:

- **Correctly size the files** – if you know that the database you are managing can expect a 2 Gig growth per month, size the data file(s) at 4G initially, not the 3 MB size that will be the default from the Model database.
- **Set correct auto grow properties** – while 10% growth for data and log files may be sufficient for low utilization databases, typically I set at least 500 MB for the auto growth settings for the data and log files. Unless I expect there to be unusually high data growth, 500 MB represents a good average growth rate, and keeps space utilization at a manageable level but allows for growth over time without heavy I/O impact.
- **Make sure only those databases that need FULL recovery are using it** – you will determine this from the business and will be part of the SLA for the application and database. If point-in-time recovery is required, make sure you have regular log backups taken of the databases in Full recovery mode.
- **Switch to bulk-logged mode for bulk insert operations** (see Chapter 3) – bulk loading is a common practice and, if done correctly, will incur minimal log growth, while reaping the performance benefits bulk loading brings. However, make sure you understand the consequences of

changing the recovery models while bulk loading data. For instance, you will be unable to perform a point-in-time recovery for the bulk transactions.

If you fail to plan properly, or are simply subject to unexpected and unpredictable file growth, what does this mean for the DBA?

Suppose a database has been inadvertently set to Full recovery with no log backups. The log file has gown massively in size and, ultimately, the drive will run out of space. If you are lucky enough, as I am to have an alerting system (see Chapter 6), the problem will be caught before that happens and I will get an alert, predictably at 2:30 AM when I have just gone to bed after resolving a different issue.

What I do in such situations, after cursing myself or other innocent people on my team for not catching this sooner, is to issue the following simple statement:

```
BACKUP LOG <databasename> WITH Truncate_Only
```

This statement has the net effect of removing all of the inactive transactions from the log file that would have otherwise been removed with a standard log backup.

Next, I shrink the log file via the GUI (or, if I am not too tired, with code) and then change the recovery model to Simple and go back to bed. Doing this will generally reclaim the necessary disk space to clear all alerts, and ensure that no further log growth will ensue. You can use DBCC to physically shrink a data or log file, as follows:

```
DBCC SHRINKFILE  (filename, target_size)
```

Many of the situations that require you to shrink a log file can be avoided simply by planning accordingly and being diligent and fastidious in your installation process (see Chapter 1), in particular by making sure the model database is always set to Simple and not Full recovery mode. It only needs to happen to you once or twice. I quote George W. Bush, "Fool me once … shame on … shame on you … Fool me can't get fooled again."

Take that, SQL Server Model Database.

Indexes and large row counts

All DBAs know that indexes are necessary for Olympic style query performance We also know that they come at a price; and that price is paid in the currency of space and maintenance time. As much as I desperately yearn for the developer's queries to work efficiently, the DBA is still the gatekeeper of the data and feels obliged to point out the specifics of why queries will and will not benefit from the indexes that the developers suggest.

Often, these index recommendations come from sources like the Database Tuning Advisor (DTA), so we DBAs often eschew them in favor of our own. I do not mean to seem high-minded on this point, my DBA nose pointed straight up in the air. However, rightly or wrongly, DBAs want to control the types of objects (triggers, temp tables, linked servers, and so on) that are added to their servers, and indexes are just another type of object that DBAs must understand, manage and maintain.

I am all in favor of a clustered index on almost every table, backed by a healthy volume of covering non-clustered indexes, but I also know from experience that indexes, for all their good, will only be utilized when proper code is executed that will take advantage of them. It is always worthwhile to explain to SQL developers why their queries do not perform as they expect, with their proposed indexes.

In this section, I am going to add indexes to the **Book_List** table in order to find out:

- How much extra space is required in order to add a clustered index to a table containing 2.9 million rows.
- Whether this space consumption is justified, by examining the proposed queries that intend to take advantage of the indexes.

Let's first get a "before" glimpse of space utilization in our **Book_List** table, using the **sp_spaceused** stored procedure, as shown in Figure 4.15. Notice the 8K of index size.

	name	rows	reserved	data	index_size	unused
1	Book_List	2902000	3318416 KB	3316808 KB	8 KB	1600 KB

Figure 4.15: index_size of Book_List table.

Before I can add a clustered index, I need to add an identity column, called **Read_ID**, on which to place the clustered index. Adding the identity column is, in itself, an expensive task for 2.9 million records. The code is as follows:

```
ALTER TABLE Book_list ADD
Read_ID INT IDENTITY
```

We can now create the clustered index on this **Read_ID** column, as shown in Listing 4.1.

```
USE [All_Books_Ever_Read]
GO
CREATE UNIQUE CLUSTERED INDEX [Read_ID] ON [dbo].[Book_List] (
[Read_Date] ASC )
    WITH (
            STATISTICS_NORECOMPUTE   = OFF,
            SORT_IN_TEMPDB = OFF,
            IGNORE_DUP_KEY = OFF,
            DROP_EXISTING = OFF,
            ONLINE = OFF,
            ALLOW_ROW_LOCKS   = ON,
            ALLOW_PAGE_LOCKS  = ON)
ON   [PRIMARY]
GO
```

Listing 4.1: Creating a clustered index on the Read_ID **column of the** Book_List **table.**

As you can see from Figure 4.16, building a clustered index on almost 3 million records takes some time and processing power.

Figure 4.16: It takes over 12 minutes to build the clustered index.

114

Also, it should be noted that users will be unable to connect to the **Book_List** table for the duration of the index build. Essentially, SQL Server has to physically order those millions of records to align with the definition of the clustered index.

Let's see what the index took out of my hide by way of space. The former index space for this table was 8K and data space was over 3 Gig. What does **sp_spaceused** tell me now? See Figure 4.17.

	name	rows	reserved	data	index_size	unused
1	Book_List	2902000	3322000 KB	3316576 KB	5376 KB	48 KB

Figure 4.17: Building the clustered index has increased the index_size **to 5376KB.**

An increase in **index_size** to 5376K does not seem too significant. When you create a clustered index, the database engine takes the data in the heap (table) and physically sorts it. In the simplest terms, both a heap and a clustered table (a table with a clustered index) both store the actual data, one is just physically sorted. So, I would not expect that adding a clustered index for the **Read_ID** column to cause much growth in **index_size**.

However, while the data size and index size for the **Book_List** table did not grow significantly, the space allocated for the database did double, as you can see from Figure 4.18.

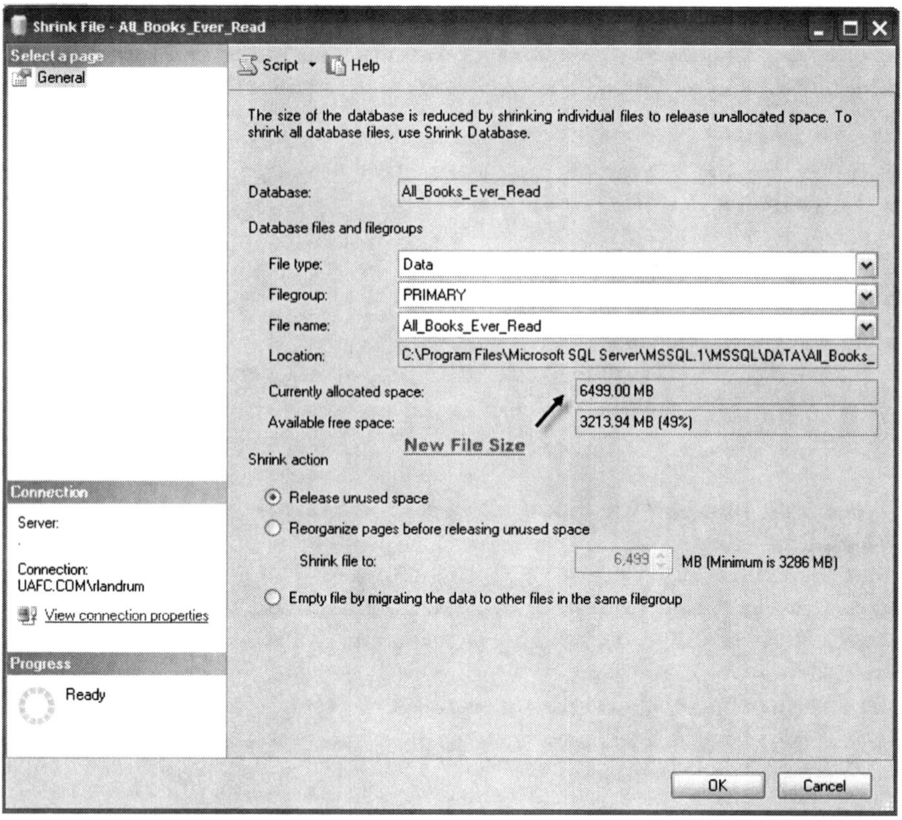

Figure 4.18: Creating the clustered index caused the data file to double in size.

So not only did the index addition take the table offline for the duration of the build, 12 minutes, it also doubled the space on disk. The reason for the growth is that SQL Server had to do all manner of processing to reorganize the data from a heap to a clustered table and additional space, almost double, was required to accommodate this migration from a heap table to a clustered table. Notice, though, that after the process has completed there is nearly 50% free space in the expanded file.

The question remains, did I benefit from adding this index, and do I need to add any covering non-clustered indexes? First, let's consider the simple query shown in Listing 4.2. It returns data based on a specified range of **Read_ID** values (I know I have a range of data between 1 and 2902000 records).

```
Select  book_list.Read_ID,
  book_list.Read_Date,
      book_list.Book,
```

```
           book_list.Person
from       book_list
where      Read_Id between 756000 and 820000
```

Listing 4.2: A query on the Read_ID column.

This query returned 64,001 records in 2 seconds which, at first glance, appears to be the sort of performance I'd expect. However, to confirm this, I need to examine the execution plan, as shown in Figure 4.19.

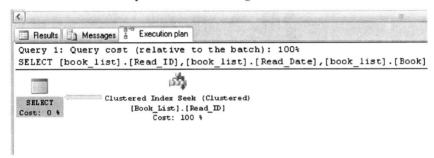

Figure 4.19: Beneficial use of clustered index for the Book_list table.

You can see that an Index Seek operation was used, which indicates that this index has indeed served our query well. It means that the engine was able to retrieve all of the required data based solely on the key values stored in the index. If, instead, I had seen an Index Scan, this would indicate that the engine decided to scan every single row of the index in order to retrieve the ones required. An Index Scan is similar in concept to a table scan and both are generally inefficient, especially when dealing with such large record sets. However, the query engine will sometimes choose to do a scan even if a usable index is in place if, for example, a high percentage of the rows need to be returned. This is often an indicator of an inefficient **WHERE** clause.

Let's say I now want to query a field that is not included in the clustered index, such as the **Read_Date**. I would like to know how many books were read on July 24th of 2008. The query would look something like that shown in Listing 4.3.

```
Select     count(book_list.Read_ID),
           book_list.Read_Date
from       book_list
where      book_list.Read_Date between '07/24/2008 00:00:00'
                               and     '07/24/2008 11:59:59'
Group By book_list.Read_Date
```

Listing 4.3: A query that is not covered by the clustered index.

Executing this query, and waiting for the results to return, is a bit like watching paint dry or, something I like to do frequently, watching a hard drive defragment. It took 1 minute and 28 seconds to complete, and returned 123 records, with an average count of the number of books read on 7/24/2008 of 1000.

The execution plan for this query, not surprisingly, shows that an index scan was utilized, as you can see in Figure 4.20.

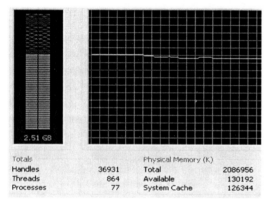

Figure 4.20: Clustered index scan for field with no index.

What was a bit surprising, though, is that the memory allocation for SQL Server shot up through the roof as this query was executed. Figure 4.21 shows the memory consumption at 2.51G which is pretty drastic considering the system only has 2G of RAM.

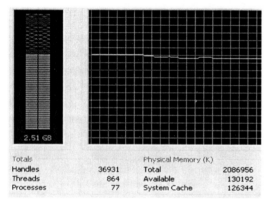

Totals		Physical Memory (K)	
Handles	36931	Total	2086956
Threads	864	Available	130192
Processes	77	System Cache	126344

Figure 4.21: Memory utilization resulting from date range query.

The reason for the memory increase is that, since there was no available index to limit the data for the query, SQL Server had to load several million records into the buffer cache in order to give me back the 123 rows I needed. Unless you have enabled AWE, and set max server memory to 2G (say) less than total server memory (see memory configurations for SQL Server in Chapter 1), then the server is going to begin paging, as SQL Server grabs more than its fair share of memory, and thrashing disks. This will have a substantial impact on performance.

If there is one thing that I know for sure with regard to SQL Server configuration and management, it is that once SQL Server has acquired memory, it does not like to give it back to the OS unless prodded to do so. Even though the query I ran has completed many minutes ago, my SQL Server instance still hovers at 2.5G of memory used, most of it by SQL Server.

It's clear that I need to create indexes that will cover the queries I need to run, and so avoid SQL Server doing such an expensive index scan. I know that this is not always possible in a production environment, with many teams of developers all writing their own queries in their own style, but in my isolated environment it is an attainable goal.

The first thing I need to do is restart SQL Server to get back down to a manageable level of memory utilization. While there are other methods to reduce the memory footprint, such as freeing the buffer cache (**DBCC DROPCLEANBUFFERS**), I have the luxury of an isolated environment and restarting SQL Server will give me a "clean start" for troubleshooting. Having done this, I can add two non-clustered indexes, one which will cover queries on the **Book** field and the other the **Read_Date** field.

Having created the two new indexes, let's take another look at space utilization in the **Book_List** table, using sp_spaceused, as shown in Figure 4.22.

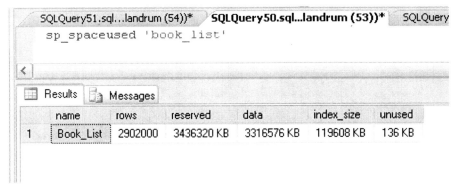

Figure 4.22: Increased index size for 2 non clustered indexes.

The **index_size** has risen from 5MB to 119MB, which seems fairly minimal, and an excellent trade-off assuming we get the expected boost in the performance of the **read_date** query.

If you are a DBA, working alongside developers who give you their queries for analysis, this is where you hold your breath. Breath held, I click execute. And ... the query went from 1 minute 28 seconds to 2 seconds without even a baby's burp in SQL Server memory. The new execution plan, shown in Figure 4.23, tells the full story.

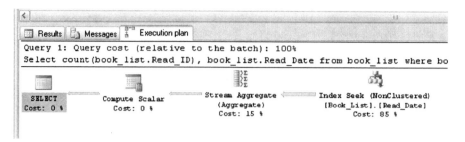

Figure 4.23: Addition of covering indexes leads to an efficient index seek operation.

So, while indexes do indeed take space, this space utilization is usually more than warranted when they are used correctly, and we see the desired pay-off in query performance.

The issue with indexes arises when development teams adopt a scattergun approach to indexes, sometimes to the point of redundancy and harm to the database. Adding indexes arbitrarily can often do as much harm as good, not only because of the space that they take up, but because each index will need to be maintained, which takes time and resources.

TempDB

No DBA who has been working with SQL Server for long will have been immune to runaway TempDB growth. If this growth is left unchecked, it can eventually fill up a drive and prohibit any further activity in SQL Server that also requires the use of the TempDB database.

SQL Server uses the TempDB database for a number of processes, such as sorting operations, creating indexes, cursors, table variables, database mail and user defined functions, to name several. In addition to internal processes, users have the ability to create temporary tables and have free reign to fill these tables with as much data as they wish, assuming that growth of the TempDB data file is not restricted to a specific value, which by default it is not.

I do not recommend restricting growth for TempDB files, but I do recommend that you be aware of what will happen if TempDB does fill up. Many SQL Server processes, including user processes, will cease and an error message will be thrown, as I will show.

The TempDB database is created each time SQL Server is restarted. It is never backed up nor can it be. It is always in Simple mode and the recovery model cannot be changed.

There are a couple of TempDB "properties", though, that you can and should change when configuring your server:

- Its location
- Its autogrowth rate

By default, TempDB is created in the default data folder, which is set during SQL installation. It is highly recommended that, if possible, this location be changed so that TempDB resides on its own disk. Many DBAs also create multiple TempDB files, typically one per processor, with the aim of boosting performance still further. However, be warned that you will need to spread the load of these multiple files across multiple disks, in order to achieve this.

Like all other databases, TempDB adopts the default configuration of the model database, which means that it will grow in 10% increments with unrestricted growth, unless you specify otherwise. In my opinion, having an autogrowth of 10% on TempDB is a bad idea because when rogue queries hit your server, calling for temporary tables, as they will do eventually, you do not want the TempDB database filling up the drive. Let's assume that you have a 30G TempDB database sitting on a 50G drive and autogrowing in 10% (i.e. 3G) increments. It would take only 6 growth events to fill the drive. Ideally, you will want to set a fixed growth rate of 3G for TempDB and use multiple TempDB data files across multiple disks.

When loading multiple tens of millions of records into TempDB, bearing in mind that 1 million records is roughly equivalent to 1G, you can see how this can happen fairly easily. So, what happens when TempDB fills up? Let's find out!

I'd have to generate a lot of TempDB activity to fill up 50GB of disk, so I am going to artificially restrict the data file for TempDB to a size of 200 MB, via the "maximum file size" property. Figure 4.24 shows the configuration.

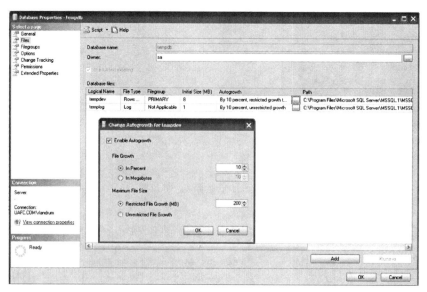

Figure 4.24: Changing the TempDB maximum file size to 2 Gigabytes for simulation.

Now that I've set the maximum file size for TempDB, it is time to fill it up and for that I will turn to our old friend, the endless loop. I have seen only a few of these in the wild but they do exist, I promise, and when you combine an endless loop with data or log space limitation, something has to give. Listing 4.4 shows the loopy code.

```
CREATE TABLE #HoldAll
    (
       Read_ID INT,
       Read_Date DATETIME,
       Person VARCHAR(100)
    )
GO
DECLARE @cnt int = 1
WHILE @cnt = 1
    BEGIN

        INSERT   INTO #HoldAll
                 SELECT   Read_ID,
                          Read_Date,
                          Person
                 FROM     All_Books_Ever_Read.dbo.book_List
                 WHERE Read_Date > '05/21/08'
    END
GO
```

Listing 4.4: The dreaded endless loop.

Notice that **@cnt** is given the value of 1, but nowhere subsequently is the value changed, so this query will run and run until it fills up a drive or surpasses a file size threshold, whichever comes sooner. In this example, the query runs for 3 minutes before we hit the 200MB file size limit, as shown in Figure 4.25, and get an error that the filegroup is full.

```
CREATE TABLE #HoldAll

    Read_ID INT,
    Read_Date DATETIME,
    Person VARCHAR(100)

GO
DECLARE @cnt int = 1
WHILE @cnt = 1
    BEGIN

        INSERT  INTO #HoldAll
                SELECT  Read_ID,
                        Read_Date,
                        Person
                FROM    All_Books_Ever_Read.dbo.book_List
                WHERE   Read_Date > '05/21/08'
    END
GO
```

```
Messages
Table 'Book_List'. Scan count 1, logical reads 415242, physical reads 2841, read-ahead reads 350782, lob logical reads 0, lob physical reads 0, lob

(2900150 row(s) affected)
Msg 1105, Level 17, State 2, Line 5
Could not allocate space for object 'temporary system object: 100580631706579520' in database 'tempdb' because the 'PRIMARY' filegroup is full.
```

Figure 4.25: Filling up TempDB.

At this point the query fails, obviously, as will any other queries that need to use TempDB. SQL Server is still functioning properly, but as long as the temp table **#HoldAll** exists, TempDB will stay filled.

Hopefully, you've got notifications and alerts set up to warn you of the imminent danger, before the file actually fills up (I will cover notifications, alerts and monitoring in depth in Chapter 6). In any event, you are likely to experience that DBA:M feeling, having spent half the night trying to track down the problem query and resolve the issue.

Your three options, as a DBA, are to:

- Restart SQL Server.
- Try to shrink the TempDB database.
- Find the errant query and eradicate it.

Generally speaking, restarting is not always an option in a production system. Shrinking TempDB is a valid option, assuming that it can be shrunk. Sometimes, when there are open transactions, it is not possible. Therefore, finding and killing the offending query is the more likely course of action. The techniques you can use to do this are the focus of the very next chapter, on Troubleshooting.

For now, I am going to simply close the query window which should force the temp table to be deleted and so allow the shrink operation to go ahead. Sure enough, once I'd closed the connection I was able to select Tasks | Shrink |Database from within SSMS, and so shrink TempDB from 200 MB back down to its original size of 8K. Problem solved.

Now, back to bed with a sleepy note to self to find the developer who wrote this code, and chastise him or her. Wait, I am the DBA who let this get into production in the first place, so new list ... chastise self, get back to sleep, find the developer tomorrow and chastise him or her anyway; if they ask how it got into production ... change subject.

A query to determine current space utilization

I have written a few articles about various queries that help me with my day to day job as a DBA. The following query is one that I use every single day to monitor potential space issues on my servers. If I notice a "danger signal" I can then dig deeper and determine the root cause, which is usually one of the issues discussed in this chapter i.e. log file growth due to incorrect recovery models, too many indexes, TempDB filling up, or just poor capacity planning.

The **SizeQuery** query, shown in Listing 4.5, combines output from several sources, such as **sp_MSForEachDB** and **xp_fixeddrives**, and merges them to show how much data and log space is used, what drive that space is used on, and how much free space is available.

```
Set NoCount On
--Check to see the temp table exists
IF EXISTS ( SELECT  Name
            FROM    tempdb..sysobjects
            Where   name like '#HoldforEachDB%' )
--If So Drop it
    DROP TABLE #HoldforEachDB_size
--Recreate it
CREATE TABLE #HoldforEachDB_size
    (
        [DatabaseName] [nvarchar](75) COLLATE
SQL_Latin1_General_CP1_CI_AS
                                NOT NULL,
        [Size] [decimal] NOT NULL,
        [Name] [nvarchar](75) COLLATE
SQL_Latin1_General_CP1_CI_AS
                                NOT NULL,
        [Filename] [nvarchar](255) COLLATE
SQL_Latin1_General_CP1_CI_AS
                                NOT NULL,

    )
ON  [PRIMARY]
```

```
IF EXISTS ( SELECT   name
            FROM     tempdb..sysobjects
            Where    name like '#fixed_drives%' )
--If So Drop it
   DROP TABLE #fixed_drives
--Recreate it
CREATE TABLE #fixed_drives
    (
       [Drive] [char](1) COLLATE SQL_Latin1_General_CP1_CI_AS
                         NOT NULL,
       [MBFree] [decimal] NOT NULL
    )
ON [PRIMARY]
--Insert rows from sp_MSForEachDB into temp table
INSERT  INTO #HoldforEachDB_size
        EXEC sp_MSforeachdb 'Select ''?'' as DatabaseName, Case
When [?]..sysfiles.size * 8 / 1024 = 0 Then 1 Else
[?]..sysfiles.size * 8 / 1024 End
AS size,[?]..sysfiles.name,
[?]..sysfiles.filename From [?]..sysfiles'
--Select all rows from temp table (the temp table will auto
delete when the connection is gone.

INSERT  INTO #fixed_drives
        EXEC xp_fixeddrives


Select  @@Servername
print '' ;
Select  rtrim(Cast(DatabaseName as varchar(75))) as
DatabaseName,
        Drive,
        Filename,
        Cast(Size as int) AS Size,
        Cast(MBFree as varchar(10)) as MB_Free
from    #HoldforEachDB_size
        INNER JOIN #fixed_drives ON
LEFT(#HoldforEachDB_size.Filename, 1) = #fixed_drives.Drive
GROUP BY DatabaseName,
        Drive,
        MBFree,
        Filename,
        Cast(Size as int)
ORDER BY Drive,
        Size Desc
print '' ;
Select  Drive as [Total Data Space Used |],
        Cast(Sum(Size) as varchar(10)) as [Total Size],
        Cast(MBFree as varchar(10)) as MB_Free
from    #HoldforEachDB_size
```

```
            INNER JOIN #fixed_drives ON
LEFT(#HoldforEachDB_size.Filename, 1) = #fixed_drives.Drive
Group by Drive,
        MBFree
print '' ;
Select   count(Distinct rtrim(Cast(DatabaseName as
varchar(75)))) as Database_Count
from     #HoldforEachDB_size
```

Listing 4.5: Size query.

Example results of the Size query are shown in Figure 4.26.

	DatabaseName	Drive	Filename	Size	MB_Free
1	All_Books_Ever_Read	C	C:\Program Files\Microsoft SQL Server\MSSQL.1\MSSQL\DATA\All_Books_Ever_Read.mdf	6499	61366
2	DBA_Rep	C	C:\Program Files\Microsoft SQL Server\MSSQL.1\MSSQL\DATA\DBA_Rep.mdf	2381	61366
3	DBA_Rep	C	C:\Program Files\Microsoft SQL Server\MSSQL.1\MSSQL\DATA\DBA_Rep_log.LDF	1744	61366
4	AdventureWorks2008	C	C:\Program Files\Microsoft SQL Server\MSSQL.1\MSSQL\DATA\AdventureWorks2008_Data.mdf	226	61366
5	dba_rep_test_native	C	C:\Program Files\Microsoft SQL Server\MSSQL.1\MSSQL\DATA\dba_rep_test_native.mdf	182	61366
6	AdventureWorks	C	C:\Program Files\Microsoft SQL Server\MSSQL.1\MSSQL\DATA\AdventureWorks_Data.mdf	170	61366
7	DCDW	C	C:\Program Files\Microsoft SQL Server\MSSQL.1\MSSQL\DATA\DCDW.mdf	100	61366
8	AdventureWorksDW2008	C	C:\Program Files\Microsoft SQL Server\MSSQL.1\MSSQL\DATA\AdventureWorksDW2008_Data.mdf	68	61366
9	AdventureWorksDW	C	C:\Program Files\Microsoft SQL Server\MSSQL.1\MSSQL\DATA\AdventureWorksDW_Data.mdf	66	61366
10	dba_rep_test_native	C	C:\Program Files\Microsoft SQL Server\MSSQL.1\MSSQL\DATA\dba_rep_test_native_1.LDF	61	61366
11	All_Books_Ever_Read	C	C:\Program Files\Microsoft SQL Server\MSSQL.1\MSSQL\DATA\All_Books_Ever_Read_log.ldf	56	61366
12	Pro_SSRS	C	C:\Program Files\Microsoft SQL Server\MSSQL.1\MSSQL\DATA\Pro_SSRS.mdf	39	61366
13	Pro_SSRS	C	C:\Program Files\Microsoft SQL Server\MSSQL.1\MSSQL\DATA\Pro_SSRS.ldf	38	61366
14	msdb	C	C:\Program Files\Microsoft SQL Server\MSSQL.1\MSSQL\DATA\MSDBData.mdf	24	61366
15	msdb	C	C:\Program Files\Microsoft SQL Server\MSSQL.1\MSSQL\DATA\MSDBLog.ldf	23	61366
16	AdventureWorks2008	C	C:\Program Files\Microsoft SQL Server\MSSQL.1\MSSQL\DATA\AdventureWorks2008_Log.ldf	18	61366
17	DCDW	C	C:\Program Files\Microsoft SQL Server\MSSQL.1\MSSQL\DATA\DCDW_log.ldf	10	61366
18	SELECT	C	C:\Program Files\Microsoft SQL Server\MSSQL.1\MSSQL\DATA\SELECT_1.ldf	9	61366
19	AdventureWorksLT2008	C	C:\Program Files\Microsoft SQL Server\MSSQL.1\MSSQL\DATA\AdventureWorksLT2008_Data.mdf	8	61366
20	tempdb	C	C:\Program Files\Microsoft SQL Server\MSSQL.1\MSSQL\DATA\tempdb.mdf	8	61366
21	AdventureWorksLT	C	C:\Program Files\Microsoft SQL Server\MSSQL.1\MSSQL\DATA\AdventureWorksLT_Data.mdf	5	61366
22	dbDBA	C	C:\Writing\Simple Talk Book\dbDBA_Data.MDF	5	61366

	Total Data Space Used	Total Size	MB_Free
1	C	11787	61366

	Database_Count
1	21

Figure 4.26: Output of Size query.

You can see that the **All_Books_Ever_Read** database has 6.4G of allocated space on the **C:** drive. Since my sample databases reside only on the **C:** drive, all allocation is for this drive. However, if I were to have my log files on **E:** and TempDB on **F:**, for example, then query output would show the breakdown for each drive that actually stores any database file. You can see there is 61G free on the **C:** drive and of that 11G consists of database files.

126

Summary

In this chapter, I have explored some of the scenarios where disk space is consumed by processes, in many cases because of incorrect configurations for recovery models, data growth for large objects and queries that overtax TempDB resources. Many of these scenarios can be avoided with proper planning. However, it can be expected that, at some point, there will arise a situation that requires the DBA team to jump in and rescue the SQL Server.

When this happens, and it happens quite frequently, DBAs need to have an arsenal of troubleshooting tools at their disposal. In the next chapter I am going to introduce some of the tools and techniques that I have used to quickly troubleshoot common problems that crop up for DBAs.

Hey, there was no monster at the end of this chapter after all. Surely it will be in the next chapter.

CHAPTER 5: DBA AS DETECTIVE

If you consider it fun to find and fix SQL Server problems then I can say without fear of contradiction that this chapter is going to come at you in a clown suit.

I always feel better at the end of the day if I've been able to isolate a problem and offer a fix. Being a SQL Server DBA, overseeing terabytes of critical business data, can be both highly stressful and highly rewarding. Frightening? Yes, like a horror movie with suspect code lurking in every shadow. Fulfilling? Absolutely, when you discover that you are only one temp table or sub-query away from being the day's hero or heroine.

This chapter is all about sleuthing in SQL Server, peeling back layer after layer of data until you've uncovered the bare metal of the problem. It can be both fun and painstaking. Words like "Deadlock" and "Victim" are common, so we must tread with care through this twilight world. And, if worse comes to worse, we may have to "Kill" something. These murderous tendencies in a DBA make many, mainly developers, fearful to approach us. They creep up to our cubicle and tempt us with their feigned courtesy; "Can you please kill me?" they ask expectantly.

"Absolutely" is our reply.

System tables versus DMVs

Before I start troubleshooting, it is important to note that the steps that I take as a DBA, at this point in my career, are ones that allow for querying across multiple versions of SQL Server: 2000, 2005 and 2008. While I certainly can appreciate the utility of the Dynamic Management Views (DMVs) in SQL 2005 and 2008, there are many companies in the real world that still use SQL 2000. As much as I would love to say that all of the servers that I manage are SQL 2005, that is just not the case. The reason that companies may be slow to upgrade are many-fold, although cost and third party application support are the two primary reasons.

However, the system tables that I use here will be deprecated in a few years, and I surely will as well. For this reason, I would strongly recommend that anyone who works primarily with SQL Server 2005 and higher should use the DMVs. With slight modification, the queries I present here can utilize DMVs in lieu of system tables or system stored procedures.

For additional information on mapping Distributed Management Views to system tables in 2000, 2005 and 2008, please see Books Online topic "Mapping System Tables to System Views."

Tracking down database performance issues

You are a DBA sitting at your cubicle, or if you are fortunate, your corner office with wrap around tinted windows overlooking a flowing brook with squirrels and hibiscus, the rustling of nothing special blowing through your perfectly set A/C vent … OK, your cubicle … and your phone rings. It is from the Help Desk and they are asking you to take a look at application Z, because User X called and said Department Y's screens are all (W)hite and they are "frozen", presumably not because of the efficient A/C vent.

One of the users has received a timeout issue related to S.Q.L., which is why you are being called. I do not know about you, but when you have more than 100 applications that tie to the SQL Servers in your infrastructure, you do not always know what server/database combination are linked from the frontend to the backend. So you have to do some upfront interrogation:

"What SQL Server are they connecting to?" you ask.

"I am not really sure, let me find out," Help Desk says. Pause. "They do not know what that is."

"OK, what is the application?"

"Oh, um, it is **Accounts_Receivable_Generation1.4**."

"That is server 'G' you say confidently." Some DBA, long before you arrived, decided it would be fun to name all servers on letters of the alphabet, one letter at a time. "G" in this case is, of course, the intuitive name for where the A.R.G application must reside because it is an accounts receivable application and "G" stands for "Gold", from the DBA's favorite online game. After jotting down a note to change that server name in the next maintenance weekend, you tell the Help Desk that you will look into the matter and get right back with them. You are on.

What follows is an example of how I track down and resolve such issues, often misdiagnosed as "database performance" issues.

Using sp_who2

The first troubleshooting tool in every DBA's tackle box is the tried-and-true stored procedure, **sp_who2**. Granted there is Activity Monitor, which is also quite handy, but I have found that there are two things wrong with Activity Monitor. Firstly, when the server is heavily burdened with locks or temporary tables, Activity Monitor often cannot be launched, and you generally receive an error message to this effect. Secondly, Activity Monitor for SQL Server 2008 is radically different and, in my opinion, too difficult to maneuver when trying to home in on a problem as quickly as possible. That is primarily the reason I am compelled to run both 2005 and 2008 versions of the client tools.

Sp_who2, on the other hand, always works and the results are generally instantaneous. It displays, among many other things, any blocking on the SQL Server instance on which the problem has been reported. Running **sp_who2** on the affected server reveals that there are indeed blocked processes, as is evidenced by the **BlkBy** field in the results, see Figure 5.1.

SPID	Status	Login	H..	BlkBy	DBName	Command	CPUTime	DiskIO	LastBatch	ProgramName	SPID	REQUESTID
6	6	BACKGROUND	sa			master	SIGNAL HANDLER	0	0	05/03 18:11:04		6	0
7	7	BACKGROUND	sa			NULL	LOCK MONITOR	0	0	05/03 18:11:04		7	0
8	8	sleeping	sa			master	TASK MANAGER	0	0	05/03 18:11:04		8	0
9	9	BACKGROUND	sa			master	FSAGENT TASK	0	0	05/03 18:11:04		9	0
10	10	BACKGROUND	sa			master	FSAGENT TASK	0	0	05/03 18:11:04		10	0
11	11	BACKGROUND	sa			master	FSAGENT TASK	0	0	05/03 18:11:04		11	0
12	12	BACKGROUND	sa			master	FSAGENT TASK	0	1	05/03 18:11:04		12	0
13	13	BACKGROUND	sa			master	FSAGENT TASK	0	3	05/03 18:11:04		13	0
14	14	BACKGROUND	sa			master	TRACE QUEUE TASK	0	0	05/03 18:11:04		14	0
15	15	BACKGROUND	sa			master	BRKR TASK	0	0	05/03 18:11:04		15	0
16	16	BACKGROUND	sa			NULL	CHECKPOINT	0	0	05/03 18:11:04		16	0
17	17	BACKGROUND	sa			master	TASK MANAGER	0	0	05/03 18:11:04		17	0
18	18	BACKGROUND	sa			master	BRKR EVENT HNDLR	0	37	05/03 18:11:04		18	0
19	19	BACKGROUND	sa			master	BRKR TASK	0	0	05/03 18:11:04		19	0
20	20	BACKGROUND	sa			master	BRKR TASK	0	0	05/03 18:11:04		20	0
21	21	sleeping	sa			master	TASK MANAGER	0	0	05/03 18:11:04		21	0
22	22	sleeping	sa			master	TASK MANAGER	0	0	05/03 18:11:04		22	0
23	23	sleeping	sa			master	TASK MANAGER	0	2	05/03 18:11:04		23	0
24	24	sleeping	sa			master	TASK MANAGER	0	0	05/03 18:11:04		24	0
25	25	sleeping	sa			master	TASK MANAGER	0	0	05/03 18:11:04		25	0
26	26	sleeping	sa			master	TASK MANAGER	0	0	05/03 18:11:04		26	0
27	27	sleeping	sa			master	TASK MANAGER	0	0	05/03 18:11:04		27	0
28	28	sleeping	sa			master	TASK MANAGER	0	0	05/03 18:11:04		28	0
29	29	sleeping	sa			master	TASK MANAGER	0	0	05/03 18:11:04		29	0
30	30	sleeping	sa			master	TASK MANAGER	0	0	05/03 18:11:04		30	0
31	31	sleeping	sa			master	TASK MANAGER	0	0	05/03 18:11:04		31	0
32	51	RUNNABLE	sa	G..		DBA_Rep	EXECUTE	0	0	05/03 18:30:22	Microsoft S..	51	0
33	52	sleeping	sa	G..		DBA_Rep	AWAITING COMMAND	31	0	05/03 18:26:44	Microsoft S..	52	0
34	54	SUSPENDED	sa	G..	55	master	SELECT	32	0	05/03 18:35:08	Microsoft S..	54	0
35	55	SUSPENDED	sa	G..	51	master	SELECT	0	0	05/03 18:35:13	Microsoft S..	55	0
36	56	RUNNABLE	sa	G..		DBA_Rep	SELECT INTO	62	2	05/03 18:33:19	Microsoft S..	56	0
37	57	sleeping	sa	G..		master	AWAITING COMMAND	0	0	05/03 18:25:56	Microsoft S..	57	0

Figure 5.1: Blocked processes uncovered by sp_who2 .

I can tell at first glance that SPID 55 is blocked by SPID 51, and that SPID 54 is blocked by 55. I can also see that the database context of the blocking SPID is the **DBA_Rep** database, which ironically and for argument's sake is the same database that the fictitious A.R.G application uses.

With **sp_who2**, I have discovered a blocking process and it has been blocking for quite some time now. Users are getting frantic, and soon this will escalate and there will be three or four people at my cubicle, who otherwise would not give the SQL Server infrastructure a second glance, laser beam focused on my every action, and fully expecting me to solve the problem quickly.

In order to do so, I am going to have to find fast answers to the following questions:

- Who is running the query and from where?
- What is the query doing?
- Can I kill the offending query?
- If I kill the query, will it rollback successfully and will this free up the blocked processes?

Who is running the query?

Finding out who is running the query, and from where, is usually easy and, in fact, may be readily apparent from the output of **sp_who2**. In this case, Figure 5.1 tells me that the query is being executed by **sa** from Microsoft SQL Server Management Studio and it is coming from the local server "G".

However, in the real world, it might not always be quite so straightforward to answer the "who" question. Some applications use a generic login as an abstraction from the user. The user may possess a valid login account, but this account is not used to directly connect to the database. Instead, the account is controlled by the application, and usually stored in a table within the application database. In these cases, you will often see the generic application login and not the user's login.

What you may also find is that the query is issued by an application residing on another server, potentially a web server, in which case the **ProgramName** field from the **sp_who2** results will likely show ".Net Client". That does not tell you much. You may also see the Web server name but, again, this may be expected. Occasionally, you may strike lucky and see an unexpected application, like Management Studio, Query Analyzer, Microsoft Access or some other application that should not be connecting to production data directly, outside of the front end application. If so, then you have made progress and can continue with the confidence that you now have a user name, program name and location. If you have not captured anything out of the ordinary, that is OK; you will still be able to find the answer to the next most important question, "What is the query doing?"

DBCC: What is the query doing?

Microsoft has been kind enough to provide us with many tools to diagnose such issues. One such tool is the DBCC set of commands. DBCC, which if you are a SQL Server DBA you are very familiar with, can be used for a variety of important tasks, from checking for and fixing corrupt databases (**DBCC CHECKDB**), which I cover in Chapter 8, to checking how memory is being used on your SQL Server instance (**DBCC MEMORYSTATUS**). There is another DBCC command, **INPUTBUFFER**, which allows you to see the underlying query that a specific SPID is executing. It is quite helpful, nay, indispensible, for the sleuthing DBA.

Using **DBCC INPUTBUFFER** is as easy as passing in the SPID number, as shown in Figure 5.2, to uncover the "Bad Query" that is blocking the other process.

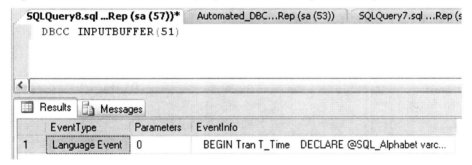

Figure 5.2: Output of DBCC INPUTBUFFER.

As you can see the output lacks formatting when returned in a grid format. I could expand the **EventInfo** field to get a better look at the query, but it would still lack proper formatting. Returning the results to text, which is simply a matter of clicking the "Results to Text" button on the Management Studio toolbar, usually delivers better results, as shown in Figure 5.3.

Clearly, someone has been tasked with filling the **Important_Data** table (shown in Listing 5.1 for those who want to work through the example) with values and will do whatever it takes to get the job done!

Figure 5.3: Results to Text for DBCC INPUTBUFFER.

```
CREATE TABLE [dbo].[Important_Data](
    [T_ID] [int] IDENTITY(1,1) NOT NULL,
    [T_Desc] [nchar](40) NOT NULL,
    [T_Back] [datetime] NULL,
    [T_Square] [uniqueidentifier] NULL
) ON [PRIMARY]
GO
```

Listing 5.1: CREATE statement for `Important_Data` **table.**

Let's take a look at this "Bad Query" in all its ugly glory, as shown in Listing 5.2.

```
BEGIN Tran T_Time

DECLARE @SQL_Alphabet varchar(26)
SET @SQL_Alphabet = '
ABCDEFGHIJKLMNOPQRSTUVWXYZ'
DECLARE @rnd_seed int
SET @rnd_seed = 26
DECLARE @DT datetime
SET @DT = '05/21/1969'
DECLARE @counter int
SET @counter = 1
DECLARE @tempVal NCHAR(40)

WHILE @counter < 100
    BEGIN
            SET @tempVal = SUBSTRING(@SQl_alphabet, Cast(RAND()
* @rnd_seed as int) + 1, CAST(RAND() * @rnd_seed as int) + 1)

        Insert  Into Important_Data WITH ( XLOCK )
        Values  (
                    @tempVal,
                    DATEDIFF(d, cast(RAND() * 10000 as int) + 1,
@DT),
                    NewID()
                )
        WAITFOR DELAY '00:00:01'
        SET @counter = @counter + 1


    END
    Exec  xp_cmdshell 'C:\Windows\notepad.exe'

Commit Tran T_Time
```

Listing 5.2: Really "Bad Query".

If I saw this query on a real system, my concern would begin to build at around line 15, and by line 24 I think I would be a bit red-faced. At line 29, where I see the query call **xp_cmdshell** and execute Notepad.exe, I would need a warm blankie and soft floor where I would lie in a fetal position for a few hours thinking about happy things.

Of course, at this stage I should make it clear that this query is an exercise in the ridiculous; it is one that I specifically designed to cause locking and blocking so that I could demonstrate how to resolve similar issues on your servers. The "bad query" is not the work of a reasonable person but that does not mean that something similar will never occur on one of your servers (although it would probably never occur twice). Wrapped in a transaction called **T_Time**, it inserts

135

one row at a time, 1,000 times, into the **Important_Data** table, based on random patterns for **T_Desc** and **T_Back**. It does this insert every 1 second. While doing so, it explicitly locks out the **Important_Data** table using a table hint (**XLock**) so that no other query can access the **Important_Data** table until it is complete, which will not be until 1020 seconds, or 17 minutes, passes.

Finally, we have the heinous call to **xp_cmdshell**. Again, one would think that no one would really do this in the real world. Unfortunately, I know for a fact that some developers make liberal use of **xp_cmdshell**. Sometimes, it is the path of least resistance to kicking off another process that will return a value to the calling query. But what if, at some point, the expected value is not returned and a dialogue box appears instead, awaiting user input? Suffice it to say that it would be very bad, but I am getting ahead of myself. All we need to know right now is that, for the sake of our example, this query is "happening" and I do not have a few hours or soft floor, and the warm blankie was wrenched from my grasp by my boss who is standing over me. So, it is best to just proceed ahead to resolution.

Killing the offending query

At this point, my goal is simply to kill the blocking SPID so that any queries backing up behind it can start to flow through. So, after confirming that the business has signed off on killing the offending SPID (trust me, eventually, you will get the OK to KILL this SPID), the next step seems easy enough, and the command would look something like this:

```
KILL SPID 51
```

And that is it, right? If you issue this command in SSMS, you will receive the usual reassuring "success" message, as shown in Figure 5.4.

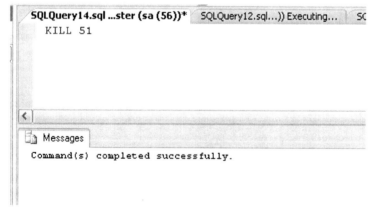

Figure 5.4: Killing the Bad Query process (51).

However, that message can be misleading. In some cases, the SPID will indeed be killed but there may be a significant time lag while the offending statement is being rolled back. An option of the **KILL** command exists that I was not aware of at one point in my career, and that is **WITH STATUSONLY**. After killing a SPID you can issue the **KILL** command again with this option and get a status of how long SQL Server estimates that a **ROLLBACK** will take. If you have been rebuilding an index for 10 minutes, for example, and kill that process, you can see the "% completion of rollback" counting up to 100%.

In other cases, it may be that, despite issuing the **KILL** command, the SPID will not be dead at all and the blocking will still be evident. If you issue the **KILL WITH STATUSONLY** command for the Bad Query, you will see something similar to Figure 5.5.

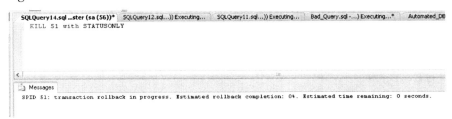

Figure 5.5: SPID that will not be killed.

As you can see, the SPID shows an estimated time rollback completion of 0%, and an estimated time remaining for rollback of 0 seconds, indicating that it is not going to be possible to kill this SPID directly. This situation can occur for the reason that I foreshadowed earlier: the blocking process has kicked off another process, such as an executable, and SQL Server is waiting, indefinitely, for that other process to complete. The only way to kill the blocking SPID is either to restart SQL Server or find and kill the executable that SQL Server is waiting for.

In this example, I know that the Bad Query launched Notepad.exe so I have a head start. Figure 5.6 shows the culprit in Task Manager.

Figure 5.6: Offending Notepad.exe preventing killing SPID 51.

Remember that Notepad is only an example; this could have been any other process that got called from **xp_cmdshell** and was waiting for user input to finish.

All I should have to do is end the Notepad.exe process and the blocking will be cleared and the resources freed. Notice that the user name for Notepad.exe is **SYSTEM**. When SQL Server issued the command to the OS, via **xp_cmdshell**, Notepad was launched as a System process, not as a user process. Right-clicking Notepad.exe and selecting "End Process" finishes off the Notepad executable, allowing SPID 51 to be killed, and all previously blocked processes to move forward.

Any **INSERT** statements that were issued as part of the transaction, before Notepad was executed, should be considered discarded, as Figure 5.7 shows.

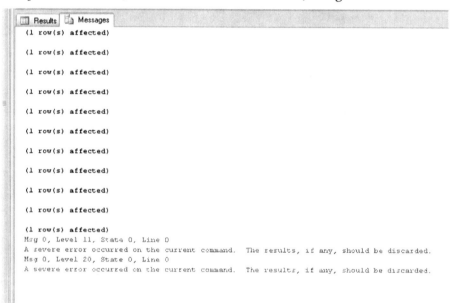

Figure 5.7: Discard any transaction for the killed SPID.

This can be confirmed by issuing a quick query against the **Important_Data** table, as shown in Figure 5.8, to verify that no records exist after the **KILL** statement was run and Notepad.exe was terminated.

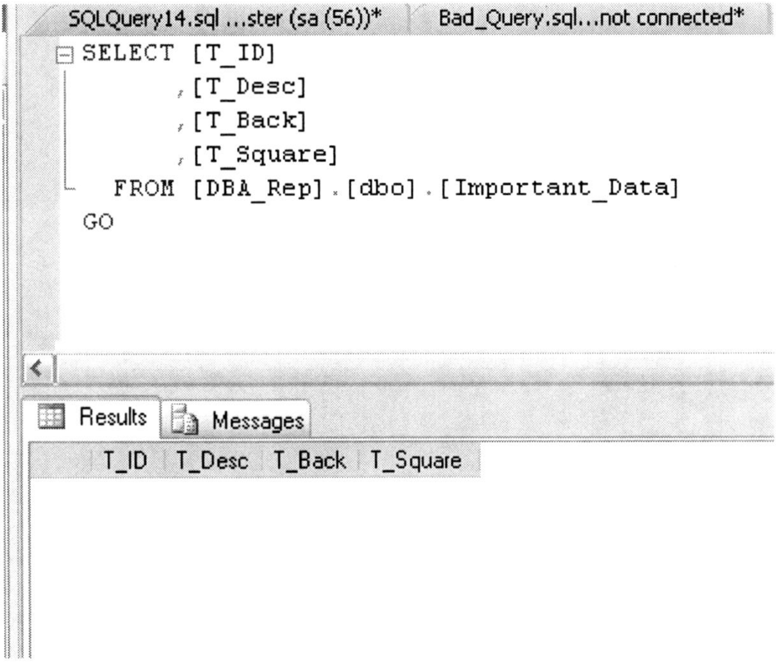

```
  SQLQuery14.sql ...ster (sa (56))*      Bad_Query.sql...not connected*
  SELECT [T_ID]
        , [T_Desc]
        , [T_Back]
        , [T_Square]
     FROM [DBA_Rep] . [dbo] . [Important_Data]
   GO
```

Results   Messages

T_ID	T_Desc	T_Back	T_Square

Figure 5.8: No committed records in Important_Data after KILL.

Using sp_lock

Before I deliver a query that is going to automate the discovery of problem queries (there I go foreshadowing again), I want to talk about another important characteristic of poorly performing queries, namely their rampant use of resources.

It is very important to monitor usage of CPU and I/O resources and I will cover those in great detail in the next chapter, on Performance Monitoring and Notifications. However, here I want to focus on locking resources. While sp_who2 gives you a good picture of processes that may be blocking other processes, and some initial insight in to the resource utilization via CPU and Disk I/O, it does not give you any details about the various locks that have been acquired in order to execute the process.

Locking is a "normal" activity in SQL Server, in that it is the mechanism by which SQL Server mediates the concurrent access of a given resource by several "competing" processes. However, as a DBA you will come to recognize certain locking behavior that is an immediate tell-tale sign of something being intrinsically wrong.

Some common lock types are:

- RID – single row lock
- KEY – a range of keys in an index
- PAG – data or index page lock
- EXT – Extent Lock
- TAB – Table Lock
- DB – Database Lock

In addition to lock types that refer to resources or objects that can be locked, SQL Server has common lock modes:

- S – Shared lock
- U – Update Lock
- X – Exclusive lock
- IS – Intent shared
- IU – Intent Update
- IX – Intent Exclusive
- BU – Bulk update

In the above list of lock types and modes, combinations of resources and modes can be created. So, for example, you can have a table lock (TAB) that has a mode of "X" for exclusive. This means that a process has requested or been granted an exclusive lock on a table. Of course, this may indeed cause blocking issues if the lock is held for a substantial duration.

SQL Server provides a stored procedure, called **sp_lock**, which provides a lot of information that is useful to a DBA regarding the number and type of locks that a process has requested.

NOTE
The SQL Server 2005, and above, equivalent of sp_lock **would be the DMV** sys.dm_tran_locks.

Figure 5.9 shows the output of **sp_lock** for SPID 51, the Bad Query.

SQLQuery18.sql ...)) Executing...   **SQLQuery14.sql ...ster (sa (56))***

```
sp_lock
```

Results | Messages

	spid	dbid	ObjId	IndId	Type	Resource	Mode	Status
1	51	5	709577566	0	RID	1:173:24	X	GRANT
2	51	5	709577566	0	PAG	1:173	IX	GRANT
3	51	5	709577566	0	RID	1:175:24	X	GRANT
4	51	5	709577566	0	RID	1:173:16	X	GRANT
5	51	5	709577566	0	RID	1:175:16	X	GRANT
6	51	5	709577566	0	RID	1:175:40	X	GRANT
7	51	5	709577566	0	RID	1:173:32	X	GRANT
8	51	5	709577566	0	RID	1:175:32	X	GRANT
9	51	5	709577566	0	RID	1:175:56	X	GRANT
10	51	5	709577566	0	RID	1:175:48	X	GRANT
11	51	5	709577566	0	RID	1:175:65	X	GRANT
12	51	5	709577566	0	RID	1:173:9	X	GRANT
13	51	5	709577566	0	RID	1:175:9	X	GRANT
14	51	5	709577566	0	RID	1:173:1	X	GRANT
15	51	5	709577566	0	RID	1:175:1	X	GRANT
16	51	5	709577566	0	RID	1:173:25	X	GRANT

Figure 5.9: Number of locks from Bad Query.

You can see that there are many locks acquired, mostly exclusive locks at the row level, as indicated by the mode "X" and the type "RID". When I see one SPID that has acquired this number of locks, especially exclusive locks, I get very concerned that something is definitely not as it should be.

Often, a simple count of the locks and, more importantly, the types of locks for a specific SPID, is enough to help me locate a poorly performing query, even if there is no obvious blocking. Acquiring locks, just like acquiring connections, requires memory resources and even shared locks, which may not block others from accessing data, can sometimes have a major performance impact due to memory or other resource pressures.

Automating discovery of problems

Up to this point we have used **sp_who2** to seek out SPIDs that are causing blocking issues, **DBCC INPUTBUFFER** to elicit the SQL being executed by such a blocking SPID, and then **sp_lock** to discover some information about the locks being acquired by the offending process. All of this took quite a bit of time to manually discover and resolve, and when a query is locking out an entire table, and depleting any number of other precious resources, this is time you don't necessarily have.

What is missing is a single query that will tell all in a single execution. Faced with this pressing need, I have developed just such a query. It returns all of the previously discovered information, and more, in an easily-digestible format,

While **sp_who2** gives good "at a glance" information, my query dives into the underlying system table, called **sysprocesses**, in order to retrieve some additional information regarding the blocking and blocked processes.

With **sp_lock,** the underlying system table is **syslockinfo**. This table does not display intuitive information in the manner of **sysprocesses**. Specifically, the type of locks have to be identified,via a join to the **spt_values** table in the **Master** database. When developing the query, I found it much easier to create a table to store the output of **sp_lock** and then do a simple count of lock types per SPID.

> TIP
> The stored procedure, sp_helptext, is one of those "hidden gems" that I
> have used many times over the years. When passed any object, such as a view
> or stored procedure, it will display the code that makes up that object.
> Running sp_lock through sp_helptext will show the join to the
> spt_values table.

Listing 5.3 shows the query that will, in one fell swoop, find and report on blocked and blocking processes and the number of locks that they are holding. First it creates a temp table to store the output of **sp_lock** and then it lists all locked and blocked processes, along with the query that each process is currently executing, or that is waiting on resources before it can be executed.

```
SET NOCOUNT ON
GO

-- Count the locks

IF EXISTS ( SELECT   Name
            FROM     tempdb..sysobjects
```

```
                WHERE    name LIKE '#Hold_sp_lock%' )
--If So Drop it
    DROP TABLE #Hold_sp_lock
GO
CREATE TABLE #Hold_sp_lock
    (
       spid INT,
       dbid INT,
       ObjId INT,
       IndId SMALLINT,
       Type VARCHAR(20),
       Resource VARCHAR(50),
       Mode VARCHAR(20),
       Status VARCHAR(20)
    )
INSERT   INTO #Hold_sp_lock
       EXEC sp_lock
SELECT   COUNT(spid) AS lock_count,
       SPID,
       Type,
       Cast(DB_NAME(DBID) as varchar(30)) as DBName,
       mode
FROM     #Hold_sp_lock
GROUP BY SPID,
       Type,
       DB_NAME(DBID),
       MODE
Order by lock_count desc,
       DBName,
       SPID,
       MODE

--Show any blocked or blocking processes

IF EXISTS ( SELECT  Name
            FROM    tempdb..sysobjects
            Where   name like '#Catch_SPID%' )
--If So Drop it
    DROP TABLE #Catch_SPID
GO
Create Table #Catch_SPID
    (
       bSPID int,
       BLK_Status char(10)
    )
GO
Insert   into #Catch_SPID
       Select Distinct
                SPID,
                'BLOCKED'
       from    master..sysprocesses
       where   blocked <> 0
```

```
        UNION
        Select Distinct
                blocked,
                'BLOCKING'
        from    master..sysprocesses
        where   blocked <> 0

DECLARE @tSPID int
DECLARE @blkst char(10)
SELECT TOP 1
        @tSPID = bSPID,
        @blkst = BLK_Status
from    #Catch_SPID

WHILE ( @@ROWCOUNT > 0 )
    BEGIN

        PRINT 'DBCC Results for SPID ' + Cast(@tSPID as
varchar(5)) + '( '
            + rtrim(@blkst) + ' )'
        PRINT '---------------------------------'
        PRINT ''
        DBCC INPUTBUFFER (@tSPID)


        SELECT TOP 1
                @tSPID = bSPID,
                @blkst = BLK_Status
        from    #Catch_SPID
        WHERE   bSPID > @tSPID
        Order by bSPID

    END
```

Listing 5.3: Automated discovery query.

There is nothing overly complicated about this query. It is a base starting point from which you can quickly analyze locking and blocking issues in SQL Server. In the case of non-blocking locks, it will show you any query that is a potential issue with regard to other resources such as memory or I/O.

Figure 5.10 shows the output of this query, captured while the "Bad Query" was executing.

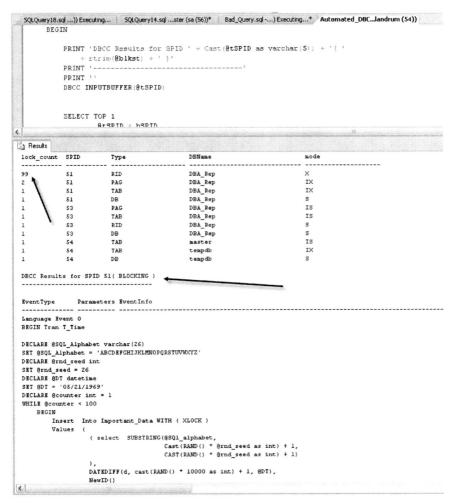

Figure 5.10: Output of SPID count and Blocking query in Automated Discovery.

Notice the high lock count of 99 for SPID 51, the culprit query. The next output section shows that, in this case, SPID 51 is indeed causing blocking, and the code that the SPID is executing follows, as we have seen previously from **DBCC INPUTBUFFER**.

In addition, the Automated Discovery Query also lists all of the blocked SPIDs behind the main blocking SPID. Figure 5.11 shows the queries, in this case simple select statements against the **Important_Data** table, which are blocked by SPID 51.

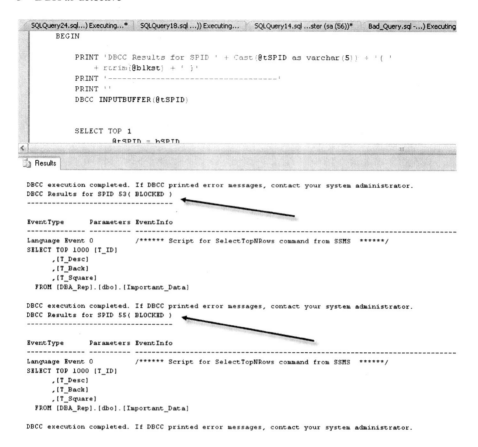

Figure 5.11: Blocked SPIDs found using Automated Discovery query.

You might decide that you would like to take this query, and make it into a stored procedure. You can then load it into a maintenance database on each server so that you have it always available. It also means that you can parameterize it to control its behavior. For example, you may decide that you do not want to execute the portion of the query that counts locks, which on a very busy system could take quite a bit of time.

Listing 5.4 shows the code to create this stored procedure, named **usp_Find_Problems**, with a flag to execute the lock count portion based on need.

```
USE [DBA_Rep]
GO
/****** Object:  StoredProcedure [dbo].[usp_Find_Problems]
Script Date: 06/22/2009 22:41:37 ******/
```

```
SET ANSI_NULLS ON
GO
SET QUOTED_IDENTIFIER ON
GO

CREATE PROCEDURE [dbo].[usp_Find_Problems] ( @count_locks BIT =
1 )
AS
    SET NOCOUNT ON
-- Count the locks
    IF @count_locks = 0
        GOTO Get_Blocks
    ELSE
        IF @count_locks = 1
            BEGIN

                CREATE TABLE #Hold_sp_lock
                    (
                        spid INT,
                        dbid INT,
                        ObjId INT,
                        IndId SMALLINT,
                        Type VARCHAR(20),
                        Resource VARCHAR(50),
                        Mode VARCHAR(20),
                        Status VARCHAR(20)
                    )
                INSERT   INTO #Hold_sp_lock
                         EXEC sp_lock
                SELECT   COUNT(spid) AS lock_count,
                         SPID,
                         Type,
                         CAST(DB_NAME(DBID) AS VARCHAR(30)) AS
DBName,
                         mode
                FROM     #Hold_sp_lock
                GROUP BY SPID,
                         Type,
                         CAST(DB_NAME(DBID) AS VARCHAR(30)),
                         MODE
                ORDER BY lock_count DESC,
                         DBName,
                         SPID,
                         MODE

--Show any blocked or blocking processes

                Get_Blocks:

                CREATE TABLE #Catch_SPID
                    (
```

```
                                bSPID INT,
                                BLK_Status CHAR(10)
                        )

                INSERT  INTO #Catch_SPID
                        SELECT DISTINCT
                                SPID,
                                'BLOCKED'
                        FROM    master..sysprocesses
                        WHERE   blocked <> 0
                        UNION
                        SELECT DISTINCT
                                blocked,
                                'BLOCKING'
                        FROM    master..sysprocesses
                        WHERE   blocked <> 0

                DECLARE @tSPID INT
                DECLARE @blkst CHAR(10)
                SELECT TOP 1
                        @tSPID = bSPID,
                        @blkst = BLK_Status
                FROM    #Catch_SPID


                WHILE( @@ROWCOUNT > 0 )
                    BEGIN

                        PRINT 'DBCC Results for SPID '
                            + CAST(@tSPID AS VARCHAR(5)) + '( '
+ RTRIM(@blkst)
                            + ' )'
                        PRINT '------------------------------
---'
                        PRINT ''
                        DBCC INPUTBUFFER (@tSPID)


                        SELECT TOP 1
                                @tSPID = bSPID,
                                @blkst = BLK_Status
                        FROM    #Catch_SPID
                        WHERE   bSPID > @tSPID
                        ORDER BY bSPID

                    END

        END
```

Listing 5.4: Statement to create `usp_Find_Problems`.

Executing **usp_Find_Problems** with no parameters will return the lock counts as
well as the blocked and blocking SPIDs, whereas executing it with a value of 0 as
the input parameter will exclude the lock counts. Figure 5.12 shows both
executions in SSMS, using vertical tab groups.

**Figure 5.12: Executing the usp_Find_Problems stored procedure with
parameters.**

Summary

In this chapter I demonstrated how I go about detecting SQL Server problems in
the form of excessive locking and blocking. While this is a good start for the DBA
detective, there is much more ground to cover. I mentioned CPU and I/O in this
chapter only peripherally, as it relates to problem code. In the next chapter, I will
continue on the path of analyzing performance issues, but will extend the topic to
explain how to make sure you get notified immediately of performance, and other,
issues.

After all, if you do not know about the problem, you can't fix it. I would much
rather be notified of a potential issue from a system that is monitoring such events
than from an irate application user, or from the Help Desk. Granted, you will be
hard pressed to totally escape emails from users and that is OK, generally they are
understanding. It is their bosses that are not. If you can find and fix, or even just

149

report, an issue before anyone else, it appears that you are ahead of the game. And you are … you are a DBA after all. Now let's delve into performance monitoring and notifications for SQL Server before someone beats us to it.

CHAPTER 6: MONITORING AND NOTIFICATIONS

As is probably clear by this stage, there are many potential monsters, lurking around corners, waiting to pounce upon the unwary DBA as he goes about his day-to-day duties. Often, however, the biggest problem is not the monster itself but the fact that the DBA is unaware that it exists.

Imagine a problem as trivial as a SQL Agent Service that fails to start; a very easy problem to fix once you know about it. But what if you don't know about it and then suddenly find out that the backup process that this service was supposed to be running has not been executed for over two weeks! The feeling at this moment for a DBA, or DBA manager, is one of frustration and disbelief. These emotions are quickly displaced however, perhaps after a few minutes alone with the warm blankie and a soft floor, by an unswerving confidence. This confidence derives from that fact that you know that positive steps will be taken to ensure that this never happens again.

In this chapter, I will describe how I use monitoring tools and techniques to make sure that my Blackberry will *always* buzz whenever a backup fails, a disk drive fills up, or a rogue process is threatening the performance of a SQL Server.

When the inevitable happens, and the e-mail notification hits your mobile device, probably at some awful hour of the morning, I'll show what you can do to easily ascertain the problem and be notified, using a mix of third party tools, such as Red Gate's SQL Response, and standard tools like Database Mail l.

Types of monitoring and notifications

The DBA's life is one of vigilantly overseeing not only the SQL Servers themselves, but all of the events that take place on the servers. When I say events, I am not specifically referring to error events that cause entries to be added to the Windows Event log or SQL Server Error log, though these are certainly included in an overall monitoring and notification strategy. Here, I am referring to events such as SQL Server Agent job failure, or an abnormal SQL Server performance condition, or excessive resource (e.g. disk space) utilization, or SQL Services availability.

It is not possible for a DBA team, no matter how large, to keep this vigil by themselves. They need automated notifications that will let them know when something goes awry, so that they can respond to the event and resolve any issues arising from it. There are many ways that DBAs can set up such notifications, either using native SQL Server tools, such as Database Mail or SQL Agent Mail (two separate entities), or a third party monitoring and notification system. There are quite a number of such applications on the market.

In my career, I have generally employed a hybrid solution of both native and third-party monitoring, because of the benefits and limitations of each. For example, a third-party application may not be able to retrieve the internal error messages of a failed SQL Agent database backup job. Conversely, it would be impractical to set up performance monitoring, say for a sustained level of high CPU utilization, for each instance of a 200-strong SQL Server farm, when a centralized third party solution could easily be maintained.

In this chapter, I will expound upon the types of events that would require such a monitoring and notification system to be in place and then give examples of solutions for each.

SQL Agent Job failures

We all know that failures occur and that the reasons for the failures are many-fold. SQL Agent Jobs, which kick off SSIS packages or maintenance tasks, such as database backups or integrity checks, are common points of failure. It is your job as DBA to respond to the failure, overcome it, and finally to understand why the failure occurred in the first place and make sure it does not happen again.

In this chapter, I will cover only one such type of failure, but it is one close to the DBA's heart and that is database backup failure. Regardless of whether you run your database and transaction log backup jobs via a third party tool or natively, perhaps using a Database Maintenance Plan, they are scheduled processes and if there is a failure you must be made aware of it. I happen to use Red Gate's SQL Backup utility (not a plug, just reality), which has built-in notifications for backup failures. However, being a duly cautious DBA, I do not rely on this notification mechanism being fail proof. I will show how to setup notifications for failed backup jobs at several different points, so that if one notification fails, others will not.

Adverse performance conditions

SQL Server is adept at managing memory, I/O requests and multi-threading across multiple CPUs. Occasionally, however, a "rogue" query will push the SQL Server to its very limits and it becomes unresponsive, as if its feelings have been hurt by the indignity of it all.

By the time we enter the unresponsive phase, it may be too late to glean what nefarious query it was that caused the problem in the first place. What is needed, in order to ensure a DBA's restful sleep, is an application that can monitor the server, using a time-based algorithm, and fire a notification when a specific threshold is crossed. For example, we may request a notification if CPU utilization exceed 85% for a set number of minutes.

There are many such third-party applications that will handle this very well, Idera Diagnostic Manager, Argent Guardian and Microsoft Operations Manager (MOM) are a few that come to mind. I will show how to use one such application, Red Gate's SQL Response, to trigger these performance alerts.

Further, once notified of the performance issue at hand, I will demonstrate how to use two indispensable tools, Performance Monitor and SQL Profiler, to quickly and easily analyze and resolve the problem.

Service availability

It should go without saying that a SQL service, such as SQL Server service (the database engine) or SQL Server Agent service, stopping is an event to which the sleepy DBA should be notified (I make it sound like these alerts always happen at night; they don't. It's just the ones that do tend to stay with you).

So, how does SQL Server notify you that it is down? It doesn't. It is down, and so cannot send a notification. This, again, would be the work of a third party monitoring application. Such monitoring solutions should also have the ability to take corrective action when encountering a stopped service, such as trying to restart the service.

I'll show how to use a third party tool, such as SQL Response, to monitor these services, and also how to configure the SQL services to have some resilience when they stop unexpectedly.

Disk space shortage

Chapter 4 discussed how to manage data growth, and the space issues that can be caused by bulk loads, errant indexing, abuse of TempDB, and so on. I can state unequivocally that disk space alerts are the most common type of alert that the DBA will face.

Disk space is not cheap, despite what you might be told by some IT managers. SCSI and fiber channel drives, which are the core storage devices for most SANs, are still quite expensive on a "per Meg" basis, compared to the slower SATA or ATA drives that are commonly used in development, staging or QA SQL Server installations.

For production servers that require many hundreds of Gigs of storage, it is essential that you analyze growth trends to make sure you will not be caught naked in the front yard when the application crashes because there is no more space (naked in the front yard? Forget that analogy). The bottom (ugg) line is that you need to be alerted not when you are completely out of disk space but when you have a specified percentage of remaining space, so that there is still time to act. In this chapter I will cover how to be alerted to uncontrolled .

Enabling notifications

Enabling notifications in SQL Server is a straightforward process that simply entails setting up a mechanism by which to send the notification emails, and then defining who it is who should receive them.

Setting up database mail I

Database mail is an essential first component in enabling the delivery of notifications in SQL Server, and its set up is included in the Automated Configuration Script in Chapter 1.

While there are other options for being notified of events, such as by Pager or Net Send, they are not really viable in today's world of mobile devices. Thankfully, SQL Server 2005 and beyond offers an SMTP mail client for both SQL Server (database engine) and the SQL Agent (job scheduler).

If you have to set up mail for SQL 2000, which a lot of people still do due to the cost of upgrading and/or lack vendor support (yes, this still happens, even in 2009 as I write this very sentence) then my heart goes out to you. Having to install and test a MAPI client like Outlook just to send mail from SQL 2000 is beyond frustrating.

> **NOTE**
> **A website still exists to assist you in your SQL Server 2000 mail woes and that is http://www.sqldev.net/xp/xpsmtp.htm. It offers an SMTP mail client for SQL Server 2000. It does not, sadly, address the SQL Agent mail, but it is worth a look.**

Setting up Database Mail 1 in SQL Server 2005 or 2008 is very straightforward. You just need to configure:

- The default profile that will be used to send mail
- An SMTP server address
- An account from which the mail will be sent

Figure 6.1 shows the profile information from the Database Mail Configuration Wizard, launched by double-clicking **Database Mail** under the Management tab in SQL Server Management Studio.

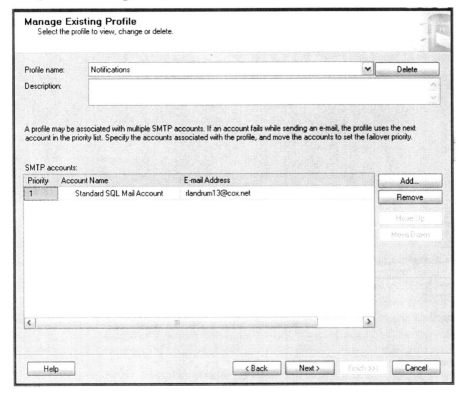

Figure 6.1: Profile for Database Mail in SQL Server 2005.

Notice that the Profile name is "Notifications" and it is associated with the Account called "Standard SQL Mail Account". It is this profile and account association that allows Database Mail to send true SMTP mail, using a standard email stored procedure, **sp_send_dbmail**.

The account information, which stores the SMTP server address, is set up separately from the profile. The account properties, which are directly associated with a profile, can be seen in Figure 6.2.

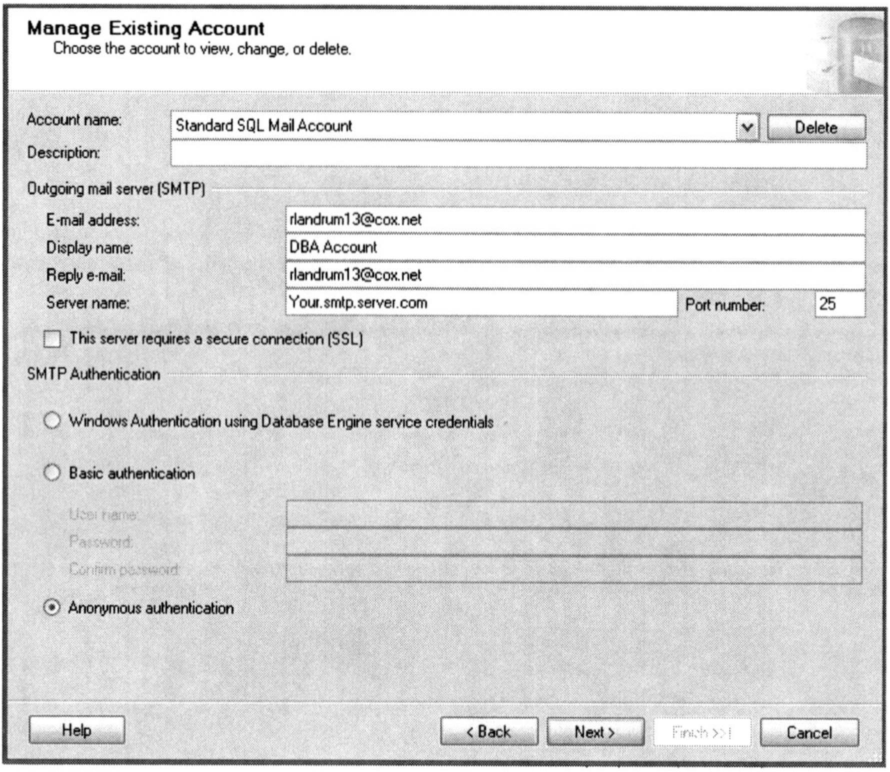

Figure 6.2: Database Mail account settings associated with the Notifications profile.

Having configured Database Mail 1 with a default profile and account, both tasks thankfully having guided wizards, you can send a test mail using the stored procedure, **sp_send_dbmail**. The options for this stored procedure are many but a simple test can be performed with the code shown in Listing 6.1.

```
msdb..sp_send_dbmail
 @recipients = N'rlandrum13@cox.net',
 @subject = N'Mail must work or else...',
 @body = N'This is a level 1 alert....please wake up to
failure.'
```

Listing 6.1: Sending a test mail using sp_send_dbmail.

NOTE
You may notice that sp_send_dbmail is now located in the MSDB database, whereas xp_sendmail, in versions prior to SQL Server 2005, was located in the Master database.

If all went well with the test, you should receive a test message similar to that shown in Figure 6.3 (and yes, that is Outlook Express. I will not apologize).

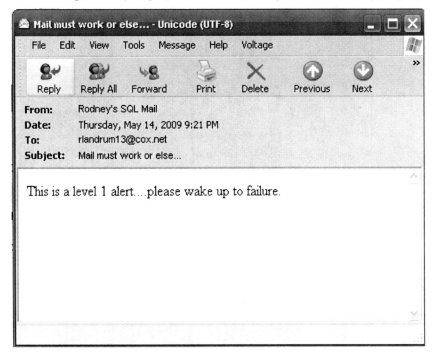

Figure 6.3: Mail received from sp_send_dbmail.

While Database Mail 1 is certainly important for sending mail from code, such as maintenance stored procedures, it is only one part of the notification system that the DBA will use, if he or she is diligent. You will also want to configure SQL Agent to use Database Mail, for scheduled jobs that execute the code. In this way, you will have built in redundancy of notifications, one message coming from the code and one message coming from the SQL Agent service that executed the job code.

To configure SQL Agent notifications, right-click SQL Server Agent in SSMS, select "Properties" and then choose the **Alert System** page, as shown in Figure 6.4.

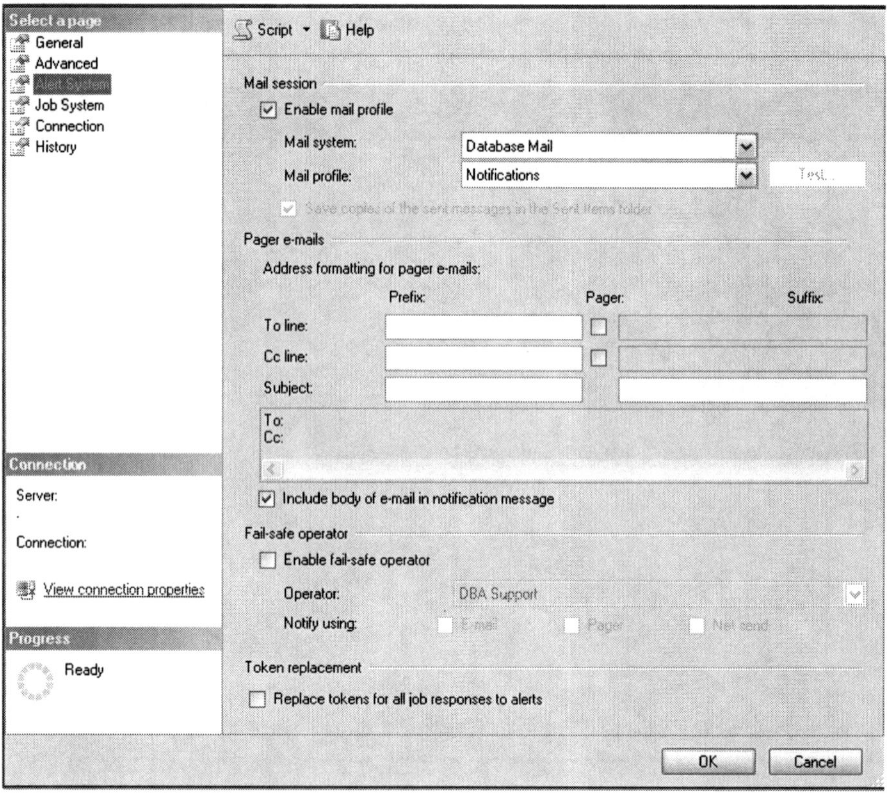

Figure 6.4: Configuration for SQL Server Agent mail.

Here, I have chosen to enable the mail profile and selected "Database Mail" 1 as the mail system, along with the "Notifications" profile created previously.

Setting up an operator

Having configured Database Mail and SQL Server Agent, the final step is to setup an operator i.e. the person (or people) who will receive the messages from any failures, either internally in the code or from the SQL Agent job. This can be a single email address but it is far better to use a distribution list, such as **DBATeam@companyname.com**, so that every member of the team receives the notification messages.

> **NOTE**
> Of course, you should use a single account to validate everything works, prior to setting this server to production, so that other team members do not get inundated with false alarms during testing.

158

It's important that the whole team is aware of any errors or failures that occur, even if they are not on-call. Generally, the on call DBA will have his or her mobile device configured in such a way that a "fail" or "error" will cause a raucous and marriage-damaging alert to scream forth when the fated message hits it, while other DBAs can continue to sleep soundly, having set their devices to a phone-only profile. However, it does also mean that if the on-call DBA does not respond, for whatever reason, someone else can.

Setting up an operator is as easy as right-clicking Operators in SSMS and selecting "New Operator". This opens the dialogue shown in Figure 6.5. Here is where you will set the e-mail address for the operator.

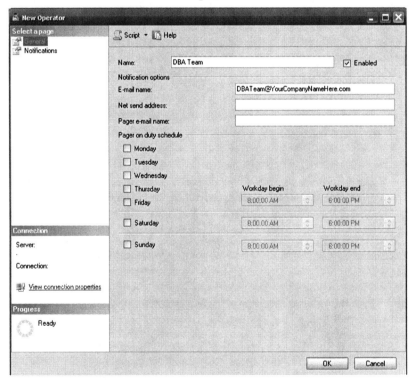

Figure 6.5: Setting up an operator group mail account.

With SQL Agent configured for mail, and Database Mail 1 successfully tested with the operator, all I need to do is configure each job about which the team needs to be notified. This can be done from the "Notifications" section of the Properties page of each job. Having done this, I can rest assured that any jobs that fails will notify me at 2:34 AM so that I can be jolted from dreaming about work into actually doing some work.

NOTE
It is important to remember to restart the SQL Agent Service after you enable mail. Otherwise you may receive an error that states that attempt to send mail failed because no email session has been established.

Backup failure notification

As much as we might not like it, or are astonished to see it, failures do happen and happen regularly. The goal of attaining the 4 9s availability looks good on paper but to pull it off costs exorbitantly. Database backups are certainly not immune from failure. There are many problems that cause backup failures, such as network outages (don't tell the network admin this as he or she will say everyone always tries to blame the network), SAN issues or other general failures, such as backup shares disappearing or filling up.

Database backups are probably, no, certainly the most important aspect of the DBA's job. Without good backups, you cannot recover business-critical data in the event of a disaster. Whether you're performing a full, differential or log backup, success has to be guaranteed. If a failure occurs during a backup, the DBA has to respond quickly, especially on production servers. If an error occurs at 1 AM, waiting until the next day is not generally deemed acceptable, as it would probably violate the Service Level Agreement (SLA) that IT has agreed with the organization in regard to the maximum acceptable number of hours of data loss.

If it is agreed upon that 6 hours is the maximum acceptable amount of data loss, then the backup schedule can be setup to accommodate this. The shorter the period the more diligence and expense it entails. If, for example, the SLA dictates a maximum of 15 minutes data loss then this will require log backups to be taken every 15 minutes, increasing the risk of failure due to outages or some other unforeseen circumstance.

As noted earlier, I perform the bulk of my backups using Red Gate's SQL Backup tool. Besides the benefits of compression, speed and security via encryption, it has the added bonus of a built-in SMTP mail client. Back in the days of SQL 2000, where no such SMTP client existed natively, Red Gate's SMTP mail client proved to be invaluable for notifications.

I have a backup script that rolls through a set-based list of databases to be backed up, taking account of the fact that databases like TempDB should be omitted. The script runs as a scheduled SQL Agent job, and sequentially backs up every database on the list, one at a time, using SQL Backup.

With this set up, I am interested in two different types of notification, in the event of a backup job failing. I want to see "redundant" notifications of the failure both from the SQL Agent backup job itself *and* the code that performs the backup.

In order to demonstrate notifications for backup failures, I will need to set up a backup job and intentionally make it fail, which is something that makes me squeamish even when it's just for demonstration purposes. To keep things, simple, for this demonstration, I'm going to use a script that backs up just a single database, using the Red Gate extended stored procedure **sql_backup**. The script is shown in Listing 6.2.

```
DECLARE @exitcode INT
DECLARE @sqlErrorCode INT
EXECUTE master..sqlbackup N'-SQL "BACKUP DATABASE [DBA_Rep] TO
DISK = ''D:\Backups\<AUTO>.sqb'' WITH COMPRESSION = 1,
MAILTO_ONERROR = ''rlandrum13@cox.net''"', @exitcode OUTPUT

IF( @exitCode > 0 OR @sqlErrorCode > 0 )
BEGIN
   -- Raise Error
   RAISERROR ('SQL Backup failed', 16, 1)
END
```

Listing 6.2: Red Gate SQL Backup statement.

An important point to note about the backup code is use of the **Mailto_Onerror** parameter. This tells the Red Gate extended stored procedure to use its own native SMTP client to send an email notification, if there are any errors with the backup. This is first line of defense for the DBA. If I were to run this code and produce an error, I should immediately receive a detailed notification telling me not only what database failed to backup (in this case, **DBA_Rep**) but also what the cause of the failure was. That information is critical to resolving the issue going forward so that is does not happen again.

If instead of using a third party tool I were to use native T-SQL code, for example **BACKUP DATABASE**, I would capture any errors in a variable string and then email the failures when the backup job completed using **sp_send_dbmail**, which I have mentioned previously. This type of backup code requires some additional scripting, of course. If you are familiar with SSIS, it is also possible, via a Database Maintenance Plan, to add a step in to send mail upon failure. There are really many options available to the DBA to get notifications from failed jobs.

OK, now to produce the backup failure. This is not actually quite as easy as it might sound as it's generally a pretty robust process, and I would venture that 98% of backups succeed. To produce the required failure, I simply started a backup of the **DBA_Rep** database to my 350G USB external hard drive and then pulled out the connecting USB cable (subtle, I know).

In my dream world, the resulting error would say "Rodney Pulled the Plug on the USB Hard Drive". It doesn't, of course, but the error message still provides some useful information, as you can see from Figure 6.6, which states that a "non-recoverable I/O error occurred".

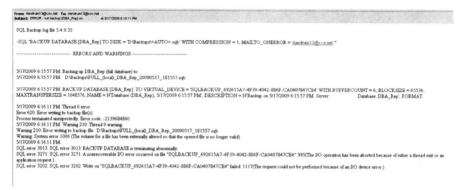

Figure 6.6: Error mail message from Red Gate SQL Backup.

At this point, I know that it was an I/O error that caused the failure, and I can respond by attempting to backup the database again, and then looking deeper into the issue.

If this error were caused by lack of disk space , as it often is, I would need to free up enough disk space on the destination to accommodate the backup file, and then re-run the backup. The failure message also contains key words like "error" that I can use to trigger a higher level alert on my mobile device, associated with a really obnoxious ring tone of the sort you will want to avoid in theatres or quiet dinners with your loved one.

However, what if this message did not get delivered for whatever reason … who knows, we might have changed mail servers and forgotten to update the Red Gate mail client properties. I still need to get a notification if the backup fails. You will have seen in Listing 6.2 that I intentionally wrapped error checking around the backup statement. If the backup script fails, it should report this fact to the calling process, which is generally a SQL Agent job, which can then send a notification, via Database Mail. l

In order to enable this notification mechanism, we first need to create a SQL Agent job that will run our custom backup script. To do this, simply right-click on "SQL Server Agent" in SSMS and select New | Job. In the "General" section, remember to name the job, in my case "Backup Database Test Failure" and then give the job a valid category, in this case "Database Maintenance". Use of meaningful job categories is valuable for reporting. In the DBA Repository, for example, I run job reports based on each category of job.

Next, in the "Steps" section, select "New" and paste in the backup code from Listing 6.2, so that your step looks as shown in Figure 6.7.

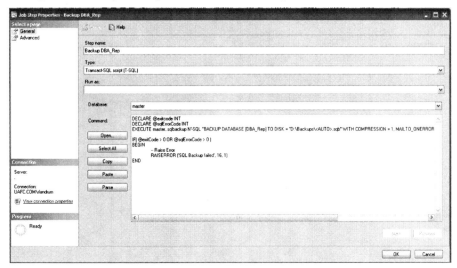

Figure 6.7: Creating Job Step for backup code.

Click OK and then select the "Notifications" section. Click the box to enable the E-mail action, and then from the drop down select the "DBA Team" operator that we created earlier. The default action, which we'll accept, is to notify "When the Job Fails," as shown in Figure 6.8.

Other options are available, such as mailing when the job succeeds or completes. Perhaps you want to receive a notification when the backup job completes, regardless of whether it fails. Click OK to create the job, and we are done.

For the sake of this demo, rather than schedule the job, I'm simply going to right-click on it and select "Start Job at Step". Once the job starts, I yank out the USB cable one more time. As expected, I have forced another backup failure, as you can see in Figure 6.9.

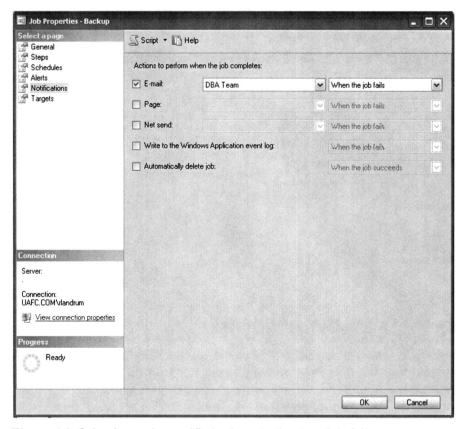

Figure 6.8: Selecting to be notified when the backup job fails.

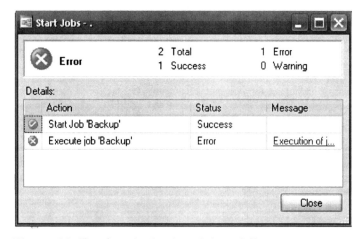

Figure 6.9: Forcing the backup job to fail.

Now, let me check my mail. Yep, everything worked as expected, and I receive, almost instantaneously, two separate email notifications; one from the SQL Agent job telling me the job itself failed and the other more detailed mail comes from the code inside the job, as shown side-by-side in Figure 6.10.

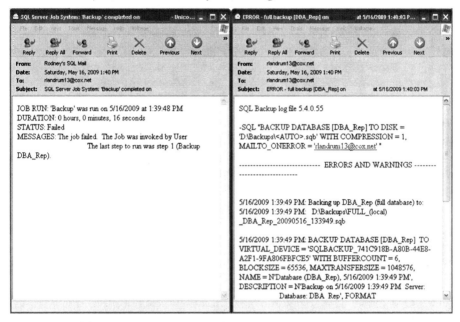

Figure 6.10: Two separate mail notifications from two separate sources.

Performance issues

If, over a sandwich, you were to ask a DBA to describe the performance issues that he or she has faced during the preceding year, you will, as the lunch drifts into the late afternoon, probably start to regret not being more focused in your line of questioning. All DBAs are faced with all manner of performance issues. If you were to ask, "What is the worst performance issue you had in the past year," you will get a contemplative stare to the ceiling, hand on chin, eyes scanning and finally, "Oh yeah, there was that one time when … I found code from a website application that was flagrantly misusing MARS (Multiple Active Result Sets) connections and instead of having an expected 300 logical connections, there were over 8500, each simultaneously eating into available RAM until the server slowed to a crawl."

In other words, the question is not *if* DBAs are going to face performance issues in their environment, but what types of problems they *are going* to encounter, and how they can deal with them.

In Chapter 5, *DBA as Detective*, I demonstrated how poorly-designed code can bring your server to a crawl, and offered some remedial measures. In this chapter, I want to shift the focus onto code that has been tested and approved and moved to production but, once there, causes resource issues with regard to CPU, RAM or Disk I/O.

It may not be that the code itself causes SQL Server to use too many resources; it may be due more to some "confluence of circumstances," for example the code running at the same time as a maintenance process, such as an index rebuild, or code that results in an excessively high number of connections, at the time the OS is also performing a memory-intensive process.

I am going to show how DBAs can be notified when such performance issues arise, and then how to proactively respond to them before the Help Desk is called or, worse, the user sends mail to you, your boss, your boss's boss and your mother and father, all of whom will shake their heads disapprovingly. OK, maybe that is just me, but you get the point.

If you are in an enterprise environment, chances are you already have a monitoring solution in place for server administrators and you can piggy back off that alerting system and, with luck, it will include SQL-specific alerts that allow you to, for example, report blocked processes.

If you don't have this luxury, then you have two choices: build your own monitoring solution, or buy in a third-party solution. While you can certainly build your own, the cost in terms of time and resources is going to be high. You can, for example, set up performance alerts using the native Windows Perfmon utility, or by setting native SQL alerts, which are part of SQL Agent. However, scripting all of these alerts requires some level of skill and patience.

Although I do not demonstrate setting native SQL Alerts in this chapter because, to be quite honest, they are not part of my overall monitoring and notification strategy, Figure 6.11 does show where you would go to do this, along with a few samples of the type of events that you can monitor.

Native SQL Alerts also allow you to capture performance metrics, but only for SQL performance counters, so disk space usage and CPU utilizations, for example, would require additional consideration. This may require use of gain Perfmon, or esoteric Windows Management Instrumentation (WMI) queries.

Figure 6.11: Native SQL Alerts samples.

Alternatively, you can acquire a third-party monitoring solution that is not only SQL-centric, but can be centrally managed. Once such product is Red Gate's SQL Response. Price is definitely a consideration when choosing a monitoring solution and, in my opinion, SQL Response works out to be much more affordable than rolling your own. This is not a sales pitch; it is just a demonstration of a product that is available to DBAs and one that happens to have become part of my tackle box for performance monitoring and diagnostics.

The main performance metrics that you will want to monitor are CPU, Memory and I/O. As an example of a typical performance alert, I am going to configure an alert in SQL Response to monitor CPU utilization and then run a query that should push the CPU utilization above a set threshold. Figure 6.12 shows the SQL Response alert configuration window.

For this demonstration, I have customized the standard "CPU utilization unusual" alert so that should fire if CPU utilization exceeds 70% for at least 5 seconds. The default is 90% for 10 seconds, which is more in line with what you would normally use to trigger this alert.

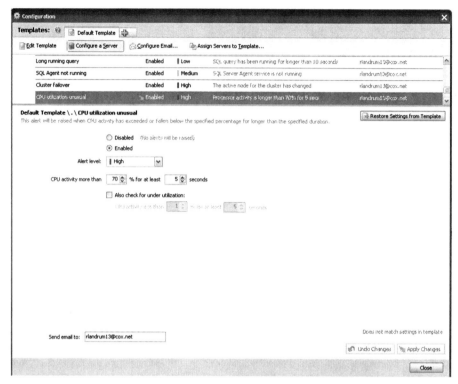

Figure 6.12: Configuring CPU utilization alert in SQL Response.

Notice also that there is a "send email to:" box where you can enter a single or group email address. Email notifications can be setup for all alerts or individually. To set up the email server, simply click on "Configure Email", in the same alerts window, and enter your SMTP email information, such as server name and reply to account.

Now all I need to do is kick off a query that will raise the CPU above 70% for more than 5 seconds. The code from the previous chapter, with a slight modification to remove the "bad" code will work just fine, see Listing 6.3. After all, some otherwise "acceptable" code will still require a lot of resources to process.

```
DECLARE @SQL_Alphabet varchar(26)
SET @SQL_Alphabet = 'ABCDEFGHIJKLMNOPQRSTUVWXYZ'
DECLARE @rnd_seed int
SET @rnd_seed = 26
DECLARE @DT datetime
SET @DT = '05/21/1969'
DECLARE @counter int
SET @counter = 1
DECLARE @tempVal NCHAR(40)
```

```
WHILE @counter < 10000000000
    BEGIN
        SET @tempVal = SUBSTRING(@SQl_alphabet,
            Cast(RAND() * @rnd_seed as int) + 1,
            CAST(RAND() * @rnd_seed as int) + 1)
        SET @counter = @counter + 1
    END
```

Listing 6.3: Modified code to raise CPU levels for testing.

Of course, you won't generally know what code is causing the issue beforehand, so we'll also need a way to find out what code is causing the spike in resource utilization, so that it can be fine tuned to use fewer resources and so speed performance for other contending processes.

I execute the query and wait. As the query is executing, I can monitor CPU utilization using the System Information application, which can be launched from Sysinternals Process Explorer (http://technet.microsoft.com/en-us/sysinternals/bb896653.aspx), as shown in Figure 6.13.

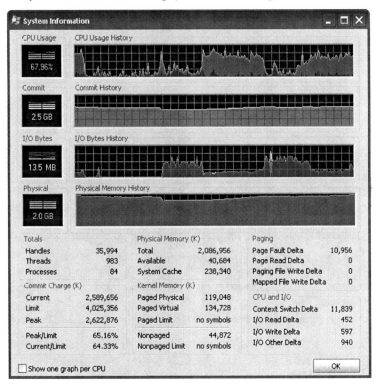

Figure 6.13: Watching CPU utilization with System Information.

You can certainly use Task Manager instead but I just happen to like the added eye candy of System Information and Process Explorer. Once the CPU utilization has hit 70% for 5 seconds, the alert is generated and emailed to me, as shown in Figure 6.14.

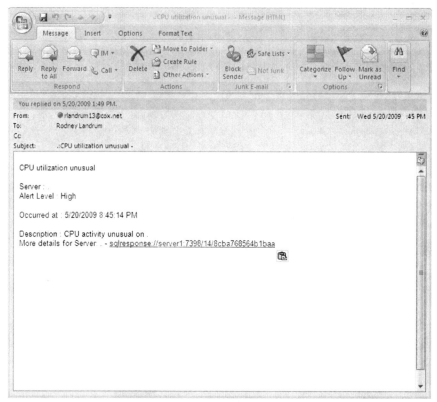

Figure 6.14: Email notification from SQL Response of "unusual" CPU utilization.

The alert contains limited information, but it would be easy to include in the mail message a key word, such as "unusual", to trigger a Level 1 alert (a high level alert for Blackberry users), since it is "unusual" to receive mail with the word "unusual" in it. However, perhaps you might want to be more specific and use something like "CPU activity unusual" to set the alert. At any rate, the alert did fire and so I was made aware of a potential issue before users complained or processes failed.

With SQL Response, you can find out what caused the CPU spike simply by turning on the tracing option that instructs SQL Response to capture the code that was executing at the time that alert was generated. In order to enable this feature, simply click on "Server Properties" and select "Enable collection of trace data" for the monitored server, as shown in Figure 6.15 (most other monitoring solutions offer similar query gathering features).

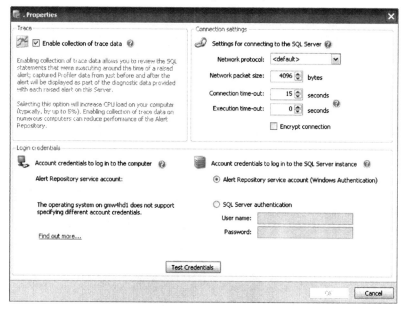

Figure 6.15: Enabling the capture of trace data.

The trace data allows you to see what code is associated with the alert, or at least to correlate the notification to the query that was running at the time the alert was fired. Figure 6.16 shows the query that SQL Response collected with the alert, which is indeed the query that I ran to trigger the high CPU utilization alert in the first place.

Figure 6.16: Capturing the query that triggered high CPU.

With the query in hand you can begin the arduous task of tracking down the user or process that has caused the issue. And once you find them you will have the further unenviable task of informing them that their query has caused you much pain and suffering. However, I have found that, as a team, everyone is open to suggestions and few I have met in my travels through the data world really take offence at your scrutiny of their code. They have a job to do and they want to excel just like you. If you tell them there is a problem they will genuinely listen and try to fix it. As a DBA you have the ability to help and this team work is truly what is required. You may not like being awoken at 2:00AM by an alert for high CPU utilization, but it is important to not let that resentment spill over to other team members. Use the knowledge to fix the issue so that it will not happen again.

Stopped services and disk space shortage

Low disk space and failing SQL Services are probably the two most prevalent issues that a DBA will encounter. Stopped services are generally an issue when there is a maintenance window that requires a restart of a server and the SQL Agent service, for example, was not set to auto start. While this may happen once, it generally does not happen again, because it usually means that other jobs have not run, and if one of those jobs is a backup job things get ugly very quickly.

Fortunately, SQL Response can monitor and alert for both of these special conditions. Figure 6.17 shows the SQL Response alerts for Disk Space and stopped services, either the SQL Agent service or SQL Server service, or both.

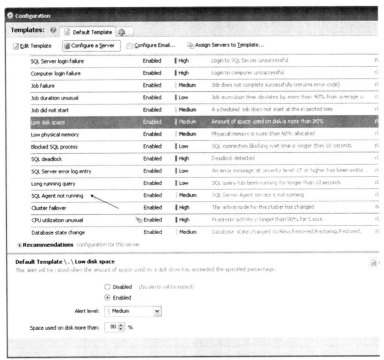

Figure 6.17: Low disk space and SQL Server Agent not running.

172

One of the things that I really like about SQL Response is that it alerts on the jobs scheduled by the SQL Agent, even if the SQL Agent is not running. What this means to me is that if I know I have a backup job set to run at 10:00 PM and the SQL Agent, which has a job to execute that backup, is not running, then SQL Response will not only notify me that the SQL Agent is not running but that that job did not run as scheduled.

Disk space, as we have learned in previous chapters, can be compromised for a number of reasons, including uncontrolled log growth, TempDB filling up, and so on. As noted earlier, the DBA needs to be warned of the imminent danger while there is still time to act, not when all space is gone. Figure 6.18 shows the threshold setting for disk space in SQL Response.

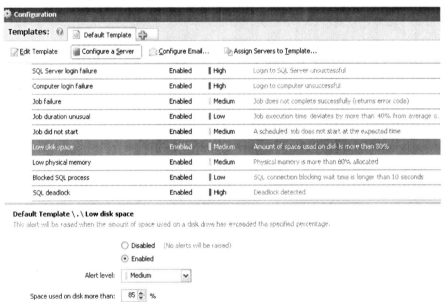

Figure 6.18: Disk space notification for 85%.

Notice the alert is set to trigger when the disk has filled to 80% (and not 100%) full, which gives you no time to plan a strategy, such as investigating log or TempDB growth, or perhaps any large data file that is set to auto-grow by a very high percentage.

Summary

In most of the IT world, being a DBA is not a 9 to 5 job. Many organizations have tens or hundreds of servers that must work around the clock and so, sometimes, must DBAs. Notifications are necessary evils of the DBA world and you will be asked to carry mobile devices that will go off at all times of the day, and predictably at night, minutes after you have dozed off.

Servers do not sleep and nor do their scheduled jobs. Backup failures, though not common, do happen and if you miss a backup because you were not notified of the failure, then you run the risk of data loss. To the DBA and those who manage DBAs and up the chain, data loss is unacceptable. You do not want to be the one to tell your boss that a failed backup occurred and no one responded and someone is desperately waiting for you to restore from the previous night's backup.

Performance notifications are nearly as important. Time lost waiting for queries to complete, especially those queries that block other queries, is not acceptable to business. They do not want to know about the details of the code, they only want it to work and work correctly. Finding the issue, as I have said, is the first step to resolving it. With the tools and techniques outlined in this chapter, you should be able to quickly find issues and resolve 95% of them before others are even aware of them, which is what you ultimately desire. If you must bring up the problem, you can safely do it after the fact, when it has been eradicated. Telling your boss there was a problem and you were able to respond to it and resolve it is much better than him or her asking you about a problem that you were totally unaware of.

Chapter 7: Securing access to SQL Server

Thus far in the book we have covered a lot of ground in terms of automating processes, battling data growth, troubleshooting code and getting notification of impending danger. Now, I want to turn to a subject that is also sure to be near and dear to every DBA's heart, and that is security.

Securing SQL Server is a broad topic, worthy of an entire book in its own right. However, when securing access to a SQL Server instance, most DBAs think first of logins, users, or credentials; in other words, the mechanisms by which they control access to their databases. Such mechanisms are certainly the first line of defense when it comes to restricting access to the sensitive data that your databases store and it is these "outer defenses" that are the focus of this chapter.

Of course, this aspect of security alone is a huge topic, and there is much work to be done by the DBA, or security administrator, in creating and managing users, logins and roles, assigning permissions, choosing authentication schemes, implementing password policies, and so on. Here, however, I am going to assume that this security infrastructure is in place, and instead focus on the techniques and scripts that DBAs can use on a day-to-day basis to monitor and maintain the users that have access to their databases, and their activity. Specifically, I'll show you how to:

- Find out who has access to data.
- Find out when and how they accessed the data.
- Use a DDL trigger (created in Listing 1.2, in Chapter 1) to capture activity on database objects, such as deleting a table.
- Implement a server-side trace to capture exactly what the users have been doing on a SQL instance.

These scripts, collectively, can be rolled into our SQL Server tacklebox (otherwise known as the DBA Repository) so that you will know at a glance what accounts or groups have been granted access to the data on each of the servers you manage.

Overview of security challenges

As DBAs, believe it or not, we may not even be fully aware of exactly what data is being housed within the walls or, more accurately, pages of the databases we manage. We may know, for example, that the databases contain confidential

175

financial or healthcare data. However, without some investigation, we may not be able to give you a granular description of the data or tell you exactly where it is stored ("social security numbers are stored in the SSN field on table X"). More often than not, the DBA, unless specifically requested, did not design the underlying database.

What we do know is that there are many avenues leading to that data, and that we have to defend every one of them; it is a heavy burden to bear. This data nestles snuggly in the lower depths of indexes and tables, all potentially brought to light by stored procedures written by developers and report writers that we have to trust to write code that will prevent SQL Injection attacks, for example, or to store passwords in encrypted form within the database.

DBAs not only have to be concerned about who has access to what resources, and how, the primary topic of what I will cover in this chapter, but also about the security of that data at rest and in transit. As we know and have covered previously, data is migratory, so the data that resides on a server you manage will not stay there for long. It will wind up in text files, possibly on the laptop of a developer or log shipped to another location that you are also responsible for where security is just as important. As data guardian (commonly now referred to as Data Steward), you have to be familiar with all aspects of keeping that data safe from unapproved viewers. Knowing all of the residences, even temporary, of the data is vital; it could be on a network, on a tape, on a physical disk, in a report or accessible to users who are writing ad hoc queries.

The introduction of Transparent Data Encryption (TDE) in SQL Server 2008 is a welcome feature for many DBAs who heretofore had relied on non-SQL native features to encrypt data and log files.

Encrypting network packets is another concern for companies with sensitive data to protect. DBAs need to understand how to configure SQL Server to use secure channel communications, via Secure Sockets Layer (SSL), in much the same way you would configure a certificate for use on a Web application.

SQL Injection attacks are also a common concern for DBAs. If a breach of security does occur, then the DBA needs to know about it immediately, and have a means to close the security hole, and then track the path of the intrusion and assess the damage caused. What's needed, assuming you don't run full C2-level auditing on all of your servers, is a Server-side tracing solution, with filtering on a range of criteria, and the ability to consolidate that collected data into a central location for analysis, as I will demonstrate later in the chapter.

Though I cannot cover encryption techniques, or preventing SQL Injection attacks or server side tracing, in this chapter I would like to provide several links that I have found useful on these topics.

- **Encryption using TDE**
  http://msdn.microsoft.com/en-us/library/bb934049.aspx
- **Encrypting Network Connections to SQL Server**
  http://msdn.microsoft.com/en-us/library/ms189067.aspx
- **Preventing SQL Injection Attacks**
  http://msdn.microsoft.com/en-us/magazine/cc163917.aspx

Finding SQL logins, Windows users and groups

In this section I will share many queries from the tacklebox that I have used over the years for discovering what accounts have been granted access to the SQL Server instances I manage.

One of the earliest "security" scripts that I wrote was essentially just a simple query that provided me with enough information that I could, at a glance, see what Windows users and Windows groups, as well as SQL logins, had access to a given server, and at what level of privilege. It is the privilege that is important to me. You may think that, as a DBA, I would be intimately familiar with which users had access to which servers, and with which permissions. This is certainly true if I am managing 10 or even 20 servers. It only becomes a concern when I am asked to manage 50 or more servers, many of which may have been in existence long before my arrival on the scene.

The script is shown in Listing 7.1. It was originally written for SQL Server 2000 and 2005, but still works well for SQL Server 2008. I should note that, in SQL Server 2005 and 2008, there are a few Security Catalog Views that can assist with interrogating login information, like **sys.sql_logins** and **sys.sql_principals**. However, I have found that, for my needs the query in Listing 7.1, against the old **syslogins** system table, provides everything I need in one go.

```
SELECT   CONVERT(char(100), SERVERPROPERTY('ServerName')) AS
Servername,
         sid,
         status,
         createdate,
         updatedate,
         accdate,
         totcpu,
         totio,
         spacelimit,
         timelimit,
         resultlimit,
         name,
         dbname,
         password,
```

```
          language,
          denylogin,
          hasaccess,
          isntname,
          isntgroup,
          isntuser,
          sysadmin,
          securityadmin,
          serveradmin,
          setupadmin,
          processadmin,
          diskadmin,
          dbcreator,
          bulkadmin,
          loginname
FROM      master..syslogins
```

Listing 7.1: Querying Master..syslogins.

Having taken a look at the big picture, I then use a pared-down version of the same query, shown in Listing 7.2, which returns fewer columns and only those rows where the logins have **sysadmin** privileges.

```
SELECT    loginname,
          sysadmin,
          isntuser,
          isntgroup,
          createdate
FROM      master..syslogins
WHERE sysadmin = 1
```

Listing 7.2: The scaled down Syslogins query.

This query returns the name of each login that has **sysadmin** privileges, indicates whether the login is a Windows user (**isntuser**), or a Windows Group (**isntgroup**), and shows the date the login was created. Table 7.1 shows some sample results.

loginname	sysadmin	isntuser	isntgroup	createdate
BUILTIN\Administrators	1	0	1	8/24/07
Server1\SQLServer2005 MSSQLUser $Server1$MSSQLSERVER	1	0	1	8/24/07
Server1\SQLServer2005 SQLAgentUser $Server1$MSSQLSERVER	1	0	1	8/24/07

loginname	sysadmin	isntuser	isntgroup	createdate
NT AUTHORITY\SYSTEM	1	1	0	8/24/07
Apps1_Conn	1	0	0	9/9/08
sa	1	0	0	4/8/03
RodDom\rodney	1	1	0	1/21/09
RodDom\All_DBA	1	0	1	5/26/09

Table 7.1: Results of query for syslogins.

The results reveal that we have two SQL logins, two Windows users and four Windows groups who have **sysadmin** privileges. Let's take a look at each group in turn.

Windows users

The two Windows users are **RodDom\rodney** and **NT Authority\System**. The former is my own Windows account, and the latter is a "built-in" local system account, which is automatically a member of the SQL Server **sysadmin** fixed server role. Generally, neither of these are a primary concern. If you find you have a high number of accounts that have **sysadmin** privileges, especially in production systems, it is worth investigating further to understand why. It is much more secure to provide the users with only the privileges they need, which for anyone other than the administrators of the instance, should be read only.

SQL logins

For SQL Logins, there are two: **sa** and **Apps1_Conn**. The presence of the latter brings up an aspect of security that is tiresome for many DBAs, namely the presence of the ubiquitous "application account".

Many applications use their own mechanism for securing data or, more accurately, the functioning of the application. For example, it is common practice to have an application that makes all of its connections through a single login, usually of escalated privileges, and then controls individual access via logins that it stores in various "application tables" within the database.

As a DBA, when I discover these escalated privileges on a SQL Server instance, I start to ask questions. When it is determined that the application account does not need the escalated admin privileges and so they can be reduced, I feel I have made headway and can rest assured that one more potentially compromising hole has been plugged.

Sometimes, however, this level of access is "business justified" and there is little the DBA can do but fume silently. The problem for the DBA is that there are no individual SQL logins to audit and, unless there is an internal auditing mechanism, there is often no auditing, full stop. What is worse is that many developers know the credentials of these application accounts so can use them to login to production systems, as they see fit. The DBA is often defenseless in this scenario.

Nevertheless, the DBA should still audit connections via this account, and be on the lookout for any instances where this account information is used to initiate a connection from a source other than the application itself. I am not trying to throw a damp towel on developers, or produce a tell-all book about their nefarious deeds. However, in my time I have witnessed some "interesting" authentication techniques, and I would be remiss if I did not point out the pitfalls of some of these methods, in as much as they are not fully auditable and are prone to abuse.

Let's assume for now, though, that the application we are concerned with uses valid SQL or Windows AD accounts to connect to the database, and move on.

> **NOTE**
> **If you are interested in discovering more about how to capture and analyze connections over time, please read my article on gathering connection information at:**
> **http://www.simple-talk.com/sql/database-administration/using-ssis-to-monitor-sql-server-databases-/**

Windows groups

If a Windows user is granted access to database objects, say for running ad hoc queries, then I highly recommend granting that access though a Windows group. It makes life much easier for the DBA who is responsible for granting, revoking, and otherwise reporting on, levels of access. Instead of having to administer 20 or more individual users, all needing the same level of access, only one group is needed. Furthermore, due to segregation of duties, it is often the Windows Server Administrator who will ultimately be responsible for adding and/or removing the user to the group via Windows administrative tools such as Active Directory Users and Computers.

One of the caveats when using Windows groups, however, is that a default schema cannot be defined for a Windows group, meaning that developers or architects in a group will have to remember to qualify all objects to the schema level. So, for example, they would need to use **Create dbo.tablename**, instead of just **CREATE tablename**. I believe, though, that this caveat, which really is just best practice anyway, is not enough to stop you from pushing for access via Windows groups, where you can.

Returning to Table 7.1, we see that there are five rows that correspond to Windows Groups. Two of these are created during the installation of SQL Server, one for the SQL Agent user:

And one for SQL Server:

```
Server1\SQLServer2005MSSQLUser$Server1$MSSQLSERVER
```

I am not worried so much about these accounts because a general search of these local groups, via "Manage Computer | Local Users and Groups", reveals that there are no members other than NT Authority\System, which I already know has **sysadmin** privileges.

For the other two groups, **RodDom\All_DBA** and **Builtin\Administrators**, however, I would like to know the members. The latter is another built-in local account that I find surprising has not been removed from SQL Server instances. It is certainly best practice and, in SQL Server 2008, Microsoft finally has taken this view and does not include this group with the base install of the database engine.

I could open Active Directory Users and Computers, or even Computer Manager, two common tools for managing Windows accounts at the domain and local computer level, to see who has local administrative rights on the SQL Server I am managing. However, there surely has to be a better way, within SQL Server, to look up the members of the groups, right? Yes there is and that is what I am going to cover in the next section.

Find Windows Active Directory group membership

At this point, I have identified several logins that have **sysadmin** privileges on my SQL Server, including two Windows groups, one of which is created default in SQL Server 2000 and 2005 (**Builtin\Administrators**), and one of which was added manually at some point (**RodDom\All_DBA**). What I need to know now is: who are the members of these groups?

SQL Server has an extended stored procedure called **xp_logininfo** that will provide me with this information. However, it would be quite an arduous task to work through, server by server, group by group, executing **xp_logininfo** to retrieve the members of each these groups. Instead, I wrote a script, saved in the DBA Repository, which automatically runs through each group in turn and returns this information, to be stored in the same central location for analysis.

Before unveiling this query, it should be noted that there are certain caveats. In my experience, **xp_logininfo** does not work well if there are cross domain issues, whereby the local Active Directory cannot deliver the account information when users from external, trusted domains have been added. If you receive errors such as the one shown in Listing 7.3, then you know that there is some issue, external to SQL Server, that is preventing you from interrogating that particular group.

```
Msg 15404, Level 16, State 3, Procedure xp_logininfo, Line 42
Could not obtain information about Windows NT group/user
```

Listing 7.3: Cross domain issues when using xp_logininfo.

If you narrow the scope of your query to just **Builtin\Administrators**, it always works, in my experience.

The second "caveat" is that the query uses a ... *cursor* ... but it is limited in scope so I take this one liberty. I normally eschew cursors, but my mentor, many years ago, used cursors and never apologized, so this is an homage to her as she is no longer with us ... thank you Kelly. The query, warts, cursors and all, is shown in Listing 7.4.

```
SET NoCount ON
SET quoted_identifier OFF

DECLARE @groupname VARCHAR(100)

IF EXISTS (SELECT        *
                        FROM            tempdb.dbo.sysobjects
                        WHERE       id =
OBJECT_ID(N'[tempdb].[dbo].[RESULT_STRING]'))
 DROP TABLE [tempdb].[dbo].[RESULT_STRING];

CREATE TABLE [tempdb].[dbo].[RESULT_STRING]
( Account_Name VARCHAR(2500),
type varchar(10),
Privilege varchar(10),
Mapped_Login_Name varchar(60),
Group_Name varchar(100) )

DECLARE Get_Groups CURSOR
    FOR Select
name from master..syslogins
where
isntgroup = 1 and status >= 9 or Name= 'BUILTIN\ADMINISTRATORS'

-- Open cursor and loop through group names
OPEN Get_Groups
FETCH NEXT FROM Get_Groups INTO @groupname
```

```
WHILE ( @@fetch_status <> -1 )
    BEGIN
        IF ( @@fetch_status = -2 )
            BEGIN
                FETCH NEXT FROM Get_Groups INTO @groupname
                CONTINUE
            END

--Insert SQL Commands Here:
Insert into [tempdb].[dbo].[RESULT_STRING]
Exec master..xp_logininfo @Groupname, 'members'

        FETCH NEXT FROM Get_groups INTO @groupname
    END

DEALLOCATE Get_Groups

Alter TABLE [tempdb].[dbo].[RESULT_STRING] Add Server
varchar(100) NULL;

GO

Update [tempdb].[dbo].[RESULT_STRING] Set Server =
CONVERT(varchar(100), SERVERPROPERTY('Servername'))

-- Now Query the temp table for users.

SET NoCount OFF
SELECT [Account_Name]
     , [type]
     , [Privilege]
     , [Mapped_Login_Name]
     , [Group_Name]
     , [Server]
  FROM [tempdb].[dbo].[RESULT_STRING]
```

Listing 7.4: Get list of groups to interrogate for members.

The results of the query can be seen in Table 7.2. Notice the **Account_Name** field corresponds with the **Group_Name** field. For example, I can see that there are several users, including one called **Server1\rodlan**, who are members of the **Builtin\Administrators** group. These users would have been invisible to me without this query. The **RodDom\All_DBA** group has a single user, **Rodlan\rlandrum**. I know from the syslogins query that **RodDom\All_DBA** is a sysadmin.

183

Account_ Name	type	Privilege	Mapped_Login_ Name	Group_Name	Server
Server1\ Administrator	user	admin	Server1\ Administrator	BUILTIN\ Administrators	Server1
Server1\ ASPNET	user	admin	Server1\ ASPNET	BUILTIN\ Administrators	Server1
Server1\ rodlan	user	admin	Server1\ rodlan	BUILTIN\ Administrators	Server1
Server1\ rodlanew	user	admin	Server1\ rodlanew	BUILTIN\ Administrators	Server1
RodDom\ Domain Admins	group	admin	RodDom\ Domain Admins	BUILTIN\ Administrators	Server1
RodDom\ Server_Support	group	admin	RodDom\ System_Support	BUILTIN\ Administrators	Server1
RodDom\ rlandrum	user	admin	RodDom\ rlandrum	BUILTIN\ Administrators	Server1
RodDom\ rlandrum	user	admin	RodDom\ rlandrum	RodDom\ All_DBA	Server1

Table 7.2: Finding Windows group members with SQL.

Now I can place the emphasis not on the group but on the members of this group, and begin questioning why a particular user is a member of a group that has **sysadmin** privileges.

However, it's not only the **sysadmin** privilege that can be dangerous in the wrong hands. Any user that has more than the minimum privileges required to do their job is potentially a threat. Remember, I use words like "threat" and "danger" because, as DBA, I feel I am responsible for all activity on the SQL Servers that I manage. If a user gets into one of my databases as a result of obtaining some elevated privilege, and accidentally drops or truncates a table, I am ultimately responsible for getting the data back. It does happen.

Knowing that a user dropped or truncated a table does not undo the damage. The user should not have had access to begin with. However, if you do not even know what happened, you will be even worse off in the long run. Techniques such as DLL triggers and Server Side Traces will provide you with knowledge of

184

modifications made to database objects, such as which user account performed the action and when.

I will describe both DDL triggers and Server Side traces at the end of the chapter. Now, I move on from the Server level to the database level, and to SQL users and database roles.

Find SQL users at the database level

This next query from the security tacklebox dives into each database, looking for accounts and their access to said database. This query interrogates user information that is stored in the **sysusers** system tables, in each individual database, and so an iterative method is needed to plod through every database that we wish to investigate. The **sys.users** table is superseded by **sys.database_prinicapls** in SQL Server but still works in all current versions.

My solution, shown in Listing 7.5, uses my favorite Microsoft-provided stored procedure, **sp_MSForEachDB**, to do most of the work for me. This stored procedure takes a query as input, with "?" as a variable mapping for the database name. So, for example, **[?]..sysusers** equates to "each **sysusers** table in each database on the server".

```
IF EXISTS ( SELECT    *
            FROM      tempdb.dbo.sysobjects
            WHERE     id =
OBJECT_ID(N'[tempdb].[dbo].[SQL_DB_REP]') )
    DROP TABLE [tempdb].[dbo].[SQL_DB_REP] ;
GO

CREATE TABLE [tempdb].[dbo].[SQL_DB_REP]
    (
        [Server] [varchar](100) NOT NULL,
        [DB_Name] [varchar](70) NOT NULL,
        [User_Name] [nvarchar](90) NULL,
        [Group_Name] [varchar](100) NULL,
        [Account_Type] [varchar](22) NULL,
        [Login_Name] [varchar](80) NULL,
        [Def_DB] [varchar](100) NULL
    )
ON  [PRIMARY]

INSERT  INTO [tempdb].[dbo].[SQL_DB_REP]
        Exec sp_MSForEachDB 'SELECT   CONVERT(varchar(100),
SERVERPROPERTY(''Servername'')) AS Server,
''?'' as DB_Name,
usu.name u_name
,CASE
```

```
      WHEN (usg.uid is null) then ''public''
      ELSE usg.name
      END as Group_Name
,CASE
      WHEN usu.isntuser=1 then ''Windows Domain Account''
      WHEN usu.isntgroup = 1 then ''Windows Group''
       WHEN usu.issqluser = 1 then ''SQL Account''
      WHEN usu.issqlrole = 1 then ''SQL Role''
      END as Account_Type
      ,lo.loginname
      ,lo.dbname as Def_DB

FROM
    [?]..sysusers usu LEFT OUTER JOIN
    ([?]..sysmembers mem INNER JOIN [?]..sysusers usg ON
mem.groupuid = usg.uid) ON usu.uid = mem.memberuid
    LEFT OUTER JOIN master.dbo.syslogins  lo on usu.sid =
lo.sid

WHERE
    (usu.islogin = 1 and usu.isaliased = 0 and usu.hasdbaccess =
1) and
    (usg.issqlrole = 1 or usg.uid is null)'

SELECT    [Server],
          [DB_Name],
          [User_Name],
          [Group_Name],
          [Account_Type],
          [Login_Name],
          [Def_DB]
FROM      [tempdb].[dbo].[SQL_DB_REP]
```

Listing 7.5: Finding SQL users and roles.

This particular query does not deal so much with **sysadmin** privileges but more with high database level privileges. For example, it investigates membership of the **db_owner** database role, which can perform all configuration and maintenance activities on a database. The DBA can also use it to investigate membership of other database roles that may have been created to serve a purpose, such as the execution of stored procedures.

The results of this query will instantly let the DBA know if any users have escalated privileges of which he or she was previously unaware. Table 7.3 shows some sample results from executing this query (due to space restrictions I omitted the **Server** column; the value was **Server1** in each case).

DB_Name	User_Name	Group_Name	Account_Type	Login_Name	Def_DB
DBA_Rep	dbo	db_owner	Windows Domain Account	RodDom\rodney	master
ReportServer	dbo	db_owner	Windows Domain Account	RodDom\rodney	master
ReportServer	NT AUTHORITY\SYSTEM	RSExecRole	Windows Domain Account	NT AUTHORITY\SYSTEM	master
Custom_HW	dbo	db_owner	SQL Account	sa	master
Custom_HW	HWC Development	db_owner	Windows Group	NULL	NULL
Custom_HW	JimV	db_owner	Windows Domain Account	NULL	NULL
Custom_HW	jyoungblood	public	Windows Domain Account	NULL	NULL
Custom_HW	RN	public	Windows Group	NULL	NULL

Table 7.3: Escalated database privileges.

In addition to illuminating membership of the **db_owner** role, notice that there are also some potentially orphaned **HWC Development** users in the **Custom_HW** database, as indicated by the **NULL** value in the **Login_Name** field. This generally happens when you restore a database from one server to another server where the logins do not exist, and would warrant further investigation.

If it were determined that these are indeed orphaned users, or groups, then I would add the accounts to the target system and execute **sp_change_users_login** for SQL logins, or add the Windows user or group account for non-SQL login accounts.

Loading up the DBA repository with security data

As described in Chapter 2, I use the DBA repository as a central documentation tool, where I store all relevant information regarding my servers. I use an SSIS package to execute my maintenance scripts against all of the servers in my care, and store the results in the central repository, for analysis. Security information is a vital part of this. Figure 7.1 shows the objects in the DBA Repository SSIS package that execute the previously-described three security queries against all of the servers I specify, so that I can interrogate all potential security issues from one source.

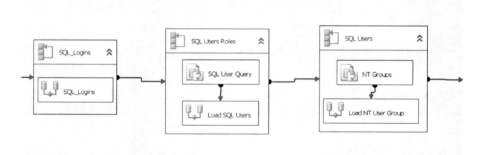

Figure 7.1: Security queries in DBA Repository SSIS package for multiple servers.

NOTE
Chapter 2 provides further details of the DBA repository, and how to use the associated SSIS package.

In addition to analysis, being able to find individual users by name makes finding and removing these users very easy. This is especially important when a user leaves the organization, for example. Yes, if the access to database objects was made via a Windows user or group then disabling the account in Windows Active Directory will alleviate the security risk. However, if the account was an SQL account that the user had access to, there is still a potential risk. Having the combined data of all three types of logins insures that a successful removal of the account occurs.

Finding service accounts with WMIC

The next query has been quite useful to me over the years. It uses WMIC (Windows Management Instrumentation Console), along with **xp_cmdshell**, and allows me to find out what service accounts are set up to run SQL Server, and other services such as Analysis Services and SQL Agent. Service credentials control access to various resources, like network shares. It is important that you know whether you are running SQL Server as "local system", which will not have access to external resources, for example, or a valid Windows service account, which will have access to said resources.

There are manual ways to obtain this information, but who wants manual when you can get the information quickly with a few simple lines of T-SQL code? Granted, this trick requires **xp_cmdshell**, the use of which is a habit I roundly condemn in others but tolerate in myself. Such is the nature of the DBA (well, this DBA anyway).

Listing 7.6 shows the fairly simple query that uses **xp_cmdshell**, Windows WMIC and a few other functions from the text parsers grab bag, like **LEN()** and **CHARINDEX()**:

```
IF  @@microsoftversion / power(2, 24) >= 9
BEGIN
    EXEC sp_configure 'show advanced options', 1
    RECONFIGURE WITH OVERRIDE

    EXEC sp_configure 'xp_cmdshell', 1

    RECONFIGURE WITH OVERRIDE

END

IF EXISTS ( SELECT  Name
            FROM    tempdb..sysobjects
            WHERE   name LIKE '#MyTempTable%' )
    DROP TABLE #MyTempTable

Create Table #MyTempTable
    (
      Big_String nvarchar(500)
    )
Insert  Into #MyTempTable
        EXEC master..xp_cmdshell 'WMIC SERVICE GET
Name,StartName | findstr /I SQL'

-- show service  accounts

Select  @@ServerName as ServerName,
        Rtrim(Left(Big_String, charindex('    ', Big_String)))
as Service_Name,
        RTrim(LTrim(Rtrim(Substring(Big_String, charindex('
', Big_String),
                                    len(Big_String)))))) as
Service_Account
```

```
from      #MyTempTable

IF   @@microsoftversion / power(2, 24) >= 9

   EXEC sp_configure 'xp_cmdshell', 0

   RECONFIGURE WITH OVERRIDE

   EXEC sp_configure 'show advanced options', 0
   RECONFIGURE WITH OVERRIDE
```

Listing 7.6: Query to show service credentials.

The first thing the script does is to check whether I am executing this query against a version of Microsoft SQL Server 2005 or higher:

```
IF   @@microsoftversion / power(2, 24) >= 9
```

The reason for this is that **xp_xmdshell** has to explicitly be enabled in 2005 and beyond, whereas in SQL Server 2000 it is enabled by default, but one has to have the required privileges to execute it.

If the version is SQL Server 2005 or higher, the script uses **sp_configure** to enable **advanced options** followed by **xp_cmdshell**. I then create a temp table, selfishly called **#MyTempTable**, and fill it with the output from the Windows Management Instrumentation Command line utility (WMIC).

I pipe (what is this, UNIX?) the output to grep, sorry I mean the **findstr** command, searching for the value "SQL" in the result set. Next, I parse the long text string that is returned, called **Big_String**, into the temporary table.

The end result, shown in Table 7.4, is a useful list of all SQL services and the accounts that have been configured as login accounts for each service.

ServerName	Service_Name	Service_Account
Server1	msftesql$SRVSAT	LocalSystem
Server1	MSSQL$SRVSAT	RodDom\rodney
Server1	MSSQLSERVER	RodDom\rodney
Server1	MSSQLServerADHelper	NT AUTHORITY\ NetworkService
Server1	MSSQLServerADHelper100	NT AUTHORITY\ NETWORK SERVICE

ServerName	Service_Name	Service_Account
Server1	MSSQLServerOLAPService	LocalSystem
Server1	SQLAgent$SRVSAT	LocalSystem
Server1	SQLBackupAgent	LocalSystem
Server1	SQLBackupAgent_SRVSAT	LocalSystem
Server1	SQLBrowser	LocalSystem
Server1	SQLSERVERAGENT	LocalSystem
Server1	NULL	NULL

Table 7.4: Service credentials query results.

While I do not use this query often, it always saves me many frustrating minutes of trying to manually find the same information, via tools such as Computer Management and Services.

Surveillance

To this point, I have focused on finding logins, users, groups and service accounts. The queries presented so far have all been useful for managing many hundreds if not thousands of accounts, all with some level of privilege to my SQL Server instances.

However, knowing who has access to the data, and what level of access they have, is only one aspect of security I want to touch on in this chapter. It is also crucial for the DBA to track such actions as failed login attempts and to audit, as far as possible, the actions of users once they are in amongst the data.

In this section, I will introduce three surveillance techniques to help with these issues: Error Log interrogation with T-SQL, DDL Triggers and Server-side Tracing.

Error log interrogation

Unlike a lot of DBAs that I know, I do not scour the SQL Error logs daily. I tend to review them when looking for a specific error, or when conducting a periodic security review. It is not that I think it is a waste of time to do it, I just think that I would much prefer to read the logs with T-SQL. Fortunately, SQL Server offers two stored procedures to make this possible, namely **sp_enumerrorlogs** and **sp_readerrolog**.

As Figure 7.2 shows, **sp_enumerrorlogs** simply lists the available SQL Server error logs.

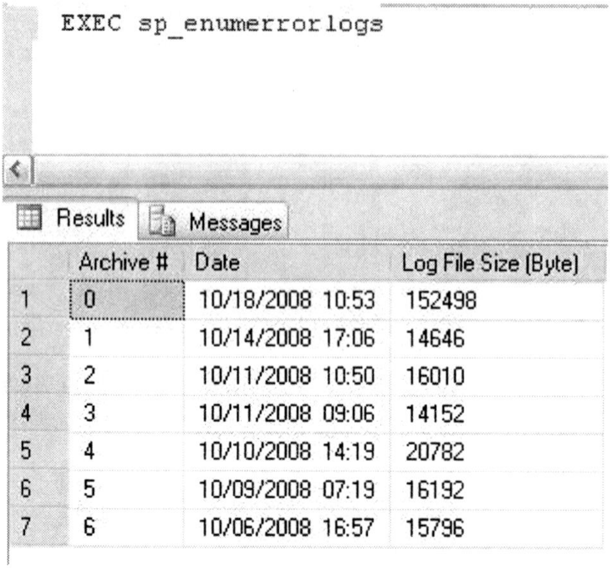

```
EXEC sp_enumerrorlogs
```

	Archive #	Date	Log File Size (Byte)
1	0	10/18/2008 10:53	152498
2	1	10/14/2008 17:06	14646
3	2	10/11/2008 10:50	16010
4	3	10/11/2008 09:06	14152
5	4	10/10/2008 14:19	20782
6	5	10/09/2008 07:19	16192
7	6	10/06/2008 16:57	15796

Figure 7.2: Querying the SQL Server error logs with sp_enumerrorlogs.

The procedure **sp_readerrorlog** accepts the **Archive #**, from **sp_enumerrorlogs**, as input and displays the error log in table form, as shown in Figure 7.3, where you can see that the first archived log file (1) is passed in as a parameter. Archive number 0 refers to the current error log.

It is possible to load and query every error log file by combining the two stored procedures with a bit of iterative code. Listing 7.7 shows the custom code used to loop through each log file, store the data in a temp table, and subsequently query that data to find more than five consecutive failed login attempts, as well as the last good login attempt.

In order for this to work, you will need to enable security logging for both successful and failed logins, as most production servers should do. This can be configured via the Security tab of the Server Properties. Finally, note that this query will only work for SQL Server 2005 and 2008.

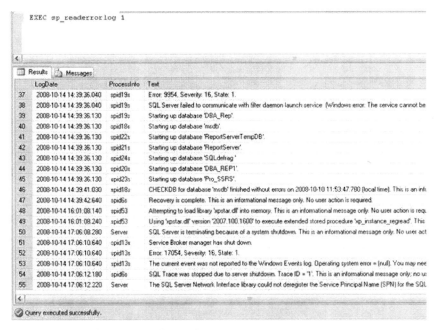

Figure 7.3: Using sp_readerrorlog.

```
DECLARE @TSQL   NVARCHAR(2000)
DECLARE @lC     INT

CREATE TABLE #TempLog (
        LogDate         DATETIME,
        ProcessInfo NVARCHAR(50),
        [Text] NVARCHAR(MAX))

CREATE TABLE #logF (
        ArchiveNumber       INT,
        LogDate             DATETIME,
        LogSize             INT
)

INSERT INTO #logF
EXEC sp_enumerrorlogs
SELECT @lC = MIN(ArchiveNumber) FROM #logF

WHILE @lC IS NOT NULL
BEGIN
        INSERT INTO #TempLog
        EXEC sp_readerrorlog @lC
        SELECT @lC = MIN(ArchiveNumber) FROM #logF
        WHERE ArchiveNumber > @lC
```

```
END

--Failed login counts. Useful for security audits.
SELECT Text,COUNT(Text) Number_Of_Attempts
FROM #TempLog where
 Text like '%failed%' and ProcessInfo = 'LOGON'
 Group by Text

--Find Last Successful login. Useful to know before deleting
"obsolete" accounts.
SELECT Distinct MAX(logdate) last_login,Text
FROM #TempLog
where ProcessInfo = 'LOGON'and Text like '%SUCCEEDED%'
and Text not like '%NT AUTHORITY%'
Group by Text

DROP TABLE #TempLog
DROP TABLE #logF
```

Listing 7.7: Searching for failed login attempts.

The results of this query are shown in Figure 7.4.

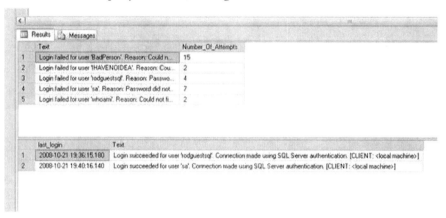

Figure 7.4: Querying for successful and unsuccessful login attempts.

We can see that there is a "BadPerson" out there who has tried 15 times to access this server. The second result set shows the st successful login for a certain account, retrieved using the **MAX()** function for the **last_login** field.

While this particular example probes login attempts for security auditing purposes, the same solution can be easily tweaked to accommodate all manner of error log analysis, from database errors to backup failures.

DDL triggers

In Chapter 1, I included in the Configuration script (Listing 1.2) code to create a DDL trigger that would alert the DBA to any database creation or deletion (drop). I'm now going to demonstrate how to use this to track DDL actions, and what you can expect to see with this DDL trigger enabled on your SQL Servers.

DDL (Data Definition Language) triggers are very similar to the DML (Data Manipulation Language) triggers, with which you are undoubtedly familiar. DDL triggers can be scoped at either the database or server level, meaning they can be set to fire when a particular statement, such as **ALTER TABLE**, is issued against a specific database, or when a DDL statement is issued at the server level, such as **CREATE LOGIN**.

Listing 7.7 shows the code to create the DDL trigger, **AuditDatabaseDDL**, which you may have missed amongst everything else going on in Listing 1.2.

Notice that the scope of the trigger, in this case, is **ALL SERVER**. The **Eventdata()** function is employed to set the values of the variables that will ultimately be mailed to the DBAs when the DDL event occurs, in this case when a database is created or dropped from the server where the trigger is created.

```
--Setup DDL Triggers
--Setup Create Database or Drop Database DDL Trigger

/****** Object:  DdlTrigger [AuditDatabaseDDL]
                 Script Date: 02/05/2009 19:56:33 ******/
SET ANSI_NULLS ON
GO

SET QUOTED_IDENTIFIER ON
GO

CREATE TRIGGER [AuditDatabaseDDL]
ON ALL SERVER
FOR CREATE_DATABASE, DROP_DATABASE
AS

DECLARE @data XML,
        @tsqlCommand NVARCHAR(MAX),
        @eventType NVARCHAR(100),
        @serverName NVARCHAR(100),
        @loginName NVARCHAR(100),
        @username NVARCHAR(100),
        @databaseName NVARCHAR(100),
        @objectName NVARCHAR(100),
        @objectType NVARCHAR(100),
        @emailBody NVARCHAR(MAX)
```

195

```
SET @data = EVENTDATA()
SET @tsqlCommand =
EVENTDATA().value('(/EVENT_INSTANCE/TSQLCommand/CommandText)[1]
','nvarchar(max)')
SET @eventType =
EVENTDATA().value('(/EVENT_INSTANCE/EventType)[1]','nvarchar(ma
x)')
SET @serverName =
EVENTDATA().value('(/EVENT_INSTANCE/ServerName)[1]','nvarchar(m
ax)')
SET @loginName =
EVENTDATA().value('(/EVENT_INSTANCE/LoginName)[1]','nvarchar(ma
x)')
SET @userName =
EVENTDATA().value('(/EVENT_INSTANCE/UserName)[1]','nvarchar(max
)')
SET @databaseName =
EVENTDATA().value('(/EVENT_INSTANCE/DatabaseName)[1]','nvarchar
(max)')
SET @objectName =
EVENTDATA().value('(/EVENT_INSTANCE/ObjectName)[1]','nvarchar(m
ax)')
SET @objectType =
EVENTDATA().value('(/EVENT_INSTANCE/ObjectType)[1]','nvarchar(m
ax)')

SET @emailBody = + '--------------------------------' +
CHAR(13)
            + '- DDL Trigger Activation Report    -' +
CHAR(13)
            + '--------------------------------' +
CHAR(13)
            + 'Sql Command: '
                + ISNULL(@tsqlCommand, 'No Command Given') +
CHAR(13)
            + 'Event Type: '
                + ISNULL(@eventType, 'No Event Type Given') +
CHAR(13)
            + 'Server Name:
                ' + ISNULL(@serverName, 'No Server Given') +
CHAR(13)
            + 'Login Name: '
                + ISNULL(@loginName, 'No LOGIN Given') +
CHAR(13)
            + 'User Name: '
                + ISNULL(@username, 'No User Name Given') +
CHAR(13)
            + 'DB Name: '
                + ISNULL(@databaseName, 'No Database Given') +
CHAR(13)
```

196

```
                + 'Object Name: '
                    + ISNULL(@objectName, 'No Object Given') +
CHAR(13)
                + 'Object Type: '
                    + ISNULL(@objectType, 'No Type Given') +
CHAR(13)
                + '- - - - - - - - - - - - - - - - - - - - - - - - - - - - - - - - - - - - - - - - - - - - - - - - - - - - ';

EXEC msdb..sp_send_dbmail @profile_name='Admin Profile',
@recipients='yourmail@yourmail.com', @subject='DDL Alteration
Trigger', @body=@emailBody

GO

SET ANSI_NULLS OFF
GO

SET QUOTED_IDENTIFIER OFF
GO

ENABLE TRIGGER [AuditDatabaseDDL] ON ALL SERVER
GO
```

Listing 7.8: DDL trigger for database creates and drops.

With the trigger enabled, it is easy enough to test, simply by creating a database on the server (**CREATE DATABASE TEST_TRIGGER**). As expected, and as shown in Figure 7.5, the mail comes in and I can see the captured events, including the username that created the database, as well as the time.

Figure 7.5: Mail from DDL trigger for database creation.

197

With only a slight modification to the DDL trigger, I can also be notified of any login creations on the server, with a simple addition of **CREATE LOGIN** to the **FOR** statement of the **CREATE TRIGGER** statement:

```
CREATE TRIGGER [AuditDatabaseDDL]
ON ALL SERVER
FOR CREATE_DATABASE, DROP_DATABASE, CREATE LOGIN
```

Listing 7.9: Tracking login creation.

With the new trigger in place I can attempt to also create a login, as shown in Listing 7.10.

```
CREATE LOGIN  RogerKennsingtonJones WITH PASSWORD =
'MyPassword12'
```

Listing 7.10: RogerKensingtonJones, we know you exist. Don't try anything funny.

Again, as expected I receive the mail notification that the account has been created. At that point, the reaction would be one of concern, but at least I know that I have several scripts available that will allow me to get to the bottom of who created this account, why, and what privileges it has.

Server-side tracing

Most DBAs will have experienced the scenario whereby a red-faced program/development manager storms up to them and demands to know why his ultra-critical tables keep getting truncated, and who is doing it.

The problem is that in order to get a complete picture of your server at a transactional level, you need either full time Profiler tracing, or to enable C2 level auditing; both of which come at a high cost. These auditing tools will not only slow down your servers considerably, but the drive space required in order to keep a record of each transaction on your server is daunting, at best.

The solution I offer here presents a "lightweight" alternative. It is rooted in the idea that issues in a system will inevitably show up more than once. If you are having consistent issues with data loss, or unwanted record modification, then this collection of stored procedures may help you out. With this set of scripts, you can:

- Capture trace information about a server, on a set schedule.
- Filter the captured data to suit your needs.
- Archive the data for future auditing.

This solution also allows the trace data to be stored in our central DBA repository so you don't have scattered auditing information cluttering up your individual instances.

Tracing stored procedures

The two stored procedures I present here offer a quick way to automatically enable customizable profiler traces on your SQL servers, as well as to centrally store trace information from any number of machines.

The code for handling the trace data is slightly different between SQL 2000 and SQL 2005, but the overall functional logic is essentially the same in each case. I provide both versions of the script in the code download for this book at http://www.simple-talk.com/RedGateBooks/ RodneyLandrum/SQL_Server_Tacklebox_Code.zip.

The first script, **usp_startTrace**, is shown in Listing 7.11 and is used to initiate the customizable trace. This stored procedure handles all the tasks of setting up the tracing events, creating the trace file, setting up filters and starting the actual trace. The script is set up to look at five different trace events, and these happen to be the same default events that Profiler monitors, which are:

- Login Events
- Logout Events
- RPC Completion Events
- SQL Batch Completion Events
- SQL Batch Start Events

The script first looks to see if a trace with the name defined is already running. This is done by querying the central data storage server. This central storage is a linked server that has a database with the tables required to store and query this information. Again, the script files to create this database on your linked server are included in the code download to this book.

Once the trace name has been checked, the script sets up a trace that matches the parameters you have supplied. This includes the ability to filter any of the trace event data columns with a keyword. The most common filter use will be on the text data column, which holds the T-SQL code run by a user.

Finally, the script stores the trace information in the central auditing database for future use.

```
USE [msdb]
GO

SET ANSI_NULLS ON
GO
SET QUOTED_IDENTIFIER ON
GO

/*
   Procedure Name : usp_startTrace
   -------------------------------
   Parameter 1 : traceName - Unique identifier of trace [Req]
   Parameter 2 : traceFile - Physical file to hold trace data
while running [Req]
   Parameter 3 : maxFileSize - Maximum size that traceFile can
grow to [Default: 5MB]
   Parameter 4 : filterColumn - Trace event data column to
filter results on [Default: 0]
   Parameter 5 : filterKeyword - Keyword used when filterColumn
is defined [Default: NULL]
*/
CREATE PROCEDURE [dbo].[usp_startTrace]
   @traceName      NVARCHAR(50),
   @traceFile      NVARCHAR(50),
   @maxFileSize    BIGINT = 5,
   @filterColumn   INT = 0,
   @filterKeyword  NVARCHAR(50) = NULL
AS

   SET NOCOUNT ON

   -- Test for trace existence in the Trace_IDs table, alert
user if trace is invalid
   -- Change linked server name here
   IF EXISTS (
      SELECT * FROM MYSERVER123.DBA_Info.dbo.Trace_IDs
      WHERE (TraceName = @traceName OR TraceFile = @traceFile)
        AND TraceServer = SERVERPROPERTY('ServerName')
   )
   BEGIN
      PRINT('Trace ' + @traceName + ' already exsists or the
file is in use, please choose another name/file')
      RETURN
   END

   /*
      Variable Declaration
      --------------------
      traceError - Will hold return code from sp_trace_create
to validate trace creation
      TraceID - Will hold the system ID of the newly created
trace
```

```
      on - Used byb sp_trace_setevent to turn on data columns
for particular events
   */
   DECLARE    @traceError    INT,
         @TraceID    INT,
         @on         BIT
     SET @on = 1

   -- Create the trace and store the output in traceError, then
test traceError for failure
   -- and alert the user if the trace cannot be started
   EXEC @traceError = sp_trace_create @TraceID output, 0,
@traceFile, @maxFileSize, NULL

   IF @traceError <> 0
   BEGIN
     PRINT('Trace could not be started: ' + @traceError)
     RETURN
   END

   -- Add events that we want to collect data on for the trace
   -- Audit Login events (14)
   exec sp_trace_setevent @TraceID, 14, 1, @on
   exec sp_trace_setevent @TraceID, 14, 9, @on
   exec sp_trace_setevent @TraceID, 14, 6, @on
   exec sp_trace_setevent @TraceID, 14, 10, @on
   exec sp_trace_setevent @TraceID, 14, 14, @on
   exec sp_trace_setevent @TraceID, 14, 11, @on
   exec sp_trace_setevent @TraceID, 14, 12, @on
   -- Audit Logout events (15)
   exec sp_trace_setevent @TraceID, 15, 15, @on
   exec sp_trace_setevent @TraceID, 15, 16, @on
   exec sp_trace_setevent @TraceID, 15, 9, @on
   exec sp_trace_setevent @TraceID, 15, 13, @on
   exec sp_trace_setevent @TraceID, 15, 17, @on
   exec sp_trace_setevent @TraceID, 15, 6, @on
   exec sp_trace_setevent @TraceID, 15, 10, @on
   exec sp_trace_setevent @TraceID, 15, 14, @on
   exec sp_trace_setevent @TraceID, 15, 18, @on
   exec sp_trace_setevent @TraceID, 15, 11, @on
   exec sp_trace_setevent @TraceID, 15, 12, @on
   -- ExistingConnection events (17)
   exec sp_trace_setevent @TraceID, 17, 12, @on
   exec sp_trace_setevent @TraceID, 17, 1, @on
   exec sp_trace_setevent @TraceID, 17, 9, @on
   exec sp_trace_setevent @TraceID, 17, 6, @on
   exec sp_trace_setevent @TraceID, 17, 10, @on
   exec sp_trace_setevent @TraceID, 17, 14, @on
   exec sp_trace_setevent @TraceID, 17, 11, @on
   -- RPC:Completed events (10)
   exec sp_trace_setevent @TraceID, 10, 15, @on
   exec sp_trace_setevent @TraceID, 10, 16, @on
```

```
   exec sp_trace_setevent @TraceID, 10, 1, @on
   exec sp_trace_setevent @TraceID, 10, 9, @on
   exec sp_trace_setevent @TraceID, 10, 17, @on
   exec sp_trace_setevent @TraceID, 10, 10, @on
   exec sp_trace_setevent @TraceID, 10, 18, @on
   exec sp_trace_setevent @TraceID, 10, 11, @on
   exec sp_trace_setevent @TraceID, 10, 12, @on
   exec sp_trace_setevent @TraceID, 10, 13, @on
   exec sp_trace_setevent @TraceID, 10, 6, @on
   exec sp_trace_setevent @TraceID, 10, 14, @on
   -- SQL:BatchCompleted events (12)
   exec sp_trace_setevent @TraceID, 12, 15, @on
   exec sp_trace_setevent @TraceID, 12, 16, @on
   exec sp_trace_setevent @TraceID, 12, 1, @on
   exec sp_trace_setevent @TraceID, 12, 9, @on
   exec sp_trace_setevent @TraceID, 12, 17, @on
   exec sp_trace_setevent @TraceID, 12, 6, @on
   exec sp_trace_setevent @TraceID, 12, 10, @on
   exec sp_trace_setevent @TraceID, 12, 14, @on
   exec sp_trace_setevent @TraceID, 12, 18, @on
   exec sp_trace_setevent @TraceID, 12, 11, @on
   exec sp_trace_setevent @TraceID, 12, 12, @on
   exec sp_trace_setevent @TraceID, 12, 13, @on
   -- SQL:BatchStarting events (13)
   exec sp_trace_setevent @TraceID, 13, 12, @on
   exec sp_trace_setevent @TraceID, 13, 1, @on
   exec sp_trace_setevent @TraceID, 13, 9, @on
   exec sp_trace_setevent @TraceID, 13, 6, @on
   exec sp_trace_setevent @TraceID, 13, 10, @on
   exec sp_trace_setevent @TraceID, 13, 14, @on

   -- If a filter has been used, setup the filter column
   -- and the keyword using sp_trace_setfilter
   IF @filterColumn > 0
   BEGIN
      EXEC sp_trace_setfilter @traceID, @filterColumn, 0, 6,
@filterKeyword
   END

   -- Set the trace to status 1, running
   EXEC sp_trace_setstatus @TraceID, 1

   -- Log all needed trace information in the Trace_IDs table
using the linked repository server
   -- Change linked server name here
   INSERT INTO MYSERVER123.DBA_Info.dbo.Trace_IDs
      ( TraceName, TraceID, TraceFile, TraceServer )
   VALUES
      ( @traceName, @TraceID, @traceFile,
CONVERT(nvarchar(128), SERVERPROPERTY('ServerName')) )
```

```
    -- Notify user of trace creation
    PRINT('Trace Started')
    SET NOCOUNT OFF
GO
```

Listing 7.11: usp_startTrace.

Remember that the structure of the **trace_data** table in version-dependent, and the one shown in Listing 7.11 is specific to SQL Server 2005 (the SQL 2000 equivalent is in the download). The central storage database can house both 2000 and 2005 data, but will use different tables depending on the version. The stored procedures are also version dependant and are respectively named. The reason for the slight difference is that the two versions handle trace data differently and have slightly differing schema.

The second script, **usp_stopTrace**, is shown in Listing 7.12 and uses the data stored about the trace to archive the data and to close the trace after completion.

```
USE [msdb]
GO

SET ANSI_NULLS ON
GO
SET QUOTED_IDENTIFIER ON
GO

/*
    Procedure Name : usp_stopTrace
    ------------------------------
    Parameter 1 : traceName - Unique identifier of trace to be
stopped [Req]
*/
CREATE PROCEDURE [dbo].[usp_stopTrace]
    @traceName NVARCHAR(50)
AS

    SET NOCOUNT ON

    /*
        Variable Declaration
        --------------------
        traceID - Will hold the ID of the trace that will be
stopped and archived
        traceFile - The physical file to export data from
        command - Variable to hold the command to clean the
traceFile from the server
    */
    DECLARE @traceID INT,
            @traceFile NVARCHAR(100),
```

```
        @command NVARCHAR(150)

   -- Test for the trace via name in the repository, if it
exsists proccess it, if not alert the user
   -- Change linked server name here
   IF EXISTS (
       SELECT * FROM MYSERVER123.DBA_Info.dbo.Trace_IDs
        WHERE TraceName = @traceName
          AND TraceServer = SERVERPROPERTY('ServerName')
   )
   BEGIN
       -- Gather the traceID and traceFile from the respository
       -- Change linked server name here
       SET @traceID  = (SELECT TraceID FROM
MYSERVER123.DBA_Info.dbo.Trace_IDs WHERE TraceName = @traceName
AND TraceServer = SERVERPROPERTY('ServerName'))
       -- Change linked server name here
       SET @traceFile = (SELECT TraceFile FROM
MYSERVER123.DBA_Info.dbo.Trace_IDs WHERE TraceName = @traceName
AND TraceServer = SERVERPROPERTY('ServerName'))

       -- Set the status of the trace to inactive, then remove
the trace from the server
       EXEC sp_trace_setstatus @traceID, 0
       EXEC sp_trace_setstatus @traceID, 2

       -- Archive the older trace data and remove all records to
make room for the new trace data
       -- Change linked server name here
       INSERT INTO MYSERVER123.DBA_Info.dbo.trace_archive SELECT
* FROM MYSERVER123.DBA_Info.dbo.trace_table

       -- Change linked server name here
       DELETE FROM MYSERVER123.DBA_Info.dbo.trace_table

       -- Change linked server name here
       INSERT INTO MYSERVER123.DBA_Info.dbo.trace_table SELECT *
FROM ::fn_trace_gettable(@traceFile + '.trc', default)

       -- Remove the existing trace file for future use
       SET @command = 'DEL ' + @traceFile + '.trc'
       EXEC xp_cmdshell @command

       -- Delete the trace information from the repository
       -- Change linked server name here
       DELETE FROM MYSERVER123.DBA_Info.dbo.Trace_IDs WHERE
TraceName = @traceName AND TraceServer =
SERVERPROPERTY('ServerName')

       -- Alert the user that the trace has been stopped and
archived
       PRINT('Trace ' + @traceName + ' Stopped and Archived')
```

```
      RETURN
   END

   -- Alert the user that the trace was not found in the
repository
   PRINT('Trace ' + @traceName + ' Not Found')

   SET NOCOUNT OFF

GO
```

Listing 7.12: usp_stopTrace.

The procedure takes only one parameter, **traceName**, which it uses to query the central server to retrieve all of the data that was stored by the **usp_startTrace** script. This information includes the name, trace id and trace file. Once the data has been received, the trace is stopped and the records from the **trace_data** table are archived into the **trace_archive** table. The new trace file is then pushed into the **trace_data** table. So, you can always find the newest trace data in the **trace_data** table and any older trace information in the **trace_archive** table.

The trace file is then deleted from the server, via **xp_cmdshell**, and the trace identity is removed from the central repository to free up the trace name and id for future use.

Implementation

There are just a few steps that you will need to take in order to get these trace procedures working correctly in your environment.

- Choose a main repository for your trace data, and modify the procedures to point to the machine on which you want to store the trace data. For example, I have my database, **DBA_Info**, residing on a test machine. Any version of SQL Server will work for the storage of data; the differences in the scripts are only due to changes in definitions of data collected in the traces.
- Create a new database for the trace data, using the create database/table scripts included in the source code zip file, to hold all of this data. You only need to run the create scripts for the version of the script you will be using, or both if you will be using the procedures on multiple machines, utilizing both SQL 2000 and SQL 2005. The results from either version are stored in separate tables so your repository database can contain both 2000 and 2005 archive trace data.

205

- Set up a user with read/write permissions on the central storage database, to be used for the linked server credentials.
- Use the new user credentials you have just made to setup a linked server on the SQL Server that you want to run an automated trace on.
- In the **usp_startTrace** and **usp_stopTrace** scripts, locate the calls (all noted in the comments) that point to a generic linked server (**MYSERVER123**) and modify them to reflect the name of your central trace data repository server.
- Run the create scripts on each of the servers that will be performing the traces.

Once these stored procedures are installed, you can begin starting and stopping traces via a query window/query analyzer or through SQL Agent jobs.

Testing

Here is a quick example that demonstrates how to find the cause of all this grief for our beloved program manager. Create a new SQL Agent job to kick off at 5:30 PM (after business hours) involving only one step, as shown in Figure 7.6. In this step, execute the start trace procedure, with the parameters needed to gather only the data relevant to the issue at hand.

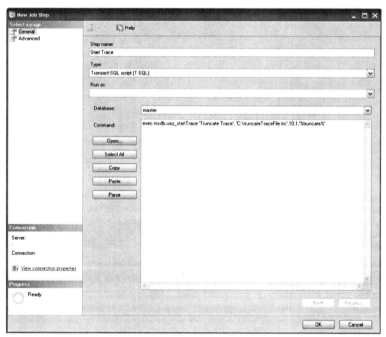

Figure 7.6: Create a SQL Agent job to run usp_startTrace.

This will produce a trace named **TruncateTrace**. The trace file will be stored in the root of the C drive. The maximum space the trace file should take is 10 MB and we will place a filter on the first column (text data) looking for any instances of the word "truncate".

The last three parameters are optional and will be defaulted to 5 (trace file size in MB), 0 (no trace column) and NULL (no filter keyword) respectively. If you do not specify these parameters then a bare bones trace will be created with a maximum file size of 5 MB, and it will perform no filtering, so you will get all available data from the trace events.

Alternatively, create another job to run at 6:00 AM, calling the **usp_stopTrace** giving the same trace name, as shown in Figure 7.7.

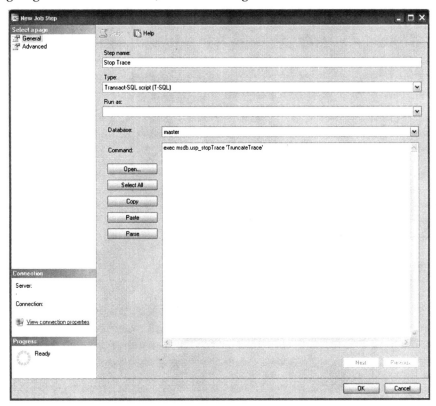

Figure 7.7: Create a SQL Agent job to run usp_stopTrace.

This will stop any trace named **TruncateTrace** on this particular server and export all of the collected data into the repository table (**trace_table** or **trace2k_table**) on the linked data collection server.

Any older information will have been archived to the **trace_archive** (or **trace2k_archive**) table. All data is marked with the server name so we can still filter the archive table to look at older data from any server. The trace file is also cleaned up from the traced server so the filename will be available for future use. This will require that **xp_cmdshell** is available for use by the SQL Agent service account. From this point, all we have to do is look through our newly acquired **trace_table** data for the suspect.

I hope that these scripts can make life a little easier for those of you out there who do not run full auditing on all of your SQL servers. The trace scripts can easily be modified to include other columns and other trace events. I am presenting this as a spring board for any DBA out there that needs an automated solution for profiler tracing. If you do want to add any event or trace columns, I would look to http://msdn2.microsoft.com/en-us/library/ms186265.aspx for a complete list of all trace events and available data columns.

In an event, the next time you encounter a red-face program manager, demanding to know who truncated his tables, much job satisfaction can be gained from being able to respond something along the lines of:

"*So <Manager Name>, we have been tracing that server all week and it seems that one of the DTS packages you wrote, and have running each night, is the problem. It is truncating the table in question each morning at 4:00 AM. Don't be too hard on yourself though. We all make mistakes.*"

Summary

All SQL Server DBAs are tasked with securing the SQL Servers they manage. While it is not the most glamorous of tasks, it is one of, if not the most, important aspects of being a DBA. This is especially true in a world where compromised data results in large fines, humiliation and potential loss of the coveted job that you were hired to do.

Knowing who has access to the data you oversee if the first step. Working to alleviate potential threats, either harmfully innocent or innocently harmful, is essential. The scripts provided here will assist you in isolating and resolving these threats. There is so much more to securing SQL Server and I have only touched on the obvious first line, user accounts and logins, error logs, DDL triggers, and server-side tracing.

Next and last up is the topic of data corruption, which ranks right up there with security in terms of threats to the integrity of the DBA's precious data. I'll show you how to detect it and how to protect yourself and your databases and most importantly what to do when you realize you have a problem … which statistically speaking, you will eventually. Be afraid; I saved the monster at the end of the book until the end of the book. Don't turn the data page.

CHAPTER 8: FINDING DATA CORRUPTION

I have mentioned a couple of times previously the monster at the end of this book. This being the final chapter, it is time for the monster to be revealed. The monster can be a silent and deceptive job killer. It can strike at once or lay in wait for weeks before launching an attack. No, I am not talking about developers; I am talking about **database corruption**.

If you have been a DBA for long enough, you will have encountered the data corruption monster in at least one of its many forms. Often corruption occurs when there is a power failure and the server, rather than shutting down gracefully, simply dies in the middle of processing data. As a result of this, or some other hardware malfunction, data or indexes become corrupt on disk and can no longer be used by SQL Server, until repaired.

Fortunately, there are several steps you can take to protect your data, and equally important your job, in the event of data corruption. First and foremost, it should go without saying that not having a good backup strategy is equivalent to playing Solitary Russian Roulette. However, I'll also demonstrate a few other techniques, based around the various DBBC commands, and a script that will make sure corruption issues are discovered and reported as soon as they occur, before they propagate through your data infrastructure. Hopefully, suitably armed, the DBA can limit the damage caused by this much-less-friendly version of the monster at the end of the book.

P.S. If you are unfortunate enough never to have read *The Monster at the End of This Book* (by Jon Stone, illustrated by Michael Smollin, Golden Books), starring the lovable Grover Monster from Sesame Street, you have firstly my sympathy and secondly my apologies, because the previous references will have meant little to you. I can only suggest you buy it immediately, along with *The Zombie Survival Guide* (by Max Brooks, Three Rivers Press), and add them both to your required reading list for all new DBAs.

Causes of corruption

There are many ways that a database can become "corrupt". Predominantly it happens when a hardware malfunction occurs, typically in the disk subsystem that is responsible for ensuring that the data written to disk is the exact same data that SQL Server expected to be written to disk when it passed along this responsibility to the operating system, and subsequently the disk controller driver and disk itself. For example, I have seen this sort of data corruption caused by a power outage in the middle of a transaction.

However, it is not just disk subsystem failures that cause data corruption. If you upgrade a database from SQL Server 2000 to SQL Server 2005 or 2008, and then interrogate it using the corruption-seeking script provided in this chapter, you may be surprised to find that you will receive what can be construed as errors in the database files. However, fortunately these are just warnings regarding space usage between versions, and there are recommended steps to address the issue, such as running **DBCC UPDATEUSAGE**.

Whatever the cause, the DBA does not want to live in ignorant bliss of possible corruption for any length of time. Unfortunately, the corruption monster is often adept at hiding, and will not rear its head until you interact with the corrupt data. By this time, the corruption may have worked its way into your backup files and, when falling through to your last resort of restoring the database, you may simply restore the same corruption. The importance of a solid, regular backup strategy cannot be overstated (so I will state it quite often). On top of that, you need a script or tool that will regularly check, and report on any corruption issues, before it's too late. I'll provide just such a script in this chapter.

Consequences of corruption

As noted in the previous section, most of the time corruption occurs due to failure in an external hardware source, like a hard disk controller or power supply. SQL Server 2005, and later, uses a feature called **Page Checksum** to detect potential problems that might arise from this. This feature creates a checksum value during writes of pages to, and subsequent reads from, disk. Essentially, if the checksum value read for a page does not match what was originally written, then SQL Server knows that the data was modified outside of the database engine. Prior to SQL Server 2005, but still included as an option, is **Torn Page Detection**, which performs similar checks.

If SQL Server detects a corruption issue, it's response to the situation will vary depending on the scale of the damage. If the damage is such that the database is unreadable by SQL Server then it would be unable to initialize and load that database. This would require a complete restore of the database in almost all cases.

If the damage is more contained, perhaps with only one or two data pages being affected, then SQL Server should still be able to read and open the database, and at that stage we can use tools such as DBCC to assess and hopefully repair the damage. Bear in mind, too, that as part of your overall backup and restore procedure, you have the ability to perform a page level restore, if perhaps you only need to restore 1 or more data pages. For additional information on restoring pages from database backups, please see: http://msdn.microsoft.com/en-us/library/ms175168.aspx

Before moving on, I should note that, while I typically leave these options enabled for all instances, both Torn Page Detection and Page Checksum incur overhead and it is possible to disable them. The idea is that if you trust your disk subsystem and power environment then you may not need to have these options turned on, if performance is the highest concern. Most disk subsystems today have battery backup to ensure write activity completes successfully.

You can use **sp_dboption** for SQL 2000 to enable or disable Torn Page Detection. For SQL Server 2005, and above, you can use the **ALTER DATABASE** command to enable either **torn page detection** or **checksum** (you are not permitted to have both on at the same time), or you can use **none** to disable them both.

Fighting corruption

Aside from having frequent and tested backups, so that you can at least return to a version of the data from the recent past, if the absolute worst happens, the well-prepared DBA will have some tools in his tacklebox that he can use to pinpoint the location of, and hopefully repair, any corrupt data.

However, before I dive in with the equivalent of a machete in a bayou, I should let you know that I am by no means an expert in database corruption. Like you, I am a just a day-to-day DBA hoping with all hope that I do not encounter corrupt databases, but wanting to be as well-prepared as I can be in case it happens.

As such, I'm going to maintain my focus on the practicalities of the tools and scripts that a DBA can use to fight corruption, mainly revolving around the use of the DBCC family of commands.

I will not dive too deeply into the bowels of the SQL Server storage engine, where one is likely to encounter all manner of esoteric terms that refer to how SQL Server allocates or maps data in the physical file, such as GAM pages (Global Allocation Map), SGAM, pages (Shared GAM), PFS pages (Page Free Space), IAM chains (Index Allocation Map), and more. For this level of detail I can do no better than to point you towards the work of Paul Randal:

http://www.sqlskills.com/BLOGS/PAUL/category/Corruption.aspx.

He has done a lot of work on the DBCC tool, is a true expert on the topic of data corruption, and is certainly the man with the most oxygen in the tank for the required dive.

DBCC CHECKDB

DBCC CHECKDB is the main command the DBA will use to test and fix consistency errors in SQL Server databases. DBCC has been around for many years, through most versions of SQL Server. Depending on who you ask, it stands for either **Database Consistency Checks** or **Database Console Commands**, the latter of which is more accurate since DBCC includes commands that fall outside the scope of just checking the consistency of a database.

For our purpose, though, we are concerned only with consistency and integrity of our databases. **DBCC CHECKDB** is actually an amalgamation of other DBCC commands, **DBCC CHECKCATALOG**, **DBCC CHECKALLOC** and **DBCC CHECKTABLE**. Running **DBCC CHECKDB** includes these other commands so negates the need to run them separately.

In order to demonstrate how to use this, and other tools, to seek out and repair data corruption, I'm first going to need to create a database, and then perform the evil deed of despoiling the data within it. If we start from scratch, it will make it easier to find and subsequently corrupt data and/or index pages, so let's create a brand new, unsullied database, aptly named "Neo". As you can see in Figure 8.1, there are no objects created in this new database. It is pristine.

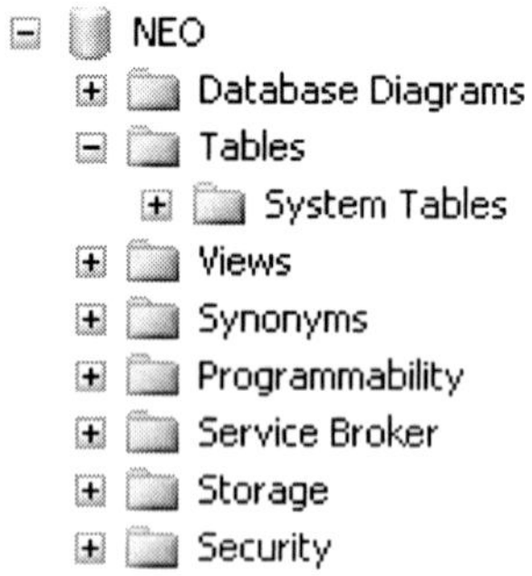

Figure 8.1: New database NEO with no objects.

Just to prove that **NEO** is not yet corrupt, we can run the **DBCC CHECKDB** command, the output of which is shown in Figure 8.2.

```
DBCC CHECKDB (NEO)
```

Messages

```
DBCC results for 'sys.sysdercv'.
There are 0 rows in 0 pages for object "sys.sysdercv".
DBCC results for 'sys.syssingleobjrefs'.
There are 146 rows in 1 pages for object "sys.syssingleobjrefs".
DBCC results for 'sys.sysmultiobjrefs'.
There are 106 rows in 1 pages for object "sys.sysmultiobjrefs".
DBCC results for 'sys.sysguidrefs'.
There are 0 rows in 0 pages for object "sys.sysguidrefs".
DBCC results for 'sys.syscompfragments'.
There are 0 rows in 0 pages for object "sys.syscompfragments".
DBCC results for 'sys.sysftstops'.
There are 0 rows in 0 pages for object "sys.sysftstops".
DBCC results for 'sys.sysqnames'.
There are 97 rows in 1 pages for object "sys.sysqnames".
DBCC results for 'sys.sysxmlcomponent'.
There are 99 rows in 1 pages for object "sys.sysxmlcomponent".
DBCC results for 'sys.sysxmlfacet'.
There are 112 rows in 1 pages for object "sys.sysxmlfacet".
DBCC results for 'sys.sysxmlplacement'.
There are 18 rows in 1 pages for object "sys.sysxmlplacement".
DBCC results for 'sys.sysobjkeycrypts'.
There are 0 rows in 0 pages for object "sys.sysobjkeycrypts".
DBCC results for 'sys.sysasymkeys'.
There are 0 rows in 0 pages for object "sys.sysasymkeys".
DBCC results for 'sys.syssqlguides'.
There are 0 rows in 0 pages for object "sys.syssqlguides".
DBCC results for 'sys.sysbinsubobjs'.
There are 3 rows in 1 pages for object "sys.sysbinsubobjs".
DBCC results for 'sys.syssoftobjrefs'.
There are 0 rows in 0 pages for object "sys.syssoftobjrefs".
DBCC results for 'sys.queue_messages_1977058079'.
There are 0 rows in 0 pages for object "sys.queue_messages_1977058079".
DBCC results for 'sys.queue_messages_2009058193'.
There are 0 rows in 0 pages for object "sys.queue_messages_2009058193".
DBCC results for 'sys.queue_messages_2041058307'.
There are 0 rows in 0 pages for object "sys.queue_messages_2041058307".
DBCC results for 'sys.filestream_tombstone_2073058421'.
There are 0 rows in 0 pages for object "sys.filestream_tombstone_2073058421".
DBCC results for 'sys.syscommittab'.
There are 0 rows in 0 pages for object "sys.syscommittab".
CHECKDB found 0 allocation errors and 0 consistency errors in database 'NEO'.
DBCC execution completed. If DBCC printed error messages, contact your system administrator.
```

Figure 8.2: No reported errors with database NEO.

As expected, there are no reported consistency or allocation errors, but that will all change very shortly. I had mentioned that there is a monster at the end of this book and it is not lovable old Grover from Sesame Street.

Please do not go on to the next page!

DBCC PAGE

Aha, you are still reading I see. Well, before we unleash the monster, I want to show you one more very important DBCC command, of which you may not be aware, namely **DBCC PAGE**. It's "officially" undocumented, in that Microsoft does not support it, but in reality I have found piles of information on this command from well known and respected sources, like Paul Randal, so I no longer consider it undocumented.

The syntax is simple:

```
dbcc page ( {'dbname' | dbid}, filenum, pagenum [,
printopt={0|1|2|3} ])
```

However, the output of the command can be quite daunting to the uninitiated DBA. So before we introduce the monster that corrupts databases, I want to run **DBCC PAGE** against the **NEO** database. The command is as follows:

```
DBCC PAGE (NEO,1,1,3)
```

The first "1" is the file number of the data file, the second "1" is the page number, and the final "3" is the print option which, depending on value chosen (0-3) returns differing levels of information. A value of "3" indicates that we want to see both page header information, as well as details. The not-very-exciting results are shown in Figure 8.3.

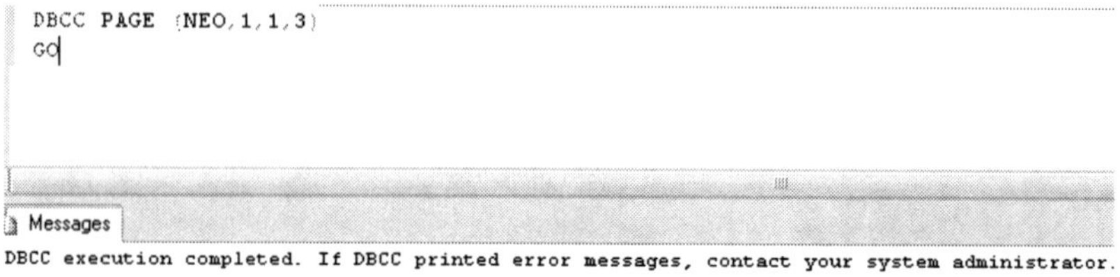

```
DBCC PAGE (NEO,1,1,3)
GO
```

Messages
DBCC execution completed. If DBCC printed error messages, contact your system administrator.

Figure 8.3: DBCC PAGE default results.

The reason that they are not very exciting is that we forgot to turn on an important trace flag (**3604**). If you are a SQL Server and not familiar with trace flags then please give me a call and we can talk over a beer or two. Really, I do not mind and I would welcome the camaraderie and chance to be pedantic.

For now, though, I'll simply note that in order to see output of the **DBCC PAGE** command, we need to run another DBCC command called **DBCC TRACEON**. Specifically:

```
DBCC TRACEON (3604)
```

Figure 8.4 shows the output from rerunning **DBCC PAGE**, with this trace flag turned on.

```
DBCC PAGE (NEO,1,1,3)
GO
```

Messages

```
(1:121)     -            =     ALLOCATED   0_PCT_FULL      IAM Page  Mixed Ext
(1:122)     -            =     ALLOCATED   0_PCT_FULL                Mixed Ext
(1:123)     -            =     ALLOCATED   0_PCT_FULL      IAM Page  Mixed Ext
(1:124)     -            =     ALLOCATED   0_PCT_FULL                Mixed Ext
(1:125)     -            =     ALLOCATED   0_PCT_FULL      IAM Page  Mixed Ext
(1:126)     -            =     ALLOCATED   0_PCT_FULL                Mixed Ext
(1:127)     -            =     ALLOCATED   0_PCT_FULL      IAM Page  Mixed Ext
(1:128)     -            =     ALLOCATED   0_PCT_FULL                Mixed Ext
(1:129)     - (1:131)    =     ALLOCATED   0_PCT_FULL      IAM Page  Mixed Ext
(1:132)     - (1:136)    =     ALLOCATED   0_PCT_FULL                Mixed Ext
(1:137)     -            =     ALLOCATED   0_PCT_FULL      IAM Page  Mixed Ext
(1:138)     - (1:140)    =     ALLOCATED   0_PCT_FULL                Mixed Ext
(1:141)     -            =     ALLOCATED   0_PCT_FULL      IAM Page  Mixed Ext
(1:142)     - (1:143)    =     ALLOCATED   0_PCT_FULL                Mixed Ext
(1:144)     - (1:149)    =     ALLOCATED   0_PCT_FULL
(1:150)     - (1:151)    = NOT ALLOCATED   0_PCT_FULL                Mixed Ext
(1:152)     - (1:153)    =     ALLOCATED   0_PCT_FULL                Mixed Ext
(1:154)     -            =     ALLOCATED   0_PCT_FULL      IAM Page  Mixed Ext
(1:155)     -            =     ALLOCATED   0_PCT_FULL                Mixed Ext
(1:156)     -            =     ALLOCATED   0_PCT_FULL      IAM Page  Mixed Ext
(1:157)     -            =     ALLOCATED   0_PCT_FULL                Mixed Ext
(1:158)     -            =     ALLOCATED   0_PCT_FULL      IAM Page  Mixed Ext
(1:159)     -            =     ALLOCATED   0_PCT_FULL                Mixed Ext
(1:160)     -            =     ALLOCATED   0_PCT_FULL      IAM Page  Mixed Ext
(1:161)     -            =     ALLOCATED   0_PCT_FULL                Mixed Ext
(1:162)     -            =     ALLOCATED   0_PCT_FULL      IAM Page  Mixed Ext
(1:163)     -            =     ALLOCATED   0_PCT_FULL                Mixed Ext
(1:164)     -            = NOT ALLOCATED   0_PCT_FULL                Mixed Ext
(1:165)     -            =     ALLOCATED   0_PCT_FULL      IAM Page  Mixed Ext
(1:166)     - (1:170)    =     ALLOCATED   0_PCT_FULL                Mixed Ext
(1:171)     -            =     ALLOCATED   0_PCT_FULL      IAM Page  Mixed Ext
(1:172)     - (1:383)    = NOT ALLOCATED   0_PCT_FULL

DBCC execution completed. If DBCC printed error messages, contact your system administrator.
```

Figure 8.4: DBCC PAGE with trace flag 3604 turned on.

At the bottom of the output I can see that pages 1:172 – 1:383 are not allocated, and all pages are 0% full. Recall, this is a database with no tables or any other objects created and with no data inserted.

So, let's now create a simple table and insert some data into it. The script to do this in is shown in Listing 8.1. It creates a table in the **NEO** database, called **ONE**, and inserts into it 1000 records (well, 999 really). Simple stuff, but the important point in the context of this example is that this data load will cause additional pages to be allocated to the database and be filled with data, and I'll be able to home in on these new pages.

```
USE [NEO]
GO

IF  EXISTS (SELECT * FROM sys.objects WHERE object_id =
OBJECT_ID(N'[dbo].[ONE]') AND type in (N'U'))
DROP TABLE [dbo].[ONE]
GO

CREATE TABLE [dbo].[ONE](
   [NEOID] [int] NULL,
   [NEOTEXT] [nchar](50) NULL
) ON [PRIMARY]

GO

BEGIN Tran T_Time

DECLARE @SQL_Alphabet varchar(26)
SET @SQL_Alphabet = 'ABCDEFGHIJKLMNOPQRSTUVWXYZ'
DECLARE @rnd_seed int
SET @rnd_seed = 26
DECLARE @counter int = 1
WHILE @counter < 1000
   BEGIN
     Insert  Into ONE
     Values (
               @counter,
              (select SUBSTRING (@SQl_alphabet,
                      Cast(RAND() * @rnd_seed as int) + 1,
                      CAST(RAND() * @rnd_seed as int) + 1)
              )
            )
     SET @counter = @counter + 1

   END
Commit Tran T_Time
```

Listing 8.1. Creating and populating the ONE table.

Figure 8.5 shows the sample data that was inserted.

218

	NEOID	NEOTEXT
1	1	STUVWXYZ
2	2	BCDEFGHIJKLMNOPQRSTUVWXY
3	3	XYZ
4	4	WXYZ
5	5	KLM
6	6	TU
7	7	ABCDEFGHIJKLMNOPQRSTUVW
8	8	DEFGH
9	9	HIJKLMNOPQRSTUVWXYZ
10	10	Z
11	11	HIJKLMNOPQ
12	12	RSTUVWXYZ
13	13	IJKLMNOPQRSTUVWXYZ
14	14	FGHIJKLMNO
15	15	OPQRSTUVWXYZ
16	16	TUVWXYZ
17	17	GHIJKLMNOPQRSTUVWXYZ
18	18	NOPQRSTUV

Figure 8.5: Sample data in the ONE table.

From Figure 8.4, I already know that, for our empty database, pages 1:172 – 1:383 were unallocated. Re-running **DBCC PAGE** should reveal that more pages have been allocated to accommodate this data, and that those pages have different percentages of fullness. Figure 8.6 shows the new results.

```
DBCC TRACEON (3604);
GO
DBCC PAGE (NEO,1,1,3)
GO
```

Messages

(1:117)	-	=	ALLOCATED	0_PCT_FULL		IAM Page	Mixed Ext
(1:118)	-	=	ALLOCATED	0_PCT_FULL			Mixed Ext
(1:119)	-	=	ALLOCATED	0_PCT_FULL		IAM Page	Mixed Ext
(1:120)	-	=	ALLOCATED	0_PCT_FULL			Mixed Ext
(1:121)	-	=	ALLOCATED	0_PCT_FULL		IAM Page	Mixed Ext
(1:122)	-	=	ALLOCATED	0_PCT_FULL			Mixed Ext
(1:123)	-	=	ALLOCATED	0_PCT_FULL		IAM Page	Mixed Ext
(1:124)	-	=	ALLOCATED	0_PCT_FULL			Mixed Ext
(1:125)	-	=	ALLOCATED	0_PCT_FULL		IAM Page	Mixed Ext
(1:126)	-	=	ALLOCATED	0_PCT_FULL			Mixed Ext
(1:127)	-	=	ALLOCATED	0_PCT_FULL		IAM Page	Mixed Ext
(1:128)	-	=	ALLOCATED	0_PCT_FULL			Mixed Ext
(1:129)	- (1:131)	=	ALLOCATED	0_PCT_FULL		IAM Page	Mixed Ext
(1:132)	- (1:136)	=	ALLOCATED	0_PCT_FULL			Mixed Ext
(1:137)	-	=	ALLOCATED	0_PCT_FULL		IAM Page	Mixed Ext
(1:138)	- (1:140)	=	ALLOCATED	0_PCT_FULL			Mixed Ext
(1:141)	-	=	ALLOCATED	0_PCT_FULL		IAM Page	Mixed Ext
(1:142)	- (1:143)	=	ALLOCATED	0_PCT_FULL			Mixed Ext
(1:144)	- (1:150)	=	ALLOCATED	0_PCT_FULL			
(1:151)	-	= NOT	ALLOCATED	0_PCT_FULL			Mixed Ext
(1:152)	- (1:153)	=	ALLOCATED	0_PCT_FULL			Mixed Ext
(1:154)	-	=	ALLOCATED	0_PCT_FULL		IAM Page	Mixed Ext
(1:155)	-	=	ALLOCATED	0_PCT_FULL			Mixed Ext
(1:156)	-	=	ALLOCATED	0_PCT_FULL		IAM Page	Mixed Ext
(1:157)	-	=	ALLOCATED	0_PCT_FULL			Mixed Ext
(1:158)	-	=	ALLOCATED	0_PCT_FULL		IAM Page	Mixed Ext
(1:159)	-	=	ALLOCATED	0_PCT_FULL			Mixed Ext
(1:160)	-	=	ALLOCATED	0_PCT_FULL		IAM Page	Mixed Ext
(1:161)	-	=	ALLOCATED	0_PCT_FULL			Mixed Ext
(1:162)	-	=	ALLOCATED	0_PCT_FULL		IAM Page	Mixed Ext
(1:163)	-	=	ALLOCATED	0_PCT_FULL			Mixed Ext
(1:164)	-	=	ALLOCATED	100_PCT_FULL			Mixed Ext
(1:165)	-	=	ALLOCATED	0_PCT_FULL		IAM Page	Mixed Ext
(1:166)	- (1:170)	=	ALLOCATED	0_PCT_FULL			Mixed Ext
(1:171)	- (1:172)	=	ALLOCATED	0_PCT_FULL		IAM Page	Mixed Ext
(1:173)	- (1:179)	=	ALLOCATED	100_PCT_FULL			Mixed Ext
(1:180)	- (1:183)	= NOT	ALLOCATED	0_PCT_FULL			
(1:184)	- (1:189)	=	ALLOCATED	100_PCT_FULL			
(1:190)	-	=	ALLOCATED	50_PCT_FULL			
(1:191)	- (1:383)	= NOT	ALLOCATED	0_PCT_FULL			

DBCC execution completed. If DBCC printed error messages, contact your system administrator.

Figure 8.6: New Pages added to NEO database after loading data.

I can see that pages 1:184 – 1:189, for example, are now allocated and are 100 percent full. Having identified one of the new pages (1:184) that contains the data that I just loaded, I can run **DBCC PAGE** again for that specific page and return a basket full of information, as shown in Figure 8.7.

Figure 8.7 Individual records from page 1:184.

I can see, for example, that it returns the actual value for both **NEOID** and **NEOTEXT**, 553 and UVWXYZ respectively. It also returns a hex dump (**10006c00 29020000...**) that specifies the specific location in the data file where the record with **NEOID** 533 is stored.

If you are not an expert in reading hexadecimal then fear not; neither am I at this point. I do know, however, that using this information I will be able to find this exact same record and modify it outside of SQL Server, which will really wreak some havoc. For that however, I will need my trusty hexadecimal editor, which I will discuss shortly.

Corruption on data pages

We know that our ONE table, in the NEO database, is a heap, so any corruption we induce is going to be directly on the data pages, rather than on any non-clustered index.

The latter case is actually more favorable as the data in the index is a "duplicate" and so it is relatively easy to repair the damage. We'll cover this latter case after we've looked at inducing, and hopefully recovering from, corruption of the data in our heap table.

Putting a Hex on the data

There are many hexadecimal editors out there in the world, many of them free or at least free to try out. For this chapter, I downloaded a trial version of one called, ironically, **Hex Editor Neo**, by HHD Software.

What a Hexadecimal editor allows the DBA to do is simply open and view the contents of a file, in this case the data file. While it is an interesting exercise, I would only recommend it for testing or training purposes as it is a very dangerous tool in inexperienced hands.

What I want to do here is use this hexadecimal editor to "zero out" data in a single database file, in fact in a single data page. This will cause the required corruption, mimicking a hardware problem that has caused inconsistent information to be written to disk, without making the database unreadable by SQL Server.

And though I have not stated it heretofore …

Do not go any further without first backing up the database!

The data that I am fixing (that is a Southern expression) to zero out resides on the data page revealed in Figure 8.7, namely **1:184**. In order to corrupt the data on this page, I first need to shutdown SQL Server, so that the parent data file, `C:\Program Files\Microsoft SQL Server\MSSQL.1\MSSQL\Data\NEO.mdf`, is not in use.

Next, I simply open Hex Editor Neo and find the location of the one record with **NEOID= 553** and **NEOTEXT ="UVWXYZ"**, that we identified using the DBCC PAGE previously.

Most hexadecimal editors, Hex Editor Neo included, have the ability to search for values within the data file. Here, referring back to the **DBBC PAGE** information for page 1:184, I simply search for the value **10006c00 29020000** to find record 553. As you can see in Figure 8.8, the record in the Hex editor looks almost identical to the output of the previous **DBCC PAGE** command.

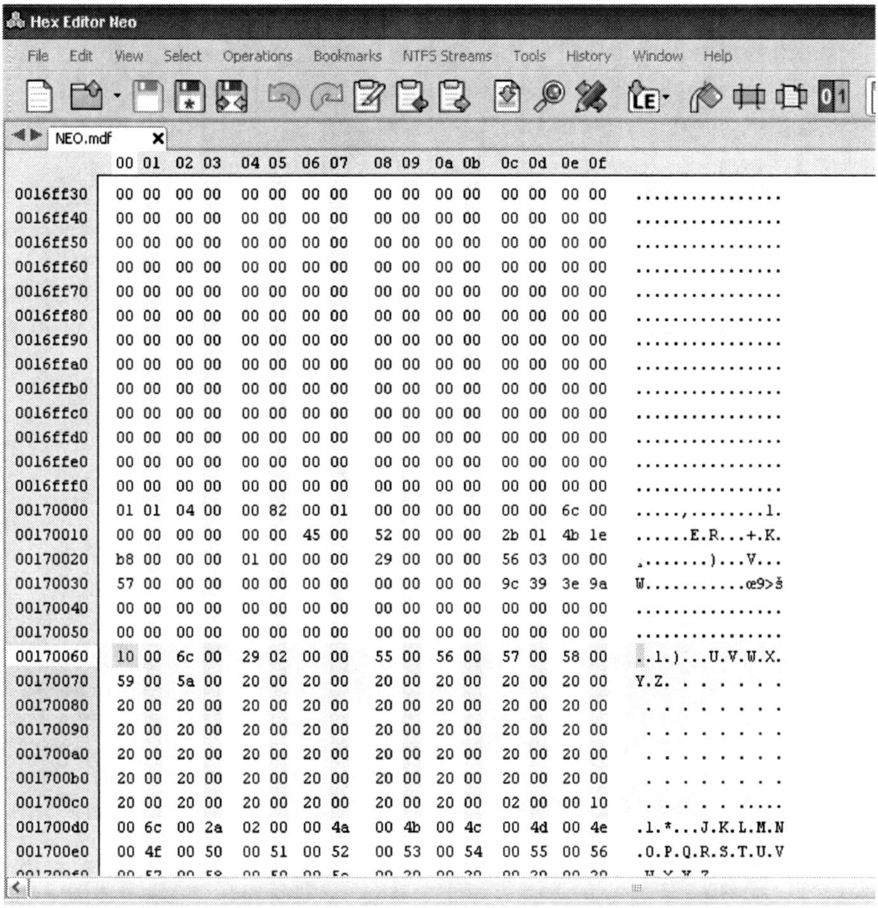

Figure 8.8: Opening the database file in Hex Editor Neo.

Next, I am simply going to make just one small change to the data, zeroing out "U" in the record, by changing 55 to 00. That is it. Figure 8.9 shows the change.

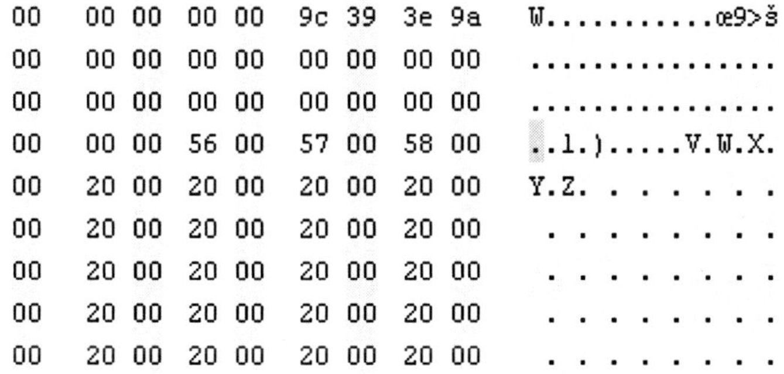

```
00   00 00  00 00   9c 39  3e 9a    W...........œ9>š
00   00 00  00 00   00 00  00 00    ................
00   00 00  00 00   00 00  00 00    ................
00   00 00  56 00   57 00  58 00    ..1.).....V.W.X.
00   20 00  20 00   20 00  20 00    Y.Z. . . . . . .
00   20 00  20 00   20 00  20 00    . . . . . . . .
00   20 00  20 00   20 00  20 00    . . . . . . . .
00   20 00  20 00   20 00  20 00    . . . . . . . .
00   20 00  20 00   20 00  20 00    . . . . . . . .
```

Figure 8.9: Zeroing out a valid data value.

223

Next I save the file, and close the Hex editor, which you have to do otherwise the date file will be in use and you will be unable to initialize the database, and start SQL Server. Now, at last, we are about to unleash the monster …

Confronting the Corruption Monster

At first glance all appears fine. The NEO database is up and available, and no errors were reported in the Event Log. In Management studio, I can drill into the objects of the database, including the ONE table, without issue. However, if I try to query the table with SELECT * FROM ONE, something frightening happens, as shown in Listing 8.2.

```
Msg 824, Level 24, State 2, Line 1

SQL Server detected a logical consistency-based I/O error:
incorrect checksum (expected: 0x9a3e399c; actual: 0x9a14b99c).

It occurred during a read of page (1:184) in database ID 23 at
offset 0x00000000170000 in file

'C:\Program Files\Microsoft SQL
Server\MSSQL.1\MSSQL\DATA\NEO.mdf'.  Additional messages in the
SQL Server error log or system event log may provide more detail.
This is a severe error condition that threatens database
integrity and must be corrected immediately.

Complete a full database consistency check (DBCC CHECKDB) . This
error can be caused by many factors; for more information, see
SQL Server Books Online.
```

Listing 8.2: Corruption strikes the ONE **table.**

This is indeed the horror show that DBAs do not want to see. It is obviously a very severe error and major corruption. This error will be thrown each time record 553 is included in the query results, and so any table scan will reveal the problem.

This has to be fixed quickly. Fortunately, we took a backup of the database prior to corrupting the data file so if all else fails I can resort to that backup file to restore the data. It is critical, when dealing with corruption issues, that you have known good backups. Unfortunately, in the real world, it's possible this corruption could have gone undetected for many days, which will mean that your backups will also carry the corruption.

If this is the case then, at some point you may be faced with accepting the very worst possible scenario, namely data loss. Before accepting that fate, however, I am going to ace down the monster, and see if I can fix the problem using DBCC CHECKDB.

There are many options for **DBCC CHECKDB** and I'll touch on only a few of them here. **DBCC CHECKDB** has been enhanced many times in its life and received major re-writes for SQL Server 2005 and above. One of the best enhancements for the lone DBA, working to resolve corruption issues, is the generous proliferation of more helpful error messages.

So, let's jump in and see how bad the situation is and what, if anything, can be done about it. To begin, I will perform a limited check of the physical consistency of the database, with the following command:

```
DBCC CHECKDB('neo') WITH PHYSICAL_ONLY;
GO
```

Figure 8.10 shows the results which are, as expected, not great.

```
Messages
DBCC results for 'NEO'.
Msg 8928, Level 16, State 1, Line 1
Object ID 2121058592, index ID 0, partition ID 72057594039042048, alloc unit ID 7205759404330188
Msg 8939, Level 16, State 98, Line 1
Table error: Object ID 2121058592, index ID 0, partition ID 72057594039042048, alloc unit ID 720
CHECKDB found 0 allocation errors and 2 consistency errors in table 'ONE' (object ID 2121058592)
CHECKDB found 0 allocation errors and 2 consistency errors in database 'NEO'.
repair_allow_data_loss is the minimum repair level for the errors found by DBCC CHECKDB (NEO).
DBCC execution completed. If DBCC printed error messages, contact your system administrator.
```

Figure 8.10: The DBCC report on the corruption.

The worst outcome is the penultimate line, which tells me that **REPAIR_ALLOW_DATA_LOSS** is the minimal repair level for the errors that were encountered. This means that we can repair the damage by running **DBCC CHECKDB** with the **REPAIR_ALLOW_DATA_LOSS** option but, as the name suggests, it will result in data loss.

There are two other repair levels that we would have preferred to see: **REPAIR_FAST** or **REPAIR_REBUILD**. The former is included for backward compatibility and does not perform repairs of 2005 database. If the minimal repair option had been **REPAIR_REBUILD**, it would have indicated that the damage was limited to, for example, a non-clustered index. Such damage can be repaired by rebuilding the index, with no chance of data loss.

In general, it is recommended that you use the repair options of **DBCC CHECKDB** that may cause data loss only as a last resort, a restore from backup being the obvious preferable choice, so that the data will remain intact. This, of course, requires that the backup itself be uncorrupt.

For this exercise, however, I am going to act on the information provided by **DBCC CHECKDB** and run the minimal repair option, **REPAIR_ALLOW_DATA_LOSS**. The database will need to be in single user mode to perform the repair, so the syntax will be:

```
ALTER DATABASE NEO SET SINGLE_USER WITH ROLLBACK IMMEDIATE
GO
DBCC CHECKDB('neo', REPAIR_ALLOW_DATA_LOSS)
GO
```

The results of running the **DBCC CHECKDB** command are as shown in Listing 8.3.

```
DBCC results for 'ONE'.

Repair: The page (1:184) has been deallocated from object ID
2121058592, index ID 0, partition ID 72057594039042048, alloc
unit ID 72057594043301888 (type In-row data).

Msg 8928, Level 16, State 1, Line 1

Object ID 2121058592, index ID 0, partition ID 72057594039042048,
alloc unit ID 72057594043301888 (type In-row data): Page (1:184)
could not be processed.  See other errors for details.

        The error has been repaired.

Msg 8939, Level 16, State 98, Line 1

Table error: Object ID 2121058592, index ID 0, partition ID
72057594039042048, alloc unit ID 72057594043301888 (type In-row
data), page (1:184). Test (IS_OFF (BUF_IOERR, pBUF->bstat))
failed. Values are 29362185 and -4.

        The error has been repaired.

There are 930 rows in 14 pages for object "ONE".
```

Listing 8.3: The error is repaired, but data is lost.

The good news is that the errors have now been repaired. The bad news is that it took the data with it, deallocating the entire data page from the file. Notice, in passing, that the output shows an object ID for the table on which the corruption occurred, and also an index ID, which in this case is 0 as there are no indexes on the table.

So, at this point, I know that I've lost data, and it was for a data page, but only one page; but how much data exactly? A simple **SELECT** statement reveals that not only have I lost the row I tampered with (**NEOID** 553), but also another 68 rows, up to row 621. Figure 8.11 rubs it in my face.

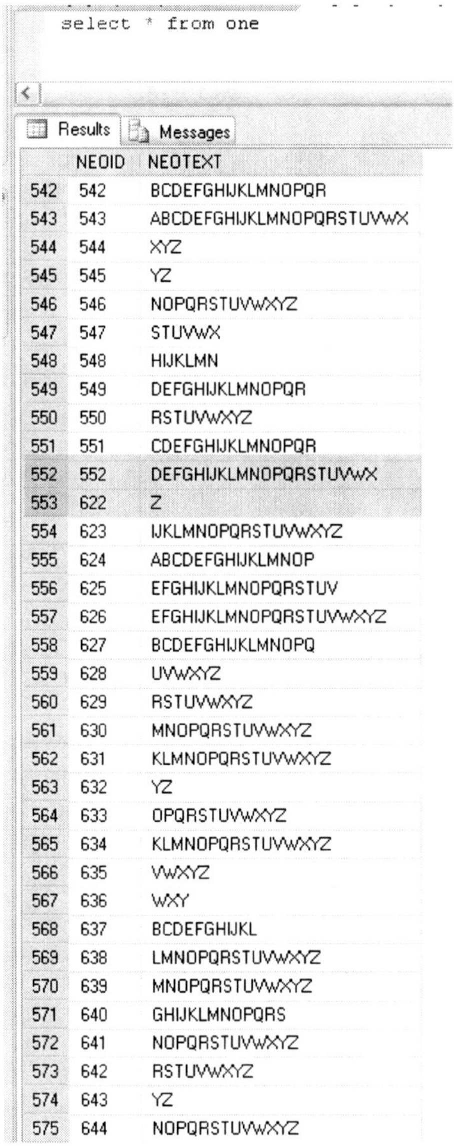

```
    select * from one
```

	NEOID	NEOTEXT
542	542	BCDEFGHIJKLMNOPQR
543	543	ABCDEFGHIJKLMNOPQRSTUVWX
544	544	XYZ
545	545	YZ
546	546	NOPQRSTUVWXYZ
547	547	STUVWX
548	548	HIJKLMN
549	549	DEFGHIJKLMNOPQR
550	550	RSTUVWXYZ
551	551	CDEFGHIJKLMNOPQR
552	552	DEFGHIJKLMNOPQRSTUVWX
553	622	Z
554	623	IJKLMNOPQRSTUVWXYZ
555	624	ABCDEFGHIJKLMNOP
556	625	EFGHIJKLMNOPQRSTUV
557	626	EFGHIJKLMNOPQRSTUVWXYZ
558	627	BCDEFGHIJKLMNOPQ
559	628	UVWXYZ
560	629	RSTUVWXYZ
561	630	MNOPQRSTUVWXYZ
562	631	KLMNOPQRSTUVWXYZ
563	632	YZ
564	633	OPQRSTUVWXYZ
565	634	KLMNOPQRSTUVWXYZ
566	635	VWXYZ
567	636	WXY
568	637	BCDEFGHIJKL
569	638	LMNOPQRSTUVWXYZ
570	639	MNOPQRSTUVWXYZ
571	640	GHIJKLMNOPQRS
572	641	NOPQRSTUVWXYZ
573	642	RSTUVWXYZ
574	643	YZ
575	644	NOPQRSTUVWXYZ

Figure 8.11: Missing data after DBCC CHECKDB Repair_Allow_Data_Loss.

These rows should be easily recovered if you have a good backup. You have a good backup, right? *Right?* Assuming you do, then you are faced with the task of restoring from backup to another database, like **NEO2**, and syncing the two tables for the missing rows. Syncing the two tables can be accomplished with a simple **INSERT INTO** statement, like that shown in Listing 8.4.

```
INSERT   INTO NEO..ONE ( NEOID, NEOTEXT )
         SELECT   NEOID,
                  NEOTEXT
         FROM     NEO2..ONE
         WHERE    NEOID NOT IN ( SELECT   NEOID
                                 FROM     NEO..ONE )
```

Listing 8.4: Syncing two tables to recover lost data rows.

In this "controlled example", the fix is fairly simple. Other scenarios, with much higher levels of corruption, may require you to turn to other measures to get the data back, after repairing with data loss. These means will almost always involve a restore of the database from backup, which is why I impress again the importance of a solid, verified and well documented database backup policy.

Corruption on non-clustered indexes

I noted earlier that corruption of a non-clustered index is much easier to deal with than corruption of an actual data page, as these indexes are just "redundancies" of the actual data and can be easily rebuilt. However, it would be interesting to prove this point. I'll use the same Hexadecimal editor technique to corrupt the non-clustered index, and not the data, and see what the outcome would be.

One indicator of whether the corruption is on an index or a table is the **IndexID** provided with the DBCC output. For our **ONE** heap table, I noted (in Listing 8.3) that the **IndexID** was 0 as there were no indexes defined for the table. An **IndexID** of 1 means a clustered index and a value of 2-250 indicates a non-clustered index.

For the sake of brevity, let's assume that I have performed the necessary repair on the **NEOID** column and created a non-clustered index on the **ONE** table, for the **NEOID** column.

First, I need to find out the page value of the index I defined for the **ONE** table. I will then plug this page of the non-clustered index into **DBCC PAGE** so that I know, again, exactly what data to modify to simulate index corruption, instead of data page corruption of the heap.

To retrieve the page value of the index, I can use another DBCC command, call it undocumented again, **DBCC INDID**. The syntax for this command is:

DBCC INDID (DBID, TABLEID,-1)

So, to execute this for my newly-indexed **ONE** table, the command will be:

```
DBCC ind(23, 2121058592, -1)
```

The results reveal several **IndexID**s, mostly zero, along with several **IndexID** values of 2, indicating a non-clustered index. Notice in Figure 8.11 the **IndexID** of 2 and the associated page of that index, 180.

```
⊟ DBCC ind(23, 2121058592, -1)
  L
```

	PageFID	PagePID	IAMFID	IAMPID	ObjectID	IndexID	PartitionNumber	PartitionID	iam_chain_type
1	1	172	NULL	NULL	2121058592	0	1	72057594039042048	In-row data
2	1	164	1	172	2121058592	0	1	72057594039042048	In-row data
3	1	173	1	172	2121058592	0	1	72057594039042048	In-row data
4	1	174	1	172	2121058592	0	1	72057594039042048	In-row data
5	1	175	1	172	2121058592	0	1	72057594039042048	In-row data
6	1	176	1	172	2121058592	0	1	72057594039042048	In-row data
7	1	177	1	172	2121058592	0	1	72057594039042048	In-row data
8	1	178	1	172	2121058592	0	1	72057594039042048	In-row data
9	1	179	1	172	2121058592	0	1	72057594039042048	In-row data
10	1	185	1	172	2121058592	0	1	72057594039042048	In-row data
11	1	186	1	172	2121058592	0	1	72057594039042048	In-row data
12	1	187	1	172	2121058592	0	1	72057594039042048	In-row data
13	1	188	1	172	2121058592	0	1	72057594039042048	In-row data
14	1	189	1	172	2121058592	0	1	72057594039042048	In-row data
15	1	190	1	172	2121058592	0	1	72057594039042048	In-row data
16	1	181	NULL	NULL	2121058592	2	1	72057594039238656	In-row data
17	1	180	1	181	2121058592	2	1	72057594039238656	In-row data
18	1	182	1	181	2121058592	2	1	72057594039238656	In-row data
19	1	183	1	181	2121058592	2	1	72057594039238656	In-row data
20	1	192	1	181	2121058592	2	1	72057594039238656	In-row data

Figure 8.12: Finding the page of the new non-clustered index.

I can now run **DBCC PAGE** again, plugging in this page information:

```
DBCC TRACEON (3604);
GO
DBCC PAGE (NEO,1,180,3)
GO
```

The results look a lot different than when looking at a data page. I see returned the Hexadecimal value (**HEAP RID**) that represents each row in the index for the page interrogated, as shown in Figure 8.12.

```
DBCC TRACEON (3604);
GO
DBCC PAGE (NEO,1,180,3)
GO
```

	FileId	PageId	Row	Level	NEOID (key)	HEAP RID (key)	KeyHashValue
1	1	180	0	0	1	0xA400000001000000	(a600ecfb3489)
2	1	180	1	0	2	0xA400000001000100	(a7005d18b1e7)
3	1	180	2	0	3	0xA400000001000200	(a800f1073957)
4	1	180	3	0	4	0xA400000001000300	(a9003fdfba3a)
5	1	180	4	0	5	0xA400000001000400	(aa0097055eee)
6	1	180	5	0	6	0xA400000001000500	(ab0026e6db80)
7	1	180	6	0	7	0xA400000001000600	(ac008af95330)
8	1	180	7	0	8	0xA400000001000700	(ad00ba57dc5b)
9	1	180	8	0	9	0xA400000001000800	(ae001a07e147)
10	1	180	9	0	10	0xA400000001000900	(af00abe46429)
11	1	180	10	0	11	0xA400000001000A00	(b00007fbec99)
12	1	180	11	0	12	0xA400000001000B00	(b100c9236ff4)
13	1	180	12	0	13	0xA400000001000C00	(b20061f98b20)
14	1	180	13	0	14	0xA400000001000D00	(b300d01a0e4e)
15	1	180	14	0	15	0xA400000001000E00	(b4007c0586fe)
16	1	180	15	0	16	0xA400000001000F00	(b500b0461199)
17	1	180	16	0	17	0xA400000001001000	(b6004104eecf)
18	1	180	17	0	18	0xA400000001001100	(b700f0e76ba1)
19	1	180	18	0	19	0xA400000001001200	(b8005cf8e311)
20	1	180	19	0	20	0xA400000001001300	(b9009220607c)
21	1	180	20	0	21	0xA400000001001400	(ba003afa84a8)
22	1	180	21	0	22	0xA400000001001500	(bb008b1901c6)
23	1	180	22	0	23	0xA400000001001600	(bc0027068976)
24	1	180	23	0	24	0xA400000001001700	(bd0017a8061d)
25	1	180	24	0	25	0xA400000001001800	(be00b7f83b01)
26	1	180	25	0	26	0xA400000001001900	(bf00061bbe6f)
27	1	180	26	0	27	0xA400000001001A00	(c000aa0436df)

Figure 8.13: Looking at the non-clustered index for the ONE table with DBCC PAGE.

I used the Hex editor again to modify, or zero out, the **HEAP RID**, and once again this does indeed corrupt the database in much the same way as changing an actual data page. However, there is one major difference: this time, when I run **DBCC CHECKDB ('neo') WITH PHYSICAL_ONLY**, the **IndexID** of the corrupt object is reported as "2" i.e. a non-clustered index.

Armed with this knowledge, I have open to me options for repairing the damage, other than restoring from backup, or running **DBCC CHECKDB** with **REPAIR_ALLOW_DATA_LOSS**, with the potential loss of data that this entails.

I can simply drop and recreate the non-clustered index using the code in Listing 8.5.

```
USE [NEO]
GO

IF  EXISTS (SELECT * FROM sys.indexes WHERE object_id =
OBJECT_ID(N'[dbo].[ONE]')
 AND name = N'NEO_ID_NC')
DROP INDEX [NEO_ID_NC] ON [dbo].[ONE] WITH ( ONLINE = OFF )
GO

USE [NEO]
GO

CREATE NONCLUSTERED INDEX [NEO_ID_NC] ON [dbo].[ONE]
(
    [NEOID] ASC
)WITH (PAD_INDEX  = OFF, STATISTICS_NORECOMPUTE  = OFF,
SORT_IN_TEMPDB = OFF,
 IGNORE_DUP_KEY = OFF, DROP_EXISTING = OFF, ONLINE = OFF,
ALLOW_ROW_LOCKS  = ON,
 ALLOW_PAGE_LOCKS  = ON) ON [PRIMARY]
GO
```

Listing 8.5: Drop and recreate corrupt non-clustered index.

Now that I have delved somewhat into corrupting, finding and fixing some problems, let's turn now to the discovery process.

Seeking out corruption

What is the best way for you to find out that you have corruption on your databases, before it propagates through numerous backups and causes bigger issues than it need do?

One option is to set up regular integrity checks using Maintenance Plans, which are useful, and certainly better than not having any integrity checks at all. However, I enjoy the level of control and flexibility I have when building custom scripts to perform the same functions as the maintenance plans. As such, rather than delve into maintenance plans, I will instead share with you a script that I use to iterate through each database, including system databases, and report on any errors returned by **DBCC CHECKDB**.

231

With this code, and an easy way to read the error logs where the **DBCC CHECKDB** results will be written (which I covered in Chapter 7), you will be comforted by the knowledge that you will not let corruption seep into your data infrastructure and go unnoticed. And that you can act thoughtfully to resolve the issue, once discovered.

The custom query, in Listing 8.6, will iterate through all databases on a SQL Server instance, capture errors and mail the top error to you so that you can look further into the matter.

```
CREATE TABLE #CheckDBTemp (
      Error          INT
    , [Level]        INT
    , [State]        INT
    , MessageText    NVARCHAR(1000)
    , RepairLevel    NVARCHAR(1000)
    , [Status]       INT
    , [DBID]         INT
    , ObjectID       INT
    , IndexID        INT
    , PartitionID    BIGINT
    , AllocUnitID    BIGINT
    , [File]         INT
    , Page           INT
    , Slot           INT
    , RefFile        INT
    , RefPage        INT
    , RefSlot        INT
    , Allocation     INT
)
-- Needed variables
DECLARE @TSQL           NVARCHAR(1000)
DECLARE @dbName         NVARCHAR(100)
DECLARE @dbErrorList    NVARCHAR(1000)
DECLARE @dbID           INT
DECLARE @ErrorCount     INT
DECLARE @EmailSubject   NVARCHAR(255)
DECLARE @ProfileName    VARCHAR(100)
DECLARE @EmailRecipient VARCHAR(255)

-- Init variables
SET @dbID = 0
SET @dbErrorList = ''
SET @EmailSubject = 'Integrity Check Failure on ' +
CAST(COALESCE(@@SERVERNAME, 'Server Name Not Available') AS
NVARCHAR)
SET @ProfileName = 'Notifications'
SET @EmailRecipient = 'rlandrum13@cox.net'
-- CYCLE THROUGH DATABASES
WHILE(@@ROWCOUNT > 0)
BEGIN
```

```
    IF( @dbID > 0 )
    BEGIN
        SET @TSQL = 'DBCC CHECKDB(''' +  @dbName  + ''') WITH
TABLERESULTS, PHYSICAL_ONLY, NO_INFOMSGS'

        INSERT INTO #CheckDBTemp
        EXEC(@TSQL)

        SELECT @ErrorCount = COUNT(*) FROM #CheckDBTemp

        IF( @ErrorCount > 0 )
        BEGIN
            SET @dbErrorList = @dbErrorList + CHAR(10) + CHAR(13)
+ 'Issue found on database : ' + @dbName
            SET @dbErrorList = @dbErrorList + CHAR(10) + CHAR(13)
+ (Select Top 1 MessageText from  #CheckDBTemp)
        END

        TRUNCATE TABLE #CheckDBTemp
    END

    IF SUBSTRING(CONVERT(varchar(50),
SERVERPROPERTY('ProductVersion')),1,1) = '8'
    BEGIN
        SELECT TOP 1 @dbName = name, @dbID = dbid
        FROM sysdatabases WHERE dbid > @dbID
            AND name NOT IN ('tempdb')
            AND DATABASEPROPERTYEX(name, 'Status') = 'Online'
        ORDER by dbid
    END
    ELSE
    BEGIN
        SELECT TOP 1 @dbName = name, @dbID = database_ID
        FROM sys.databases WHERE database_ID > @dbID
            AND name NOT IN ('tempdb')
            AND DATABASEPROPERTYEX(name, 'Status') = 'Online'
        ORDER by database_ID
    END
END
-- If errors were found
IF( @dbErrorList <> '' )
BEGIN
    IF SUBSTRING(CONVERT(varchar(50),
SERVERPROPERTY('ProductVersion')),1,1) = '8'
    BEGIN
        EXEC master..xp_sendmail @recipients = @EmailRecipient,
@subject = @EmailSubject, @message = @dbErrorList
    END
    ELSE
    BEGIN
```

```
      EXEC msdb..sp_send_dbmail @profile_name = @ProfileName,
@recipients = @EmailRecipient, @subject = @EmailSubject, @body
= @dbErrorList, @importance = 'High'
   END
END

DROP TABLE #CheckDBTemp
```

Listing 8.6: A script for seeking out and reporting database corruption.

You will notice that the code uses a **DBCC CHECKDB** option that I've not previously covered, and that is **WITH TABLERESULTS**. As the name suggests, it causes the results to be returned in table format. This option is not covered in Books Online, but is highly useful for automating error checking via SQL Agent jobs or custom code.

This code can easily be modified to return an email reporting that all databases except **NEO** are in good shape. It might soften the blow somewhat to know that of 20 databases only one is corrupt. I know it would help me somewhat. In any event, when corruption occurs you are going to receive the mail, seen in Figure 8.14, which is truly the monster that wakes you up in the middle of the night in a cold sweat.

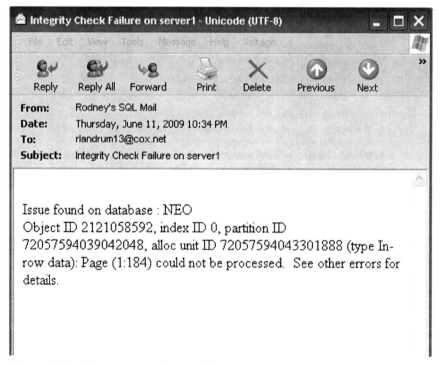

Figure 8.14: The monster in email form.

234

In this mail, I can see the **ObjectID**, the **IndexID** and the corrupted page, as well as the database name. This should be enough to go on for further investigation with the newfound tools, **DBCC PAGE**, **DBCC INDID** and **DBCC CHECKDB**, with repair options. Or, it should be a wakeup call to the fact that you might have to restore from a good backup.

Summary

In this final chapter, I have discussed how to corrupt a database and delved into several undocumented DBCC options that will assist you when corruption happens to your data. Notice I said "when". I have only touched the surface of the topic here by showing, at a very high level, how to translate pages to hexadecimal values and understand how to correlate the results of various DBCC commands, while troubleshooting corruption issues.

I cannot stress enough that having a good backup plan is the most important task for the DBA. While I did not cover backups and restores in great depth in this chapter (an entire book can be written on this topic alone), I have at least shown the best reason to have such a good backup as part of your overall high availability and disaster recovery plan. A corrupt database will indeed be a disaster and could incur much downtime. You do not want to have to go to your boss, or your bosses' boss, and tell them that you have lost data irrevocably. If you do, you might as well pull your resume out from whatever disk drive it may be on (assuming that's not corrupt as well) and update it.

There is often panic when discovering any level of corruption in your databases. Without verified backups and some basic troubleshooting tips, there is no safe place to hide when the monster rears up. All you can do is perform a repair, potentially allowing data loss for hundreds of data pages, and then duck away into the nearest cubicle, which if it was yours will soon be empty.

If you do have good backups and can repair the damage without data loss, then that cubicle may one day turn into an executive office where the wall-to-wall tinted windows reveal the flowing brook outside, where no monsters live.

The End

INDEX

SQL Tools
from **Red Gate Software**

SQL Backup

from $295

Compress, encrypt and monitor SQL Server backups

- ↗ Compress database backups by **up to 95%** for faster backups and restores
- ↗ Protect your data with up to 256-bit AES encryption (SQL Backup Pro only)
- ↗ Monitor your data with an interactive timeline, so you can check and edit the status of past, present and future backup activities
- ↗ Optimize backup performance with multiple threads in SQL Backup's engine

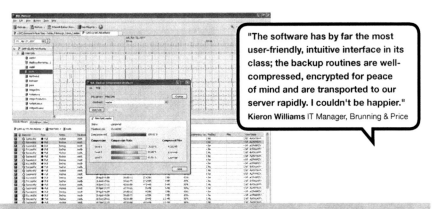

> "The software has by far the most user-friendly, intuitive interface in its class; the backup routines are well-compressed, encrypted for peace of mind and are transported to our server rapidly. I couldn't be happier."
> **Kieron Williams** IT Manager, Brunning & Price

SQL Response

from $495

Monitors SQL Servers, with alerts and diagnostic data

- ↗ Investigate long-running queries, SQL deadlocks, blocked processes and more to resolve problems sooner
- ↗ Intelligent email alerts notify you as problems arise, without overloading you with information
- ↗ Concise, relevant data provided for each alert raised
- ↗ Low-impact monitoring and no installation of components on your SQL Servers

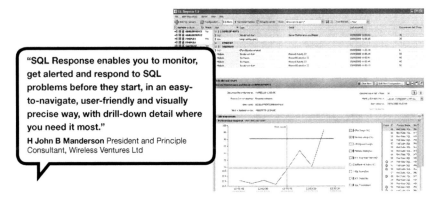

> "SQL Response enables you to monitor, get alerted and respond to SQL problems before they start, in an easy-to-navigate, user-friendly and visually precise way, with drill-down detail where you need it most."
> **H John B Manderson** President and Principle Consultant, Wireless Ventures Ltd

SQL Compare

from **$395**

Compare and synchronize SQL Server database schemas

- ↗ Automate database comparisons, and synchronize your databases
- ↗ Simple, easy to use, 100% accurate
- ↗ Save hours of tedious work, and eliminate manual scripting errors
- ↗ Work with live databases, snapshots, script files or backups

"SQL Compare and SQL Data Compare
are the best purchases we've made in the
.NET/SQL environment. They've saved us
hours of development time and the fast,
easy-to-use database comparison gives
us maximum confidence that our migration
scripts are correct. We rely on these
products for every deployment."

Paul Tebbutt Technical Lead, Universal Music Group

SQL Data Compare

from **$395**

Compare and synchronize SQL Server database schemas

- ↗ Compare your database contents
- ↗ Automatically synchronize your data
- ↗ Simplify data migrations
- ↗ Row-level restore
- ↗ Compare to backups

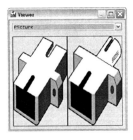

SQL Prompt

from $195

Intelligent code completion and layout for SQL Server

- ↗ Write SQL fast and accurately with code completion
- ↗ Understand code more easily with script layout
- ↗ Continue to use your current editor – SQL Prompt works within SSMS, Query Analyzer, and Visual Studio
- ↗ Keyword formatting, join completion, code snippets, and many more powerful features

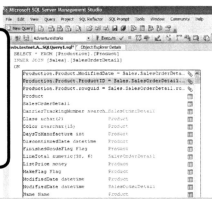

"It's amazing how such a simple concept quickly becomes a way of life. With SQL Prompt there's no longer any need to hunt out the design documentation, or to memorize every field length in the entire database. It's about freeing the mind from being a database repository - and instead concentrate on problem solving and solution providing!" **Dr Michael Dye** Dyetech

SQL Data Generator

$295

Test data generator for SQL Server databases

- ↗ Data generation in one click
- ↗ Realistic data based on column and table name
- ↗ Data can be customized if desired
- ↗ Eliminates hours of tedious work

"Red Gate's SQL Data Generator has overnight become the principal tool we use for loading test data to run our performance and load tests"
Grant Fritchey Principal DBA, FM Global

Preview of data to be generated (first 100 lines)

TitleOfCourtesy Title	BirthDate datetime	HireDate datetime	Address Address Line (Stre...	City US City	Region Region	PostalCode ZIP Code	Country Country	HomeP Phone
Dr	23/08/1963 04:0...	25/04/1992 20:0...	37 Fabien St.	Richmond	IA-CT	58907	Gibraltar	12353:
Miss	10/01/1960 23:2...	16/02/1976 11:2...	850 White Nobel...	NULL	NV-EW	39330	Tajikistan	698621
Mr	27/07/1970 13:5...	03/12/1953 15:3...	45 Green Milton	New York	TN-OH	60387	Liberia	529-89
Mr	27/01/2002 04:3...	24/07/1958 00:5...	43 Milton Bouiev	Sacramento	NM-JR	13294	Côte d'Ivoire	934-11
Mr	31/05/1994 04:1...	12/01/1964 04:4...	592 Rocky Cowl	Santa Ana	MI-UU	NULL	Jersey	417-47
Mrs	17/11/1975 10:1...	27/10/1963 18:5...	69 Clarendon Pa...	San Jose	IL-TC	41768	New Caledonia	11305!
Dr.	16/05/1974 06:1...	25/11/1998 14:5...	207 Fabien Blvd.	Houston	AL-GE	04937	Belgium	896875
Dr	27/12/1999 19:4...	03/05/1972 13:1...	53 Rocky Oak R...	Baton Rouge	MA-RT	65364	Swaziland	076-87
Dr	14/10/1971 03:1...	28/06/1978 10:0...	260 East Rocky.	Charlotte	AL-AR	97727	Benin	54684!
Mr	09/11/1981 13:2...	26/12/2001 15:0...	476 North Fabie...	Akron	MA-IU	94269	Palau	875611
Dr	26/06/1987 01:3...	30/10/1972 00:0...	48 South Hague	Norfolk	VT-UV	66385	American Samoa	89085!
Mr	20/10/1962 04:4	07/09/2005 17:1...	939 Fabien Park...	Grand Rapids	HI-YT	86033	Swaziland	58415!
Mr	25/01/2001 03:0...	18/03/1983 12:0...	348 North Green	Wichita	FL-IV	32302	Zambia	124-42
Mr	05/01/1955 10:0...	12/08/1983 22:5...	32 Cowley Boule...	Spokane	WV-DI	45980	Chile	457-22

SQL Toolbelt™ $1,795

The twelve essential SQL Server tools for database professionals

You can buy our acclaimed SQL Server tools individually or bundled.
Our most popular deal is the SQL Toolbelt: all twelve SQL Server tools in a single installer, with **a combined value of $5,240 but an actual price of $1,795**, a saving of more than 65%.

*Fully compatible with SQL Server 2000, 2005 and **2008**!*

SQL Doc

Intelligent code completion and layout for SQL Server

- ↗ Produce simple, legible and fast HTML reports for multiple databases
- ↗ Documentation is stored as part of the database
- ↗ Output completed documentation to a range of different formats.

$295

SQL Dependency Tracker

The graphical tool for tracking database and cross-server dependencies

- ↗ Visually track database object dependencies
- ↗ Discover all cross-database and cross-server object relationships
- ↗ Analyze potential impact of database schema changes
- ↗ Rapidly document database dependencies for reports, version control, and database change planning

$195

SQL Packager

Compress and package your databases for easy installations and upgrades

- ↗ Script your entire database accurately and quickly
- ↗ Move your database from A to B
- ↗ Compress your database as an exe file, or launch as a Visual Studio project
- ↗ Simplify database deployments and installations

from $295

SQL Multi Script

Single-click script execution on multiple SQL Servers

- ↗ Cut out repetitive administration by deploying multiple scripts on multiple servers with just one click
- ↗ Return easy-to-read, aggregated results from your queries to export either as a csv or .txt file
- ↗ Edit queries fast with an intuitive interface, including colored syntax highlighting, Find and Replace, and split-screen editing

$195

SQL Comparison SDK

Automate database comparisons and synchronizations

- ↗ Full API access to Red Gate comparison tools
- ↗ Incorporate comparison and synchronization functionality into your applications
- ↗ Schedule any of the tasks you require from the SQL Comparison Bundle

$595

SQL Refactor

Refactor and format your SQL code

Twelve tools to help update and maintain databases quickly and reliably, including:

- ↗ Rename object and update all references
- ↗ Expand column wildcards, qualify object names, and uppercase keywords
- ↗ Summarize script
- ↗ Encapsulate code as stored procedure

$295

How to Become an Exceptional DBA

Brad McGehee

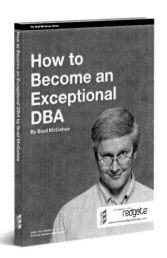

A career guide that will show you, step-by-step, exactly what you can do to differentiate yourself from the crowd so that you can be an Exceptional DBA. While Brad focuses on how to become an Exceptional SQL Server DBA, the advice in this book applies to any DBA, no matter what database software they use. If you are considering becoming a DBA, or are a DBA and want to be more than an average DBA, this is the book to get you started.

ISBN: 978-1-906434-05-2
Published: July 2008

SQL Server Execution Plans

Grant Fritchey

Execution plans show you what's going on behind the scenes in SQL Server and provide you with a wealth of information on how your queries are being executed. Grant provides a clear route through the subject, from the basics of capturing plans, through their interpretation, and then right on to how to use them to understand how you might optimize your SQL queries, improve your indexing strategy, and so on. All this rich information makes the execution plan a fairly important tool in the tool belt of pretty much anyone who writes TSQL to access data in a SQL Server database.

ISBN: 978-1-906434-02-1
Published: June 2008

Mastering SQL Server Profiler
Brad McGehee

For such a potentially powerful tool, Profiler is surprisingly underused; unless you have a lot of experience as a DBA, it is often hard to analyze the data you capture. As such, many DBAs tend to ignore it and this is distressing, because Profiler has so much potential to make a DBA's life more productive. SQL Server Profiler records data about various SQL Server events, and this data can be used to troubleshoot a wide range of SQL Server issues, such as poorly-performing queries, locking and blocking, excessive table/index scanning, and a lot more.

ISBN: 978-1-906434-15-1
Published: January 2009

Two Minute SQL Server Stumpers

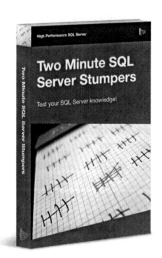

Challenge yourself in a variety of ways about the different aspects of SQL Server. Some of the questions are arcane, some very common, but you'll learn something and the wide range of questions will help you get your mind agile and ready for some quick thinking. This version is a compilation of SQL Server 2005 and SQL Server 2008 questions, to bring you up to date on the latest version of SQL Server. So read on, in order, randomly, just start going through them, but do yourself a favor and think about each before turning the page. Challenge yourself and see how well you do.

ISBN: 978-1-906434-21-2
Published: August 2009

LaVergne, TN USA
11 January 2010
169643LV00002B/10/P